Red Hat Enterprise Linux 9
Essentials

Red Hat Enterprise Linux 9 Essentials

ISBN-13: 978-1-951442-65-1

Rev: 1.0

Contents

Table of Contents

Chapter 1

1. Introduction

Arguably one of the most highly regarded and widely used enterprise level operating systems available today is the Red Hat Enterprise Linux (typically shortened to RHEL and pronounced *rell*) distribution. Not only is it considered to be among the most stable and reliable operating systems, it is also backed by the considerable resources and technical skills of Red Hat, Inc. Red Hat Enterprise Linux 9 Essentials is designed to provide detailed information on the installation, use and administration of the Red Hat Enterprise Linux 9 distribution. For beginners, the book covers topics such as operating system installation, the basics of the GNOME desktop environment, configuring email and web servers and installing packages and system updates using App Streams. Additional installation topics such as dual booting with Microsoft Windows are also covered, together with all important security topics such as configuring a firewall and user and group administration.

For the experienced user, topics such as remote desktop access, the Cockpit web interface, logical volume management (LVM), disk partitioning, swap management, KVM virtualization, Secure Shell (SSH), Linux Containers and file sharing using both Samba and NFS are covered in detail to provide a thorough overview of this enterprise class operating system.

1.1 Superuser Conventions

RHEL 9, in common with Linux in general, has two types of user account, one being a standard user account with restricted access to many of the administrative files and features of the operating system, and the other a superuser (*root*) account with elevated privileges. Typically, a user can gain root access either by logging in as the root user, or using the *su* - command and entering the root password. In the following example, a user is gaining root access via the *su* - command:

```
[neil@demo-server ~]$ su -
Password:
[root@demo-server ~]#
```

Note that the command prompt for a regular user ends with a $ sign while the root user has a # character. When working with the command-line, this is a useful indication as to whether or not you are currently issuing commands as the root user.

If the *su* - command fails, the root account on the system has most likely been disabled for security reasons. In this case, the *sudo* command can be used instead as outlined below.

Using *sudo*, a single command requiring root privileges may be executed by a non-root user. Consider the following attempt to update the operating system with the latest patches and packages:

```
[neil@demo-server ~]$ dnf update
Not root, Subscription Management repositories not updated
```

Introduction

```
Error: This command has to be run under the root user.
```

Optionally, user accounts may be configured so that they have access to root level privileges. Instead of using the *su* - command to first gain root access, user accounts with administration privileges are able to run otherwise restricted commands using *sudo*:

```
[neil@demo-server]$ sudo dnf update

We trust you have received the usual lecture from the local System
Administrator. It usually boils down to these three things:

    #1) Respect the privacy of others.
    #2) Think before you type.
    #3) With great power comes great responsibility.

[sudo] password for neil:
Updating Subscription Management repositories.
.

.
```

To perform multiple commands without repeatedly using the sudo command, a command prompt with persistent super-user privileges may be accessed as follows:

```
[neil@demo-server]$ sudo su -
[neil@demo-server]#
```

The reason for raising this issue so early in the book is that many of the command-line examples outlined in this book will require root privileges. Rather than repetitively preface every command-line example with directions to run the command as root, the command prompt at the start of the line will be used to indicate whether or not the command needs to be performed as root. If the command can be run as a regular user, the command will be prefixed with a $ command prompt as follows:

```
$ date
```

If, on the other hand, the command requires root privileges, the command will be preceded by a # command prompt:

```
# dnf install openssh
```

1.2 Opening a Terminal Window

If you are using the GNOME desktop and need to access a command prompt you will need to open a Terminal window. To do this, either press the keyboard Windows key or click on the Activities button in the top left-hand corner of the screen, then select the Terminal from the dash as shown in Figure 1-1:

Figure 1-1

1.3 Editing Files

Configuring a Linux system typically involves editing files. For those new to Linux it can be unclear which editor to use. If you are running a terminal session and do not already have a preferred editor we recommend using the *nano* editor. To launch *nano* in a terminal window simply enter the following command:

```
# nano <file>
```

Where <file> is replaced by the path to the file you wish to edit. For example:

```
# nano /etc/passwd
```

Once loaded, *nano* will appear as illustrated in Figure 1-2:

```
  GNU nano 2.9.3                        /etc/passwd

root:x:0:0:root:/root:/bin/bash
daemon:x:1:1:daemon:/usr/sbin:/usr/sbin/nologin
bin:x:2:2:bin:/bin:/usr/sbin/nologin
sys:x:3:3:sys:/dev:/usr/sbin/nologin
sync:x:4:65534:sync:/bin:/bin/sync
games:x:5:60:games:/usr/games:/usr/sbin/nologin
man:x:6:12:man:/var/cache/man:/usr/sbin/nologin
lp:x:7:7:lp:/var/spool/lpd:/usr/sbin/nologin
mail:x:8:8:mail:/var/mail:/usr/sbin/nologin
news:x:9:9:news:/var/spool/news:/usr/sbin/nologin
uucp:x:10:10:uucp:/var/spool/uucp:/usr/sbin/nologin
proxy:x:13:13:proxy:/bin:/usr/sbin/nologin
www-data:x:33:33:www-data:/var/www:/usr/sbin/nologin
backup:x:34:34:backup:/var/backups:/usr/sbin/nologin
list:x:38:38:Mailing List Manager:/var/list:/usr/sbin/nologin
irc:x:39:39:ircd:/var/run/ircd:/usr/sbin/nologin
gnats:x:41:41:Gnats Bug-Reporting System (admin):/var/lib/gnats:/usr/sbin/nolog$
nobody:x:65534:65534:nobody:/nonexistent:/usr/sbin/nologin
systemd-network:x:100:102:systemd Network Management,,,:/run/systemd/netif:/usr$
                         [ Read 44 lines ]
^G Get Help  ^O Write Out ^W Where Is  ^K Cut Text  ^J Justify   ^C Cur Pos
^X Exit      ^R Read File ^\ Replace   ^U Uncut Text^T To Spell  ^_ Go To Line
```

Figure 1-2

To create a new file simply run *nano* as follows:

```
# nano
```

When you have finished editing the file, type Ctrl-S to save the file followed by Ctrl-X to exit. To open an existing file, use the Ctrl-R keyboard shortcut.

If you prefer to use a graphical editor within the GNOME desktop environment *gedit* is a useful starting point for basic editing tasks. To launch *gedit* from the desktop press Alt-F2 to display the Enter a Command window as shown in Figure 1-3:

3

Introduction

Figure 1-3

Enter *gedit* into the text field and press the Enter key. After a short delay, gedit will load ready to open, create and edit files:

Figure 1-4

Alternatively, launch gedit from a terminal window either with or without the path to the file to open:

```
# gedit
```

```
# gedit /etc/passwd
```

1.4 Feedback

We want you to be satisfied with your purchase of this book. If you find any errors in the book, or have any comments, questions or concerns please contact us at *feedback@ebookfrenzy.com*.

1.5 Errata

While we make every effort to ensure the accuracy of the content of this book, it is inevitable that a book covering a subject area of this size and complexity may include some errors and oversights. Any known issues with the book will be outlined, together with solutions, at the following URL:

https://www.ebookfrenzy.com/errata/rhel9.html

In the event that you find an error not listed in the errata, please let us know by emailing our support team at *feedback@ebookfrenzy.com.*

2. A Brief History of Red Hat Linux

Red Hat Enterprise Linux is one of a number of variants (also referred to as *distributions*) of the Linux operating system and is the product of a U.S. company named Red Hat, Inc., based in Raleigh, North Carolina. The company was founded in the mid-1990s through the merger of two companies owned at the time by Marc Ewing and Bob Young. The origins of Linux, however, go back even further. This chapter will outline the history of both the Linux operating system and Red Hat, Inc.

2.1 What exactly is Linux?

Linux is an operating system in much the same way that Windows is an operating system (and there any similarities between Linux and Windows end). The term operating system is used to describe the software that acts as a layer between the hardware in a computer and the applications that we all run on a daily basis. When programmers write applications, they interface with the operating system to perform such tasks as writing files to the hard disk drive and displaying information on the screen. Without an operating system, every programmer would have to write code to directly access the hardware of the system. In addition, the programmer would have to be able to support every single piece of hardware ever created to be sure the application would work on every possible hardware configuration. Because the operating system handles all of this hardware complexity, application development becomes a much easier task. Linux is just one of a number of different operating systems available today.

2.2 UNIX Origins

To understand the history of Linux, we first have to go back to AT&T Bell Laboratories in the late 1960s. During this time AT&T had discontinued involvement in developing a new operating system named Multics. However, two AT&T engineers, Ken Thompson and Dennis Ritchie, decided to take what they had learned from the Multics project and create a new operating system named UNIX which quickly gained popularity and wide adoption both with corporations and academic institutions.

A variety of proprietary UNIX implementations eventually came to market, including those created by IBM (AIX), Hewlett-Packard (HP-UX), and Sun Microsystems (SunOS and Solaris). In addition, a UNIX-like operating system named MINIX was created by Andrew S. Tanenbaum and designed for educational use with source code access provided to universities.

2.3 Who Created Linux?

The origins of Linux can be traced back to the work and philosophies of two people. At the heart of the Linux operating system is something called the *kernel*. This is the core set of features necessary for the operating system to function. The kernel manages the system's resources and handles communication between the hardware and the applications. The Linux kernel was developed by

A Brief History of Red Hat Linux

Linus Torvalds, who, taking a dislike to MS-DOS and impatient for the availability of MINIX for the new Intel 80386 microprocessor, decided to write his own UNIX-like kernel. When he had finished the first version of the kernel, he released it under an open-source license that enabled anyone to download the source code and freely use and modify it without having to pay Linus any money.

Around the same time, Richard Stallman at the Free Software Foundation, a strong advocate of free and open-source software, was working on an open-source operating system of his own. Rather than focusing initially on the kernel, however, Stallman began by developing open-source versions of all the UNIX tools, utilities and compilers necessary to use and maintain an operating system. By the time he had finished developing this infrastructure, the obvious solution was to combine his work with the kernel Linus had written to create a complete operating system. This combination became known as GNU/Linux. Purists insist that Linux always be referred to as GNU/Linux (in fact, at one time, Richard Stallman refused to give press interviews to any publication which failed to refer to Linux as GNU/Linux). This is not unreasonable given that the GNU tools developed by the Free Software Foundation make up a significant and vital part of GNU/Linux. Unfortunately, most people and publications simply refer to Linux as Linux and this will probably always continue to be the case.

2.4 The Early Days of Red Hat

In 1993 Bob Young created a company named ACC Corporation which, according to Young, he ran from his "wife's sewing closet". The name ACC was intended to represent a catalog business but was also an abbreviation of a small business his wife ran called "Antiques and Collectibles of Connecticut". Among the items sold through the ACC catalog business were Linux CDs and related open-source software.

Around the same time, Marc Ewing had created his own Linux distribution company which he named Red Hat Linux (after his propensity to wear a red baseball cap while at Carnegie Mellon University).

In 1995, ACC acquired Red Hat, adopted the name Red Hat, Inc. and experienced rapid and significant growth. Bob Young stepped down as CEO shortly after the company went public in August of 1999 and has since pursued a number of business and philanthropic efforts including a print-on-demand book publishing company named Lulu and ownership of two Canadian professional sports teams. In 2018, IBM acquired Red Hat, Inc. in a deal valued at $34 billion.

2.5 Red Hat Support

Early releases of Red Hat Linux were shipped to customers on floppy disks and CDs (this, of course, predated the widespread availability of broadband internet connections). When users encountered problems with the software they were only able to contact Red Hat by email. In fact, Bob Young often jokes that this was effective in limiting support requests since, by the time a customer realized they needed help, their computer was usually inoperative and therefore unavailable to be used to send an email message seeking assistance from Red Hat's support team. In later years Red Hat provided better levels of support tied to paid subscriptions and now provides a variety of support levels ranging from "self help" (no support) up to premium support.

2.6 Open Source

Red Hat Enterprise Linux 9 is the current commercial offering from Red Hat and is primarily targeted at corporate, mission critical installations. It is also the cornerstone of an expanding ecosystem of products and services offered by Red Hat. RHEL is an open-source product in that you can download the source code free of charge and build the software yourself if you wish to do so (a task not to be undertaken lightly). If, however, you wish to download a pre-built, ready to install binary version of the software (either with or without support), you have to pay for it.

2.7 The Fedora Project

Red Hat also sponsors the Fedora Project, the goal of which is to provide access to a free Linux operating system (in both source and binary distributions) in the form of Fedora Linux. Fedora Linux also serves as a proving ground for many of the new features that are eventually adopted into the Red Hat Enterprise Linux operating system family and the CentOS derivative.

2.8 CentOS Stream - The Free Alternative

For users unable to afford a Red Hat Enterprise Linux subscription, another option is the CentOS Stream operating system. The CentOS project, initially a community-driven effort but now owned by Red Hat, takes the Red Hat Enterprise Linux source code, removes the Red Hat branding and subscription requirements, compiles it, and provides the distribution for download. Like Fedora, CentOS Stream field tests new operating system features before they are included in a future RHEL release. As such, it may lack stability but provides access to cutting-edge features.

2.9 Summary

The origins of the Linux operating system can be traced back to the work of Linus Torvalds and Richard Stallman in the form of the Linux kernel combined with the tools and compilers built by the GNU project.

Over the years, the open-source nature of Linux has resulted in the release of a wide range of different Linux distributions. One such distribution is Red Hat Enterprise Linux, created by Red Hat, Inc., a company founded by Bob Young and Mark Ewing. Red Hat specializes in providing enterprise level Linux software solutions combined with extensive technical support services.

3. Installing RHEL 9 on a Clean Disk Drive

There are now two ways in which a RHEL 9 system can be deployed. One method is to either purchase new hardware or re-purpose an existing computer system on which to install and run the operating system. Another option is to create a cloud-based operating system instance using services such as Amazon AWS, Google Cloud, or Microsoft Azure (to name but a few). Since cloud-based instances are typically created by selecting a pre-configured, ready-to-run operating system image already optimized for the cloud platform and using that as the basis for the RHEL system, there is no need to perform a manual operating system installation in this situation.

If, on the other hand, you plan to install RHEL 9 on your own hardware, the first step on the path to learning about Red Hat Enterprise Linux 9 involves installing the operating system.

RHEL can be installed either in a clean disk environment (where an entire disk is cleared of any existing partitions and dedicated entirely to RHEL) or in a dual boot environment where RHEL co-exists with another operating system on the disk (typically a member of the Microsoft Windows family of operating systems).

This chapter will cover the clean disk approach to installation from local or remote installation media. Dual boot installation with a Windows 11 system will be covered in *"Dual Booting RHEL 9 with Windows"*.

3.1 Obtaining the RHEL 9 Installation Media

Although RHEL is an open-source operating system, and as such, the source code is freely accessible, the binary installation images are only available as part of a paid Red Hat Enterprise Linux subscription. In addition to access to the installation images for RHEL, subscription levels are available that provide technical support for the operating system. If you already have a paid subscription, log into your Red Hat account to download the operating system. If you want to try RHEL before purchasing, Red Hat provides a 30-day trial. To register for a trial, visit the Red Hat website at the following address:

https://www.redhat.com/en/technologies/linux-platforms/enterprise-linux/try-it

Red Hat Developer program members are also provided access to RHEL 9. Details on joining this program can be found on the Red Hat Developers website at *https://developers.redhat.com*.

RHEL 9 is available for Intel 64-bit (x86_64) and ARM64 (AArch64) CPU architecture families. The installation media can be downloaded as a DVD or boot ISO image for each architecture. The DVD ISO image is self-contained, including all of the packages necessary to install a RHEL system, and is named using the following convention:

Installing RHEL 9 on a Clean Disk Drive

```
rhel-baseos-<version>-<architecture>-dvd.iso
```

For example, the RHEL 9.1 DVD image for 64-bit Intel systems is named as follows:

```
rhel-baseos-9.1-x86_64-dvd.iso
```

On the other hand, the boot ISO image only contains the files necessary to begin the installation and requires access to the full installation media located on a remote server. The boot image can also perform rescue operations on an existing RHEL system. The boot ISO is named using the following convention:

```
rhel-baseos-<version>-<architecture>-boot.iso
```

The RHEL 9.1 boot image for AArch64, for example, is named as follows:

```
rhel-baseos-9.1-x86_64-boot.iso
```

Having downloaded an image, either burn it to disk, or use the steps in the next section to write the media to a USB drive, configure your virtualization environment to treat it as a DVD drive or use the steps outlined later in this chapter to access the installation image over a network connection.

3.2 Writing the ISO Installation Image to a USB Drive

These days it is more likely that an operating system installation will be performed from a USB drive than from a DVD. Having downloaded the ISO installation image for RHEL 9, the steps to write that image to a USB drive will differ depending on whether the drive is attached to a Linux, macOS, or Windows system. The steps outlined in the remainder of this section assume that the USB drive is new or has been reformatted to remove any existing data or partitions:

3.2.1 Linux

The first step in writing an ISO image to a USB drive on Linux is identifying the device name. Before inserting the USB drive, identify the storage devices already detected on the system by listing the devices in */dev* as follows:

```
# ls /dev/sd*
/dev/sda  /dev/sda1  /dev/sda2
```

Attach the USB drive to the Linux system and run the *dmesg* command to get a list of recent system messages, one of which will be a report that the USB drive was detected and will be similar to the following:

```
[  406.241717] sd 6:0:0:0: [sdb] Attached SCSI removable disk
```

This output tells us that we should expect the device name to include "sdb" which we can confirm by listing device names in */dev* again:

```
# ls /dev/sd*
/dev/sda   /dev/sda1   /dev/sda2   /dev/sdb
```

This output shows that the USB drive has been assigned to /dev/sdb. The next step before writing the ISO image to the device is to run the *findmnt* command to make sure it has not been auto-mounted:

```
# findmnt /dev/sdb
TARGET                                              SOURCE     FSTYPE OPTIONS
/run/media/neil/d6bf9574-7e31-4f54-88b1             /dev/sdb ext3    rw,nosuid,no
```

If the *findmnt* command indicates that the USB drive has been mounted, unmount it before continuing:

```
# umount /run/media/neil/d6bf9574-7e31-4f54-88b1
```

Once the filesystem has been unmounted, use the *dd* command as follows to write the ISO image to the drive:

```
# dd if=/path/to/iso/<image name>.iso of=/dev/sdb bs=512k
```

The writing process can take some time (as long as 10 - 15 minutes) depending on the image size and speed of the system on which it is running. Once the image has been written, output similar to the following will appear, and the USB drive will be ready to be used to install RHEL 9:

```
5956+0 records in
5956+0 records out
3122659328 bytes (3.1 GB, 2.9 GiB) copied, 426.234 s, 7.3 MB/s
```

3.2.2 macOS

The first step in writing an ISO image to a USB drive attached to a macOS system is to identify the device using the *diskutil* tool. Before attaching the USB device, open a Terminal window and run the following command:

```
$ diskutil list
/dev/disk0 (internal, physical):
   #:                       TYPE NAME                   SIZE           IDENTIFIER
   0:        GUID_partition_scheme                     *1.0 TB         disk0
   1:                        EFI EFI                    209.7 MB       disk0s1
   2:              Apple_APFS Container disk2           1000.0 GB      disk0s2

/dev/disk1 (internal):
   #:                       TYPE NAME                   SIZE           IDENTIFIER
   0:        GUID_partition_scheme                      28.0 GB        disk1
   1:                        EFI EFI                    314.6 MB       disk1s1
   2:              Apple_APFS Container disk2            27.7 GB        disk1s2

/dev/disk2 (synthesized):
   #:                       TYPE NAME                   SIZE           IDENTIFIER
   0:        APFS Container Scheme -                    +1.0 TB        disk2
                             Physical Stores disk1s2, disk0s2
   1:              APFS Volume Macintosh HD             473.6 GB       disk2s1
   2:              APFS Volume Preboot                  42.1 MB        disk2s2
   3:              APFS Volume Recovery                 517.0 MB       disk2s3
   4:              APFS Volume VM                       1.1 GB         disk2s4
```

Having established a baseline of detected devices, insert the USB drive into a port on the macOS system and rerun the command. The same results should appear with one additional entry for the USB drive resembling the following:

```
/dev/disk3 (external, physical):
   #:                       TYPE NAME                      SIZE        IDENTIFIER
   0:                                                    *16.0 GB      disk3
```

In the above example, the USB drive has been assigned to /dev/disk3. Before proceeding, unmount the disk as follows:

```
$ diskutil unmountDisk /dev/disk3
Unmount of all volumes on disk3 was successful
```

Finally, use the *dd* command to write the ISO image to the device, taking care to reference the raw disk device (/dev/**r**disk3) and entering your user password when prompted:

```
$ sudo dd if=/path/to/iso/image.iso of=/dev/rdisk3 bs=1m
```

Once the image has been written, the USB drive is ready.

3.2.3 Windows/macOS

Several free tools are available for Windows and macOS that will write an ISO image to a USB drive, but one written specifically for writing Linux ISO images is the Fedora Media Writer tool which can be downloaded from the following URL:

https://getfedora.org/en/workstation/download/

Once installed, insert the destination USB drive, launch the writer tool, and choose the *Select .iso file* option as highlighted in Figure 3-1:

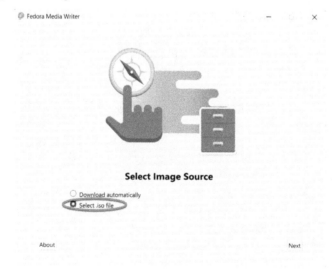

Figure 3-1

Click Next to proceed to the Write Options screen and select the USB Drive before clicking on the *Select...* button:

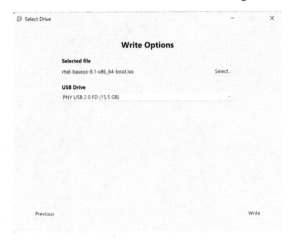

Figure 3-2

In the resulting file selection dialog, navigate to and select the RHEL 9 installation ISO image and click the *Open* button. Finally, click the Write button to start writing the image to the USB drive:

Figure 3-3

Once the image has been written to the device, the device is ready to perform the installation.

3.3 Installing Red Hat Enterprise Linux 9

Insert the RHEL 9 installation media into the appropriate drive and power on the system. If the system tries to boot from the hard disk drive, you will need to enter the BIOS set up for your computer and change the boot order so that it boots from the installation media drive first. Once the system has booted, you will be presented with the following screen:

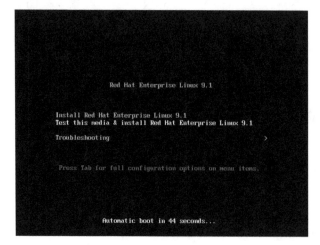

Figure 3-4

Use the arrow keys to navigate between the options and make a selection with the <Enter> key. For example, if the *Troubleshooting* option is selected, the screen shown in Figure 3-5 will appear, including options to boot from the current operating system on the local drive (if one is installed), test the system memory, or rescue an installed RHEL 9 system. An option is also available to perform the installation in basic graphics mode for systems without a graphical console:

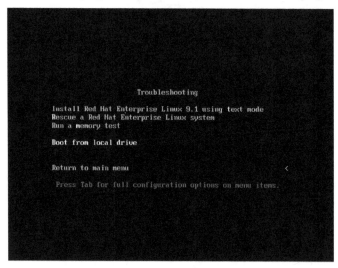

Figure 3-5

If you install the ARM64 image, the options to boot from the local drive and run a memory test may not be available on the troubleshooting screen.

Select the option on the main screen to install Red Hat Enterprise Linux and, after a short delay, the first screen of the graphical installer will appear:

Figure 3-6

Select your preferred language on the first screen before clicking *Continue* to proceed to the main installation screen as shown in Figure 3-7:

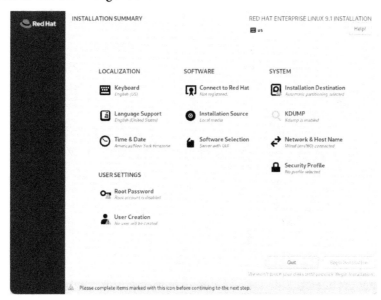

Figure 3-7

Begin by selecting the *Network & Host Name* option, enable a network device on your system, and enter a hostname before clicking the *Apply* button:

Figure 3-8

If your network connection requires additional settings, click on the *Configure...* button to access the advanced network settings screen illustrated in Figure 3-9:

Figure 3-9

Once the hostname has been defined, and a network connection enabled, click *Done* to return to the main screen.

If you wish to change the keyboard, language, or time and date settings, select the corresponding option from the Localization column of the main screen. On the *Time & Date* screen, make a selection corresponding to your geographical location. The choice is also provided to use *Network Time* which automatically synchronizes the system with external Network Time Protocol servers.

Changes to the *Installation Source* settings should not be necessary since the installation is performed from local media. To complete the installation from media located on a remote server, select *Installation Source*, enable the *On the network* option, and then specify the location of the installation media and the type of URL being used. The installation media can, for example, be an ISO image installed either on a remote web server or on a system on the local network using NFS (the topic of NFS file sharing is covered in detail in the chapter entitled *"Using NFS on RHEL 9 to Share Files with Remote Systems"*), or the URL of a remote repository (repositories are essentially online collections of the software, packages, and applications that make up the operating system from which installations onto the local system can be performed).

By default, the installer will perform a Server with GUI installation of RHEL 9. This will consist of the minimum packages necessary to run the operating system and the graphical desktop environment. To select a different installation configuration, choose the *Software Selection* option to display the screen shown below:

Figure 3-10

Use the left-hand panel to select a basic configuration and the right-hand panel to add any additional packages you know you will need after the system starts up. If the desktop environment is not required and you are unsure which packages to install on the system, use the *Minimal install* option and install additional packages as needed once the system has booted. This avoids installing any packages that may never be required.

The *Security Policy* option allows additional security packages to be installed on the system that allow security restrictions that comply with the Security Content Automation Protocol (SCAP) standards to be imposed on the system. While selecting a profile from the list installs the necessary packages, the policy restrictions are not enforced until they are enabled on the running system. Unless you work for a government entity or company that mandates this level of security, selecting a policy on this screen is optional.

The *Kdump* feature, when enabled, writes out the state of the operating system kernel in the event of a system crash. This dump file can help identify the cause of a crash but takes up system memory when enabled. Unless memory is limited on your system, this can be left in the enabled state.

Installing RHEL 9 on a Clean Disk Drive

Having configured the basic settings, the next step is to decide how the hard disk drive will be partitioned to accommodate the operating system.

3.4 Partitioning a Disk for RHEL 9

When the *Installation Destination* option is selected, the installer will present a screen similar to the one illustrated in Figure 3-11 below:

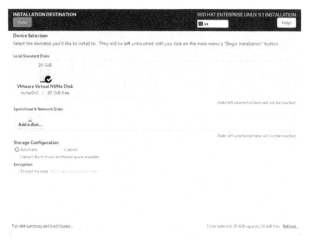

Figure 3-11

By default, the installer is configured to automatically install the operating system using the available space on the currently selected disk drive and to configure standard partition sizes. If the disk previously contained another operating system, these existing partitions will not be deleted, potentially leaving unused space on the drive after RHEL 9 has been installed. To remove any existing partitions so that they can be reclaimed and used by RHEL 9, enable the *I would like to make additional space available* option and click on the *Done* button to display the dialog shown in Figure 3-12:

Figure 3-12

To reclaim space, select a partition that is no longer needed and mark it for removal by clicking the *Delete* button. Once all the partitions to be removed have been selected, click on the *Reclaim Space* button to perform the deletion. The reclaimed space will now be used automatically by the RHEL 9 installer.

To manually configure the layout of the disk in terms of how the available space will be allocated, change the *Storage Allocation* setting from *Automatic* to *Custom* and click *Done* to display the Manual Partitioning screen (Figure 3-13):

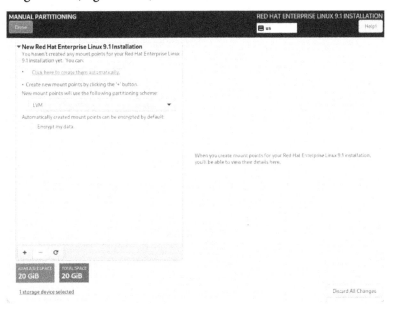

Figure 3-13

The manual partitioning screen allows configuring the disk using Logical Volume Management (LVM) or standard partitioning. LVM is the recommended option because it provides flexibility in terms of managing partition sizes once the system is up and running (LVM is covered in detail in the chapter entitled *"Adding a New Disk to a RHEL 9 Volume Group and Logical Volume"*).

Once a partitioning scheme has been selected, the last step is to decide on the sizes of the partitions and the corresponding filesystem mount points. In general, the default configuration provided by the *Click here to create them automatically* option will meet most system needs. However, to manually create partitions and allocate mount points, click the + button to declare and assign each partition manually.

Another option is to select automatic partition creation and then use the resulting screen to change the partition configuration as needed manually. Figure 3-14, for example, shows the partition configuration defined by selecting the automatic creation option and allows the settings for each partition to be modified before any changes are made to the disk:

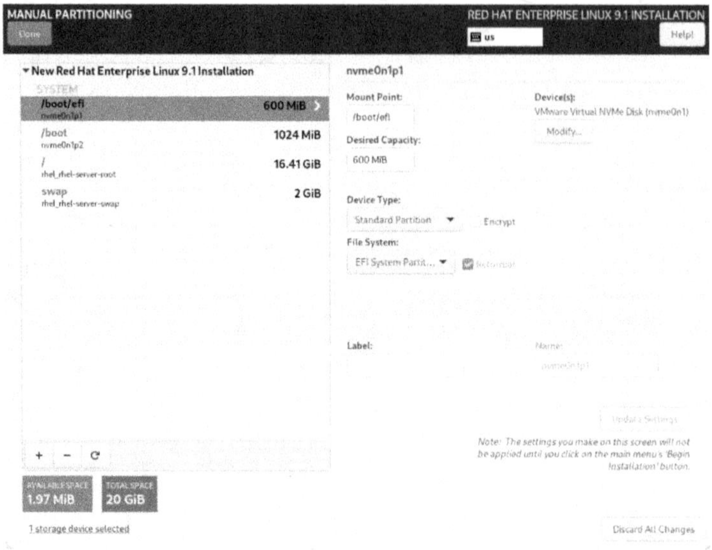

Installing RHEL 9 on a Clean Disk Drive

Figure 3-14

Once the disk has been configured, click on *Done*, review the summary of the changes to be made to the disk (Figure 3-15), followed by the *Accept Changes* button:

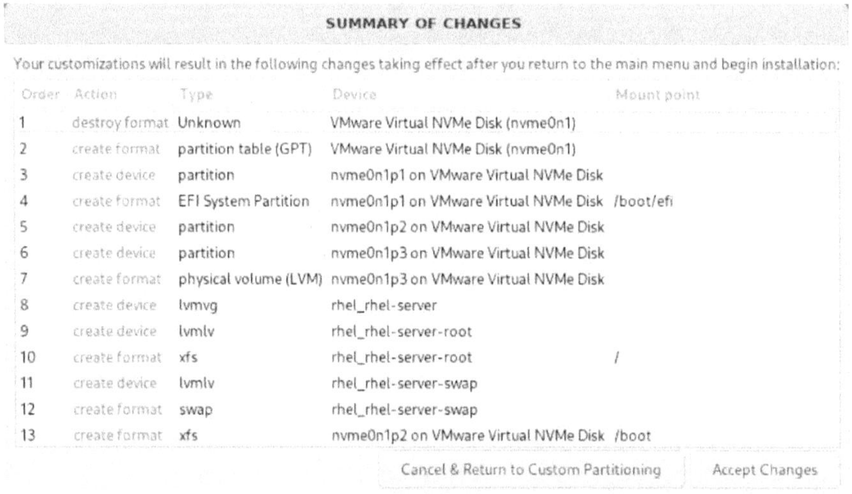

Figure 3-15

3.5 Disk Encryption

RHEL 9 also allows the disk's contents to be protected by encryption. This will require a passphrase to be entered each time the system boots. To enable encryption, select the *Encrypt my data* option on the main *Installation Destination* screen and, after clicking the *Done* button, enter the passphrase in the dialog shown in Figure 3-16:

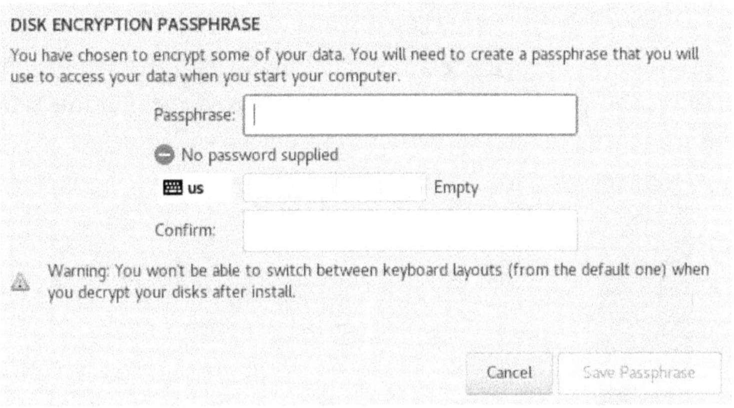

DISK ENCRYPTION PASSPHRASE

You have chosen to encrypt some of your data. You will need to create a passphrase that you will use to access your data when you start your computer.

Passphrase: |

● No password supplied

⌨ us   Empty

Confirm:

⚠ Warning: You won't be able to switch between keyboard layouts (from the default one) when you decrypt your disks after install.

Cancel   Save Passphrase

Figure 3-16

3.6 User Settings

Before the installation can be completed, you must create a root password and an optional user account. The root, or super-user account, is a special user with administrative privileges on the system. While you will generally use your own account to log into the system, you will need root privileges to configure the system and perform other administrative tasks.

Select the Root Password option and enter a suitably secure password. Options are also available to lock the root account, so it cannot be accessed and to allow access to the root account over remote connections to the system via password authentication. In general, it is recommended to leave the root account unlocked but to disallow remote SSH access using password access. If remote root access is required, it should be implemented using SSH key-based authentication, a topic we will be covering in the *"Configuring SSH Key-based Authentication on RHEL 9"* chapter of this book.

Next, select the User Creation option and enter a user name and password. If you would like this user to be able to perform administrative tasks using the *sudo* command, also enable the *Make this user administrator* checkbox. If this option is not enabled, the user must use the *su* command and enter the root password to gain root privileges (assuming that the option outlined above to lock the root account was not enabled). If the user you add will need to perform administrative tasks, sudo is the recommended option, and the checkbox should be enabled.

3.7 Registering the System

After the installation process has been completed and the system is running, the system must be registered with Red Hat before any updates, or additional packages can be installed. At the time of writing, installing the ARM64 version of RHEL 9 without first registering was possible, but the X86_64 version requires registration before installation. To register the system, select the Connect to Red Hat option and choose either the Account or Activation key option, depending on how you obtained your RHEL license. Once you have entered the information, click the Register button to complete the registration process.

3.8 The Physical Installation

Having made the appropriate package selections, clicking *Begin Installation* will start partitioning the disks and installing the packages that match the chosen installation settings. During this phase, the installation progress screen shown in Figure 3-17 will appear:

Figure 3-17

Once all the system packages have been installed and configured, remove the installation media and click *Reboot System* to restart the system.

3.9 Final Configuration Steps

What appears on the console when the system has started will depend on whether the *Workstation* or *Server with GUI* option was chosen from the Software Selection installation screen. If either of these options was selected during installation, the GNOME Display Manager (GDM) login screen will appear. On the other hand, if the minimal or server configuration options were selected, the text-based login prompt will be displayed. Regardless of the configuration, log into the system as the user created during the installation process's final steps.

In the case of a *Workstation* or *Server with GUI* installation, the GNOME initial setup tool will launch and offer a guided tour of the desktop environment.

If you did not register your system before starting the installation, you can do so at the command prompt or a Terminal window in the case of the desktop environment. To launch a Terminal session on the desktop, click *Activities* in the menu bar followed by the *Terminal* icon in the panel at the bottom of the screen, as shown in Figure 3-18:

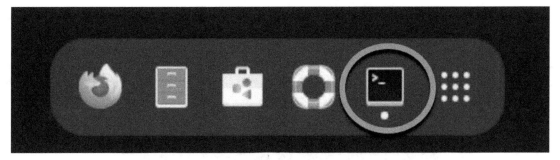

Figure 3-18

At the prompt, use the *sudo* command to gain root privileges and enter your user password:

```
$ sudo su -
```

Next, use the *subscription-manager* tool to register the system with Red Hat, entering your Red Hat Access username and password when prompted to do so:

```
# subscription-manager register
Registering to: subscription.rhsm.redhat.com:443/subscription
Username: myusername
Password:
The system has been registered with ID: 22f0ca3f-8d03-4933-be95-d6c4d8e3fe1a
The registered system name is: rhelserver1.
```

Finally, attach the system to a subscription service as follows:

```
# subscription-manager attach --auto
Installed Product Current Status:
Product Name: Red Hat Enterprise Linux for x86_64
Status:       Subscribed
```

3.10 Installing Updates

As with most operating systems today, each particular release of a RHEL distribution continues to evolve after it has been released to the public. This generally takes the form of bug fixes, security updates, and, occasionally, new features that may be downloaded over the internet and installed on your system.

Best practices dictate that the first step after installing RHEL is to make ensure any available updates are applied to the system. This can be achieved via the command-line prompt in a Terminal window using the *dnf* package manager tool. To check for the availability of updates, run the following command:

```
# dnf check-update
```

Any pending updates may be applied, once again, using the *dnf* tool:

```
# dnf update
```

Upon execution, the *dnf* tool will provide a list of available packages for update and prompt for permission to perform the update.

Installing RHEL 9 on a Clean Disk Drive

Once the update is complete, the installation is essentially finished, and RHEL 9 is ready for use.

3.11 Displaying Boot Messages

During the boot process, RHEL 9 will display the Red Hat Graphical Boot (RHGB) screen, which hides from view all of the boot messages generated by the system as it loads. To make these messages visible during the boot process (as shown in Figure 3-19), press the keyboard Esc key while the system is starting:

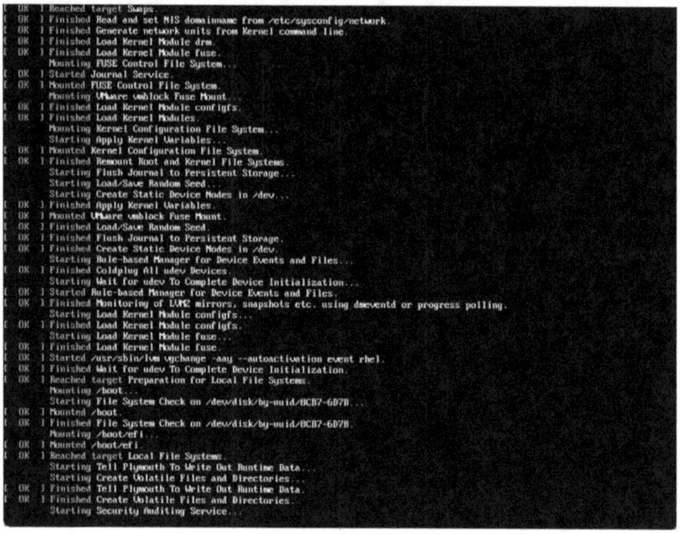

Figure 3-19

The default behavior can be changed so that messages are always displayed by default by editing the */etc/default/grub* file and changing the GRUB_CMDLINE_LINUX setting, which, by default, will resemble the following:

```
GRUB_CMDLINE_LINUX="... rhgb quiet"
```

To remove the graphical boot screen so that messages are visible without pressing the Esc key, remove the "rhgb" option from the setting:

```
GRUB_CMDLINE_LINUX="... rhgb quiet"
```

This change will cause the system to display only a subset of the boot messages generated by the system. To show all messages generated by the system, also remove the "quiet" option:

```
GRUB_CMDLINE_LINUX="... quiet"
```

Once the changes have been made, run the following command to generate a new boot configuration to take effect the next time the system starts:

```
# grub2-mkconfig --output=/boot/grub2/grub.cfg
```

3.12 Summary

The first step in working with RHEL 9 is to install the operating system. In the case of a cloud-based server, this task is typically performed automatically when an operating system image is selected for the system based on a range of options offered by the cloud service provider. Installation on your own hardware, however, involves downloading the installation media as an ISO image, writing that image to suitable storage such as a DVD or USB drive, and booting from it. Once running, the installation process allows a range of options to be configured, ranging from networking, whether the installation should proceed from the local media or via a remote server or repository, the packages to be installed, and the partitioning of the disk. Once installation is complete, it is important to install any operating system updates that may have been released since the original installation image was created.

4. Dual Booting RHEL 9 with Windows

Like most Linux distributions, Red Hat Enterprise Linux 9 will happily co-exist on a hard disk drive with just about any version of Windows up to and including Windows 11. This is a concept known as dual-booting. When you power up the system, you will be presented with a menu providing the option to boot either your RHEL 9 installation or Windows. Obviously, you can only run one operating system at a time. Still, it is worth noting that the files on the Windows partition of your disk drive will be available to you from RHEL 9 regardless of whether your Windows partition was formatted using NTFS, FAT16, or FAT32.

This installation method involves shrinking the size of the existing Windows partitions and then installing RHEL 9 into the reclaimed space. This chapter will assume that RHEL 9 is being installed on a system currently running Windows 11.

4.1 Partition Resizing

To accommodate RHEL on a disk drive that already contains a Windows installation, the first step involves shrinking the Windows partition to make some room. The recommended course of action is to use the Windows Disk Management interface to reduce the partition size before attempting to install RHEL 9.

To access Disk Management on Windows 11, right-click on the Start menu and select the option from the resulting menu as highlighted in Figure 4-1:

Figure 4-1

Dual Booting RHEL 9 with Windows

Once loaded, the Disk Management tool will display a graphical representation of the disk drives detected on the system:

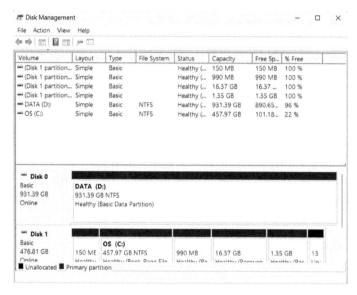

Figure 4-2

Right-click on the partition you wish to reduce in size and select *Shrink Volume...* from the popup menu. The tool will calculate the maximum amount by which the volume size can be reduced without data loss (a process that can take several minutes depending on the overall size of the partition). Once this analysis is complete, a dialog similar to the one in Figure 4-3 below will appear:

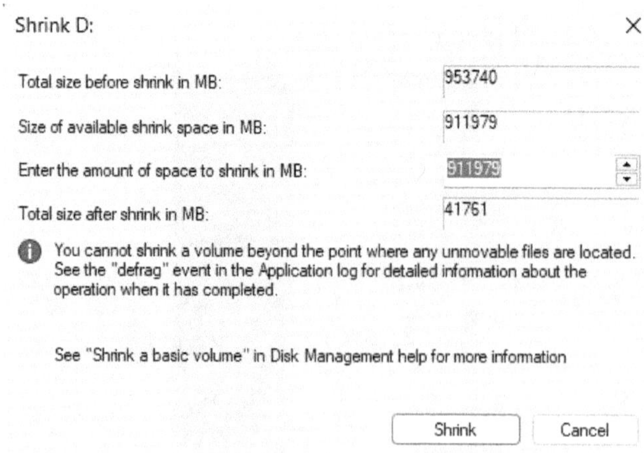

Figure 4-3

Specify a value in the *Enter amount of space to shrink in the MB* field and click the *Shrink* button to proceed. Once the resizing operation is complete, reboot using the RHEL 9 installation media (as outlined in *"Installing RHEL 9 on a Clean Disk Drive"*) and install using the new free space. During the RHEL 9 installation process, this can be achieved by selecting the Installation Destination option on the Installation Summary screen and ensuring that the Automatic storage configuration option is selected. This will automatically install RHEL 9 into the unallocated space created when the Windows partition was reduced in size.

Once installation of RHEL onto the disk is complete and the system has restarted, the standard RHEL boot menu will appear, including an additional option to boot the Windows system:

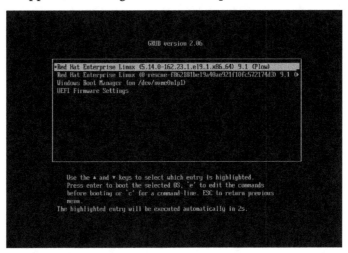

Figure 4-4

4.2 Changing the Default Boot Option

When the system starts, the boot options screen will appear, and wait 5 seconds for the user to choose an operating system. If no selection has been made before the timeout elapses, the default operating system will be started. The default operating system will be the standard (non-rescue) RHEL 9 image on a newly configured system. This default can, however, be changed from within RHEL.

A range of boot configuration options (including the 5-second timeout and the boot RHGB settings outlined in *"Installing RHEL 9 on a Clean Disk Drive"*) are declared in the */etc/default/ grub* file, which reads as follows on a new installation:

```
GRUB_TIMEOUT=5
GRUB_DISTRIBUTOR="$(sed 's, release .*$,,g' /etc/system-release)"
GRUB_DEFAULT=saved
GRUB_DISABLE_SUBMENU=true
GRUB_TERMINAL_OUTPUT="console"
GRUB_CMDLINE_LINUX="crashkernel=1G-4G:192M,4G-64G:256M,64G-:512M resume=/dev/
mapper/rhel-swap rd.lvm.lv=rhel/root rd.lvm.lv=rhel/swap rhgb quiet"
GRUB_DISABLE_RECOVERY="true"
GRUB_ENABLE_BLSCFG=true
```

The first step in changing the default boot system is to declare the GRUB_SAVEDEFAULT setting

Dual Booting RHEL 9 with Windows

within this file:

```
GRUB_TIMEOUT=5
GRUB_DISTRIBUTOR="$(sed 's, release .*$,,g' /etc/system-release)"
GRUB_DEFAULT=saved
GRUB_SAVEDEFAULT=true
.

.
```

This setting saves a new default value within the boot configuration. Next, run the *grub2-set-default* command to change the default setting using a numbering system that counts the first option as 0. For example, if the Windows 11 option is position 3 in the menu, the command to make Windows 11 the default boot option would read as follows:

```
# grub2-set-default 2
```

Check that the new setting has taken effect by running the following command:

```
# grub2-editenv list
saved_entry=f862181be19a40ae921f10fc572174d3-5.14.0-162.23.1.el9_1.x86_64
menu_auto_hide=1
boot_success=1
boot_indeterminate=0
save_default=true
```

Note that the *saved_entry* value is now set to the Linux boot partition. After changing the default, regenerate the boot configuration file as follows:

```
# grub2-mkconfig --output=/boot/grub2/grub.cfg
```

Reboot the system and verify that the boot menu defaults to the Windows option and that Windows loads after the timeout expires.

4.3 Accessing the Windows Partition from RHEL 9

When running RHEL in a dual boot configuration, it is possible to access files located on the Windows partition by manually mounting the partition from the command line. Before doing so, however, some additional packages need to be installed on the system. First, the fuse kernel module needs to be downloaded and installed:

```
# dnf install fuse
# modprobe fuse
```

Next, the Fuse NTFS driver needs to be installed. Unfortunately, this package is not included in the standard RHEL 9 repositories, so the Extra Packages for Enterprise Linux (EPEL) repository needs to be added to the system as follows:

```
# subscription-manager repos --enable codeready-builder-for-rhel-9-$(arch)-rpms
# dnf install https://dl.fedoraproject.org/pub/epel/epel-release-latest-9.noarch.
rpm
```

With the EPEL repository added, the driver can now be installed:

```
# dnf install ntfs-3g
```

Once the requisite packages are installed, the next step is to create a directory to use as the mount point for our Windows partition. In this example, we will create a directory named */mnt/windows*:

```
# mkdir /mnt/windows
```

To identify the device name that has been assigned to the Windows partition, use the *fdisk* command as follows:

```
# fdisk -l
.
.
Device                Start         End   Sectors  Size Type
/dev/nvme0n1p1         2048      206847    204800  100M EFI System
/dev/nvme0n1p2       206848      239615     32768   16M Microsoft reserved
/dev/nvme0n1p3       239616    49362943  49123328 23.4G Microsoft basic data
/dev/nvme0n1p4    132933632   134213631   1280000  625M Windows recovery environment
/dev/nvme0n1p5     49362944    51460095   2097152    1G Linux filesystem
/dev/nvme0n1p6     51460096   132933631  81473536 38.8G Linux LVM
```

In the above output, the main Windows partition containing the files we need access to is represented by */dev/nvme0n1p3*. Next, we need to run the *mount* command (assuming the Windows partition is */dev/nvme0n1p3*) as follows:

```
# mount /dev/nvme0n1p3 /mnt/windows
```

Check that the mount was successful by listing the contents of the top-level directory of the mount point:

```
# ls /mnt/windows
'$Recycle.Bin'              ProgramData              swapfile.sys
'Documents and Settings'  'Program Files'          'System Volume Information'
 pagefile.sys             'Program Files (x86)'      Users
 PerfLogs                   Recovery                 Windows
```

To automate the mount each time the system is booted, add the appropriate mount line to the */etc/fstab* file:

```
/dev/nvme0n1p3 /mnt/windows ntfs defaults 0 0
```

To unmount the Windows file system at any time:

```
# umount /mnt/windows
```

4.4 Summary

RHEL 9 can safely co-exist on the same disk drive as a Windows operating system by creating a dual boot environment. This involves shrinking the Windows system's space to make room for RHEL 9 before performing the installation. Once RHEL has been installed, the boot menu configuration must be modified to include the option to boot from Windows. To access the Windows filesystem from within RHEL, the Fuse NTFS driver needs to be installed and used to mount the Windows partitions.

5. Allocating Windows Disk Partitions to RHEL 9

In the previous chapter, we looked at installing Red Hat Enterprise Linux 9 on the same disk as Windows. This so-called "dual boot" configuration allows the user to have both operating systems installed on a single disk drive with the option to boot one or the other when the system is powered on.

This chapter is intended for users who have decided they like RHEL 9 enough to delete Windows entirely from the disk and use the resulting space for Linux. In the following sections, we will work through this process step by step.

5.1 Unmounting the Windows Partition

If the steps in the *"Dual Booting RHEL 9 with Windows"* chapter were followed to mount the Windows partition from within RHEL 9, steps should be taken to unmount the partition before continuing with this chapter. Assuming that the Windows partition was mounted as */mnt/windows*, it can be unmounted as follows:

```
# umount /mnt/windows
```

The */etc/fstab* file should also be edited to remove the */mnt/windows* auto-mount if it was previously added.

5.2 Deleting the Windows Partitions from the Disk

The first step in freeing up the Windows partition for use by RHEL is to delete that partition. Before doing so, however, any data you need to keep must be backed up from both the Windows and RHEL partitions. Having done that, it is safe to proceed with this chapter.

To remove the Windows partitions, we first need to identify the disk on which they reside using the *fdisk* tool:

```
# fdisk -l
Disk /dev/nvme0n1: 64 GiB, 68719476736 bytes, 134217728 sectors
Disk model: VMware Virtual NVMe Disk
Units: sectors of 1 * 512 = 512 bytes
Sector size (logical/physical): 512 bytes / 512 bytes
I/O size (minimum/optimal): 512 bytes / 512 bytes
Disklabel type: gpt
Disk identifier: 7A38CD86-091E-4781-BFB0-928FD383C935

Device           Start     End   Sectors   Size Type
/dev/nvme0n1p1    2048  206847    204800   100M EFI System
```

```
/dev/nvme0n1p2     206848     239615     32768    16M Microsoft reserved
/dev/nvme0n1p3     239616   49362943 49123328  23.4G Microsoft basic data
/dev/nvme0n1p4 132933632 134213631  1280000   625M Windows recovery environment
/dev/nvme0n1p5  49362944   51460095  2097152     1G Linux filesystem
/dev/nvme0n1p6  51460096 132933631 81473536  38.8G Linux LVM
```

In the above example output, the system contains one physical disk drive referenced by device name */dev/nvme0n1*. On that disk drive are six partitions accessed via the device names */dev/nvme0n1p1* through */dev/nvme0n1p6*, respectively. Based on the values in the Types column, three Windows-related partitions exist. The first is the Windows system partition, while the second, much larger, partition is the Windows boot partition containing the Windows operating system and user data, followed by the Windows recovery partition.

To remove the partitions, start the *fdisk* tool using the device name of the disk containing the partition (*/dev/nvme0n1* in this instance) and follow the instructions to display the partition and sector information once again:

```
# fdisk /dev/nvme0n1

Welcome to fdisk (util-linux 2.37.4).
Changes will remain in memory only, until you decide to write them.
Be careful before using the write command.

Command (m for help): p

Disk /dev/nvme0n1: 64 GiB, 68719476736 bytes, 134217728 sectors
Disk model: VMware Virtual NVMe Disk
Units: sectors of 1 * 512 = 512 bytes
Sector size (logical/physical): 512 bytes / 512 bytes
I/O size (minimum/optimal): 512 bytes / 512 bytes
Disklabel type: gpt
Disk identifier: 7A38CD86-091E-4781-BFB0-928FD383C935

Device             Start        End   Sectors  Size Type
/dev/nvme0n1p1      2048     206847    204800  100M EFI System
/dev/nvme0n1p2    206848     239615     32768   16M Microsoft reserved
/dev/nvme0n1p3    239616   49362943  49123328 23.4G Microsoft basic data
/dev/nvme0n1p4 132933632 134213631   1280000  625M Windows recovery environment
/dev/nvme0n1p5  49362944   51460095   2097152    1G Linux filesystem
/dev/nvme0n1p6  51460096 132933631  81473536 38.8G Linux LVM

Partition table entries are not in disk order.

Command (m for help):
```

Before proceeding, note the start and end addresses of the partitions we will be deleting (in other words, the start of */dev/nvme0n1p2* and the sector before the start of */dev/nvme0n1p5*).

At the command prompt, delete the Windows partitions (these being partitions 2, 3, and 4 on our example system):

```
Command (m for help): d
Partition number (1-6, default 6): 2

Partition 2 has been deleted.

Command (m for help): d
Partition number (1,3-6, default 6): 3

Partition 3 has been deleted.

Command (m for help): d
Partition number (1,4-6, default 6): 4

Partition 4 has been deleted.
```

Now that we have deleted the Windows partitions, we need to create the new RHEL partition in the vacated disk space. The partition number must match the number of the first partition removed (in this case, 2). It will also be necessary to enter the Start and End sectors of the partition precisely as reported for the old partition (*fdisk* will typically offer the correct values by default, though it is wise to double-check). If you are prompted to remove the NTFS signature, enter Y:

```
Command (m for help): n
Partition number (2-4,7-128, default 2): 2
First sector (206848-134217694, default 206848):
Last sector, +/-sectors or +/-size{K,M,G,T,P} (206848-49362943, default
49362943):

Created a new partition 2 of type 'Linux filesystem' and of size 23.4 GiB.
Command (m for help):
```

Having made these changes the next step is to check that the settings are correct:

```
Command (m for help): p
Disk /dev/nvme0n1: 64 GiB, 68719476736 bytes, 134217728 sectors
Disk model: VMware Virtual NVMe Disk
Units: sectors of 1 * 512 = 512 bytes
Sector size (logical/physical): 512 bytes / 512 bytes
I/O size (minimum/optimal): 512 bytes / 512 bytes
Disklabel type: gpt
Disk identifier: 7A38CD86-091E-4781-BFB0-928FD383C935

Device          Start      End  Sectors  Size Type
/dev/nvme0n1p1   2048   206847   204800  100M EFI System
```

```
/dev/nvme0n1p2   206848  49362943 49156096 23.4G Linux filesystem
/dev/nvme0n1p5 49362944  51460095  2097152   1G Linux filesystem
/dev/nvme0n1p6 51460096 132933631 81473536 38.8G Linux LVM
```

To commit the changes,we now need to write the new partition information to disk and quit from the *fdisk* tool:

```
Command (m for help): w
The partition table has been altered.
Syncing disks.
```

5.3 Formatting the Unallocated Disk Partition

To make the new partition suitable for use by RHEL 9, it needs to have a file system created on it. The recommended file system type for the current release of RHEL is XFS which will be covered in greater detail in the chapter entitled *"Adding a New Disk Drive to a RHEL 9 System"*. Creation of the file system is performed using the *mkfs.xfs* command as follows:

```
# mkfs.xfs -f /dev/nvme0n1p2
meta-data=/dev/nvme0n1p2          isize=512    agcount=4, agsize=1536128 blks
         =                        sectsz=512   attr=2, projid32bit=1
         =                        crc=1        finobt=1, sparse=1, rmapbt=0
         =                        reflink=1    bigtime=1 inobtcount=1
data     =                        bsize=4096   blocks=6144512, imaxpct=25
         =                        sunit=0      swidth=0 blks
naming   =version 2               bsize=4096   ascii-ci=0, ftype=1
log      =internal log            bsize=4096   blocks=3000, version=2
         =                        sectsz=512   sunit=0 blks, lazy-count=1
realtime =none                    extsz=4096   blocks=0, rtextents=0
```

5.4 Mounting the New Partition

Next, we need to mount the new partition. In this example, we will mount it in a directory named */data*. You are free, however, to mount the new partition using any valid mount point you desire or to use it as part of a logical volume (details of which are covered in the chapter entitled *"Adding a New Disk to a RHEL 9 Volume Group and Logical Volume"*). First, we need to create the directory to act as the mount point:

```
# mkdir /data
```

Secondly, we need to edit the mount table in */etc/fstab* so that the partition is automatically mounted each time the system starts. At the bottom of the */etc/fstab* file, add the following line to mount the new partition (modifying the */dev/nvme0n1p2* device to match your environment):

```
/dev/nvme0n1p2   /data   xfs defaults 0 0
```

Finally, we can manually mount the new partition (note that this will not be necessary on subsequent reboots as the partition will automount due to the setting we added to the */etc/fstab* file above):

```
# mount /data
```

To check the partition, run the following command to display the available space:

```
# df -h /data
Filesystem      Size  Used Avail Use% Mounted on
/dev/nvme0n1p2   24G  200M   24G   1% /data
```

5.5 Summary

The Windows partitions in a dual boot configuration can be removed anytime to free up space for an RHEL system by identifying which partitions belong to Windows and then deleting them. Once deleted, the unallocated space can be used to create a new filesystem and mounted to make it available to the RHEL system.

Chapter 6

6. A Guided Tour of the GNOME 40 Desktop

Red Hat Enterprise Linux 9 includes the GNOME 40 desktop environment. Although lacking the complexity of Windows and macOS desktops, GNOME 40 provides an uncluttered and intuitive desktop environment that provides all of the essential features of a windowing environment with the added advantage that it can be learned quickly.

In this chapter, the main features of the GNOME desktop will be covered together with an outline of how basic tasks are performed.

6.1 Installing the GNOME Desktop

If the Workstation or Server with GUI software configuration was selected during the RHEL 9 installation process, the GNOME desktop will be installed and automatically launched each time the system starts.

If any other software configuration had been selected during the RHEL 9 installation process, the GNOME desktop would not have been included in the packages installed on the system. Installing a graphical desktop environment may seem redundant on server-based systems without a display attached. It is worth noting, however, that remote access to the GNOME desktop is also possible; even on headless servers (i.e., servers lacking a monitor, keyboard, and mouse), it may still be beneficial to install the GNOME desktop packages. The topic of establishing remote desktop access will be covered in detail in this book's *"RHEL 9 Remote Desktop Access with VNC"* chapter.

If the installation configuration did not include the GNOME desktop, it can be installed at any time using the following command:

```
# dnf groupinstall workstation
```

Once the installation is complete, the desktop environment may be launched from the command prompt on a monitor as follows:

```
$ startx
```

6.2 An Overview of the GNOME 40 Desktop

The screen shown in Figure 6-1 below shows the appearance of a typical, newly launched GNOME desktop session before any other programs have been launched or configuration changes made:

A Guided Tour of the GNOME 40 Desktop

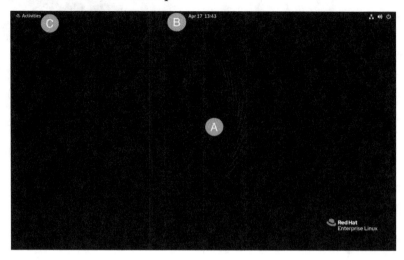

Figure 6-1

The main desktop area (marked A) is where windows will appear when applications and utilities are launched. Unlike other desktop environments, dragging and dropping files or applications onto the desktop is impossible, providing a clean and uncluttered workspace.

The bar at the top of the screen (B) is called the top bar and includes the Activities menu (C), the day and time, and a collection of buttons and icons, including network status, audio volume, battery power, and other status and account settings. In addition, the application menu for the currently active application running on the desktop will also appear in the top bar. Figure 6-2, for example, shows the application menu for the Terminal program:

Figure 6-2

6.3 Activity Overview

Applications and utilities are launched using the Activities Overview, which may be displayed by clicking the Activities button in the top bar or pressing the special key on the keyboard. On Windows keyboards, this is the Windows key; on macOS, the Command key and Chromebooks, the key displaying a magnifying glass.

When displayed, the Activities Overview will resemble Figure 6-3 below:

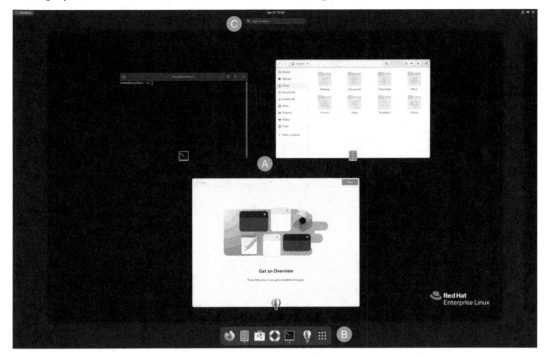

Figure 6-3

The central area of the overview (marked A in Figure 6-3 above) displays all of the currently open app windows. At the bottom of the screen (B) is the dashboard (also referred to as the *dash*) from which apps are launched. By default, the dash will display an icon for a predefined set of commonly used applications and an icon for any currently running applications. If the application is running, it will appear with a dot beneath the icon. To launch an application, simply click on the icon in the dash.

To find an application not included on the dash, one option is to select the right-most grid icon (the square comprising nine dots) to display a browsable list of applications as shown in Figure 6-4:

Figure 6-4

It is also important to be aware that some entries in the list are folders holding additional applications. Items in the grid may be repositioned by dragging and dropping the icons. To add an app to a folder, locate it in the grid and drag it into the folder. Moreover, dragging one icon and dropping it onto another will create a new folder containing both apps and to which other apps may be added.

An alternative to browsing the applications is to perform a search using the search bar (marked C in Figure 6-3 above) and shown in action in the figure below:

Figure 6-5

The list of possible matches will be refined as the text is typed into the search box.

To add an application to the dash for more convenient access, locate the icon for the application, right-click on it, and select the Add to Favorites menu option:

Figure 6-6

To remove an app from the dash, right-click on the icon in the dash and select Remove from Favorites. Alternatively, drag and drop icons to and from the dash to add and remove them.

6.4 Managing Windows

As with other desktop environments, applications run on GNOME in windows. When multiple application windows are open, the Super + Tab keyboard shortcut will display the switcher panel (Figure 6-7), allowing a different window to be chosen as the currently active window (the Super key is either the Windows key or, in the case of a Mac keyboard, the Cmd key):

Figure 6-7

If a single application has more than one window open, the switcher will display those windows in a second panel so that a specific window can be selected:

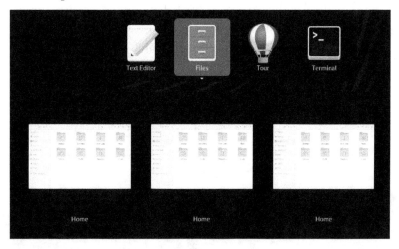

Figure 6-8

To cycle backward through the icons in the switcher, use the Shift+Tab keyboard shortcut.

To maximize a window so it fills the entire screen, click the title bar and drag the window to the top of the screen. To return the window to its original size, click on the title bar and drag it downwards. Alternatively, double-click on the title bar to toggle between window sizes. Similarly, dragging a window to the left or right side of the screen will cause the window to fill that half of the screen.

6.5 Using Workspaces

The area of the screen where the application windows appear is referred to as the workspace, and GNOME 40 allows multiple workspaces to be configured. The GNOME desktop will launch with two workspaces you can switch between using the Super+Alt+Left and Super+Alt+Right key combinations. When a window is added to a blank workspace, another blank workspace is added to the workspace panel, allowing additional workspaces to be created.

Thumbnails of the current workspaces appear beneath the search field in the Activities Overview as shown in Figure 6-9:

Figure 6-9

To switch to a different workspace, select the corresponding thumbnail. To move a window from one workspace to another, display the workspaces panel and drag and drop the application window (either the actual window from the current workspace or the thumbnail window in the workspaces panel) onto the destination workspace. To remove a workspace, close all its windows or move them to another workspace.

6.6 Calendar and Notifications

When the system needs to notify you of an event (such as the availability of system or application updates), a popup panel will appear at the top of the workspace. In addition, access to the calendar and any previous notifications is available by clicking on the day and time in the top bar, as shown in Figure 6-10:

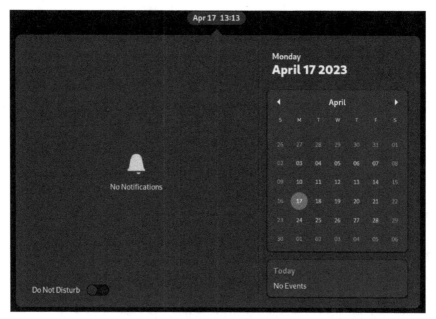

Figure 6-10

6.7 GNOME Desktop Settings

To access the Settings application, click on the row of icons on the right-hand side of the top bar and select Settings as shown in Figure 6-11:

Figure 6-11

The Settings application provides many options, such as Ethernet and WiFi connections, screen background customization options, screen locking and power management controls, and language preferences. To explore the settings available in each category, select an option from the left-hand panel in the Settings window:

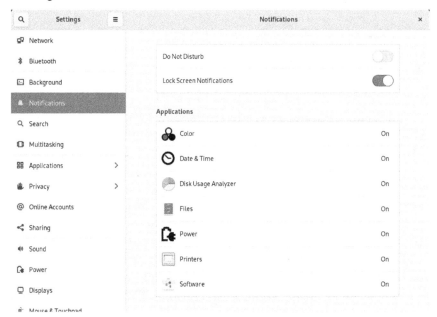

Figure 6-12

A Guided Tour of the GNOME 40 Desktop

The menu shown in Figure 6-11 above also includes options to switch users, adjust audio volume, change to a different WiFi network, and log out, restart, or power off the system.

6.8 Beyond Basic Customization

The GNOME 40 desktop is, by design, a clean and uncluttered environment with minimal customization options. However, it is possible to make additional changes to the desktop. The GNOME Project has developed a tool called GNOME Tweaks for this purpose. Use the following commands to install and run this tool:

```
# dnf install gnome-tweaks
$ gnome-tweaks
```

Once GNOME Tweaks has loaded, the interface shown in Figure 6-13 will appear:

Figure 6-13

A wide range of options for customizing the desktop is now available. Too many to cover in this chapter, so experiment with these settings before proceeding to the next chapter.

6.9 Summary

RHEL 9 includes the GNOME 40 desktop environment, which may either be included during the initial installation or installed later using the *dnf group* package installation feature. Unlike most other desktop environments, GNOME 40 is intended to provide a clean and easy-to-use windowing user interface. Key areas of the GNOME 40 desktop include the top bar, Activities overview, and dash. In addition, GNOME 40 supports multiple workspaces keeping running applications organized and the screen uncluttered. Various configuration options are available within the Settings app, including desktop background settings, audio, network configuration, and WiFi network selection.

Chapter 7

7. An Overview of the Cockpit Web Interface

Although equipped with the latest Linux desktop environment, Red Hat Enterprise Linux 9 is very much a server operating system. As such, most RHEL deployments will be to remote physical servers or as cloud-based virtual machine instances. Invariably, these systems run without a keyboard, mouse, or monitor, with direct access only available via the command prompt over a network connection. This presents a challenge in terms of administering the system from remote locations. While much can certainly be achieved via remote access to the command-line and desktop environments, there needs to be a consistent and cohesive solution to the administrative and monitoring tasks that must be performed daily on an enterprise-level operating system such as RHEL 9.

The Cockpit web-based administration interface provides this functionality. This chapter will explain how to install, configure and access the Cockpit interface while also providing an overview of the key features of Cockpit, many of which will be covered in greater detail in later chapters.

7.1 An Overview of Cockpit

Cockpit is a lightweight, web-based interface that allows general system administrative tasks to be performed remotely. When installed and configured, the system administrator opens a local browser window and navigates to the Cockpit port on the remote server. After loading the Cockpit interface into the browser and logging in, a wide range of tasks can be performed visually using administration and monitoring tools.

Behind the scenes, Cockpit uses the same tools to perform tasks typically used when working at the command line and updates automatically to reflect changes occurring elsewhere on the system. This allows Cockpit to be used with other administration tools and techniques without the risk of one approach overriding another. Cockpit can also be configured to access more than one server, allowing multiple servers to be administered and monitored simultaneously through a single browser session.

Cockpit is installed by default with a wide range of tools already bundled and allows additional extension plugins to be installed as needed. Cockpit is also designed so that you can create your own extensions using a combination of HTML and JavaScript to add missing or custom functionality.

Cockpit's modular design also allows many features to be embedded into other web-based applications.

7.2 Installing and Enabling Cockpit

Cockpit is generally not installed on RHEL 9 by default but can be set up and enabled in a few simple steps. The first step is to install the Cockpit package as follows:

```
# dnf install cockpit
```

Next, the Cockpit socket service needs to be enabled:

```
# systemctl enable --now cockpit.socket
```

Finally, the necessary ports need to be opened on the firewall to allow remote browser connections to reach Cockpit if a firewall is enabled on your system (for details on firewalls, refer to the chapter entitled *"RHEL 9 Firewall Basics"*).

```
# firewall-cmd --add-service=cockpit --permanent
# firewall-cmd --reload
```

7.3 Accessing Cockpit

If you have access to the desktop environment of the server on which Cockpit has been installed, open a browser window and navigate to *https://localhost:9090* to access the Cockpit sign-in screen. If, on the other hand, the server is remote, navigate to the server using the domain name or IP address (for example, *https://myserver.com*:9090).

When the connection is established, the browser may warn that the connection is not secure. This is because the Cockpit service uses a self-signed certificate. Select the option to proceed to the website or, to avoid this message in the future, select the advanced option and add an exception for the server address.

Once connected, the browser will load the login page shown in Figure 7-1 below:

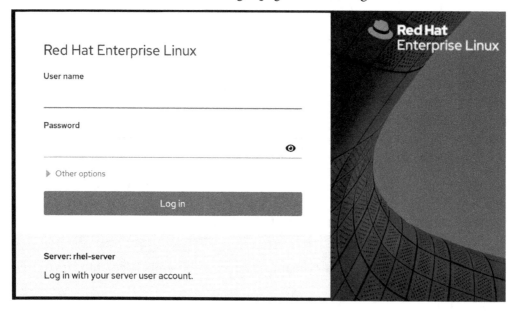

Figure 7-1

Sign in to the Cockpit interface either as root or with your user account credentials. Note that some tasks will be restricted within the Cockpit interface when signed in as a user due to permission constraints. In this situation, the Cockpit console will display a button labeled "Limited Access," as shown in Figure 7-2:

Figure 7-2

To elevate your privileges, click on the limited access button and enter your password when you are prompted to do so:

Figure 7-3

After signing in, Cockpit will display the Overview screen.

7.4 Overview

The Overview screen provides an overview of the current system, including access to CPU, memory, storage, and network activity performance metrics. This screen also includes information about the system, including the underlying hardware, hostname, system time, and whether the system software is up to date. Options are also provided to restart or shut down the system.

Figure 7-4, for example, shows the Overview page of the Cockpit interface:

An Overview of the Cockpit Web Interface

Figure 7-4

For more information on a particular category, click on the corresponding link. Figure 7-5, for example, shows the system usage and metrics screen:

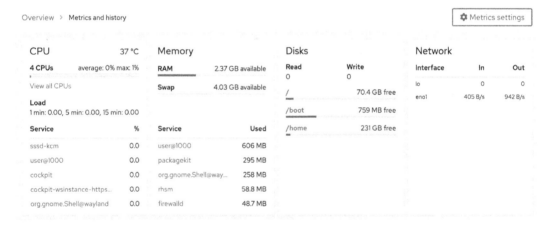

Figure 7-5

7.5 Logs

When the Logs category is selected, Cockpit displays the contents of the *systemd* journal logs. Choosing a log entry will display the entire log message. The log entries are ordered with the most recent at the top, and menus are included to filter the logs for different time durations and based on message severity.

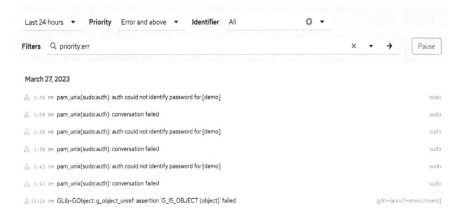

Figure 7-6

7.6 Storage

Select the Storage option to review and manage the storage on the system, including disks, partitions, and volume groups, Network File System (NFS) mounts, and RAID storage. This screen also allows disk I/O activity to be monitored in real-time and lists log output from the system *udisksd* service used to query and manage storage devices:

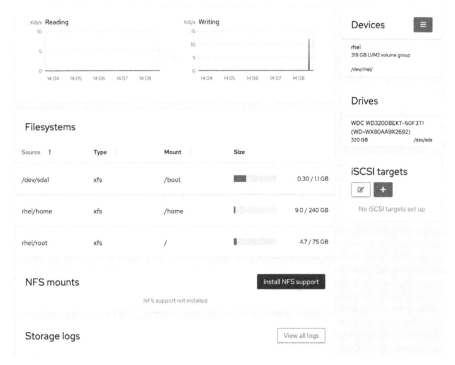

Figure 7-7

7.7 Networking

The Networking screen provides information on various network-related configurations and services, including network interfaces and firewall settings. In addition, it allows configuration changes such as creating network bridges or setting up virtual networks:

Figure 7-8

7.8 Accounts

Select this option to view the current user accounts configured on the system and create accounts for additional users. The topic of user management will be covered later in the chapter entitled *"Managing RHEL 9 Users and Groups"*:

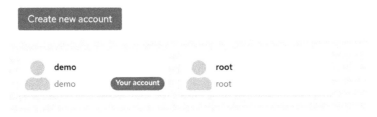

Figure 7-9

Click on an existing account to view details and make changes. The user account details page may also be used to review and add Public SSH keys to the user's account for remote access to the server, as outlined in the chapter *"Configuring SSH Key-based Authentication on RHEL 9"*.

7.9 Services

This screen displays a list of the system services running on the server and allows those services to be added, removed, stopped, and started.

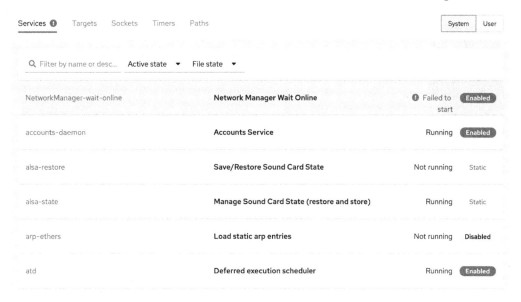

Figure 7-10

The topic of services will be covered in detail in the chapter *"Managing RHEL 9 systemd Units"*.

7.10 Applications

As previously mentioned, additional functionality can be added to Cockpit as extensions. These can either be self-developed extensions or those provided by third parties. The Applications screen lists installed extensions and allows extensions to be added or removed:

Figure 7-11

7.11 Virtual Machines

Virtualization allows multiple operating system instances to run simultaneously on a single computer system, with each system running inside its own *virtual machine*. The Virtual Machines Cockpit extension provides a way to create and manage the virtual machine guests installed on the server:

An Overview of the Cockpit Web Interface

Figure 7-12

The Virtual Machines extension is not installed by default but can be added via the Cockpit Applications screen or by running the following command:

```
# dnf install cockpit-machines
```

The use of virtualization with RHEL 9 is covered starting with the chapter *"An Overview of Virtualization Techniques"*.

7.12 Software Updates

If any software updates are available for the system, they will be listed here and can be installed from this screen:

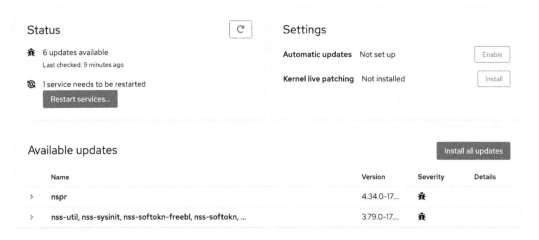

Figure 7-13

7.13 Terminal

As the name suggests, the Terminal screen provides access to the command-line prompt:

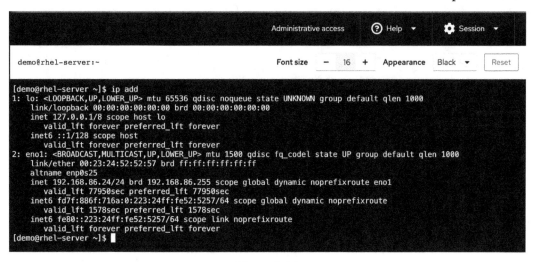

Figure 7-14

7.14 Connecting to Multiple Servers

Cockpit can be configured to administer multiple servers from within a single session. To add another host to the Cockpit session, click on the button highlighted in Figure 7-15 to display the Hosts panel:

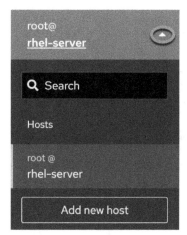

Figure 7-15

Click the *Add new host* button and enter the IP address or hostname of the other system and select a color by which to distinguish this server from any others added to Cockpit before clicking on the Add button:

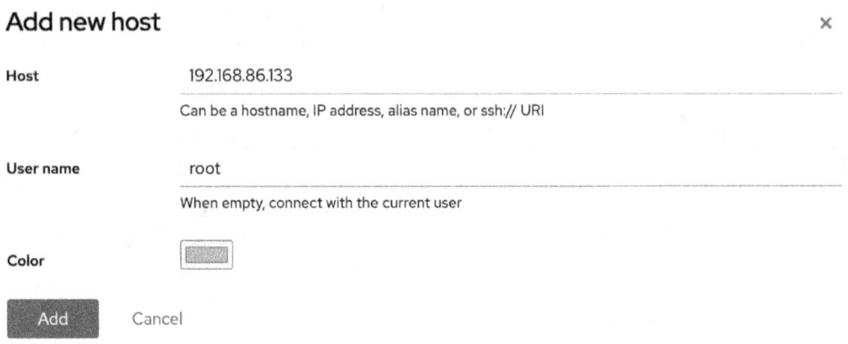

Add new host   ✕

Host	192.168.86.133
	Can be a hostname, IP address, alias name, or ssh:// URI
User name	root
	When empty, connect with the current user
Color	▭

[Add]   Cancel

Figure 7-16

Cockpit will ask you to accept a new SSH key if you are connecting to the remote server for the first time. After accepting the key, you will be prompted to enter the password for the user name specified in Figure 7-16 above. The option is also provided to set up and authorize a password-protected SSH key to enable automatic login to the second host system next time you need to access it:

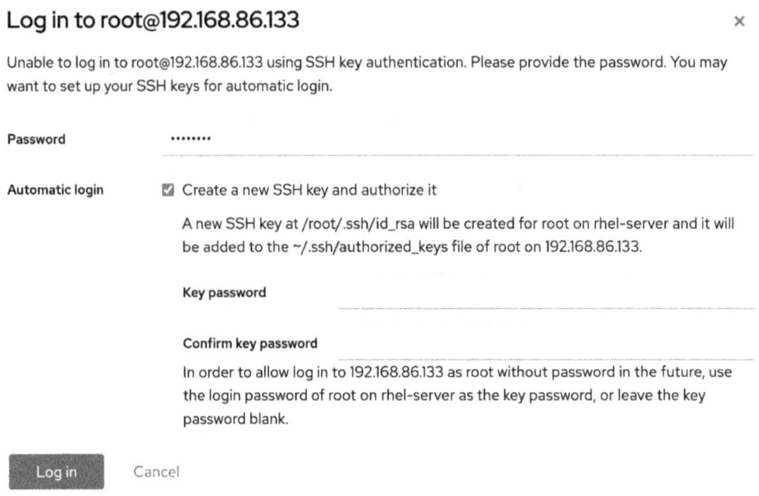

Log in to root@192.168.86.133   ✕

Unable to log in to root@192.168.86.133 using SSH key authentication. Please provide the password. You may want to set up your SSH keys for automatic login.

Password	••••••••
Automatic login	☑ Create a new SSH key and authorize it
	A new SSH key at /root/.ssh/id_rsa will be created for root on rhel-server and it will be added to the ~/.ssh/authorized_keys file of root on 192.168.86.133.
	Key password
	Confirm key password
	In order to allow log in to 192.168.86.133 as root without password in the future, use the login password of root on rhel-server as the key password, or leave the key password blank.

[Log in]   Cancel

Figure 7-17

To switch between the hosts, display the Hosts panel (Figure 7-15 above) and select the required system.

7.15 Enabling Stored Metrics

In a standard installation, Cockpit does not retain any performance metric data beyond what is displayed in the short time window covered by the graphs. To retain the data collected by Cockpit, the Cockpit Co-Pilot (PCP) package needs to be installed. Begin by installing the *cockpit-pcp* package as follows:

```
# dnf install cockpit-pcp
```

After installing cockpit-pcp, log out of the current Cockpit session and back in.

Next, display the Metrics and history screen and click on the *Metrics settings* button to display the screen shown in Figure 7-18, switch on the *Collect metrics* option, and click Save:

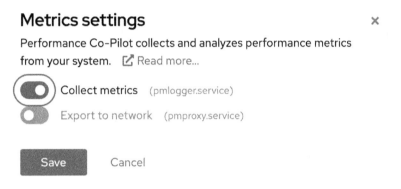

Figure 7-18

After sufficient time has elapsed for Cockpit to gather data, the metric information will appear as shown in Figure 7-19, categorized in hourly blocks:

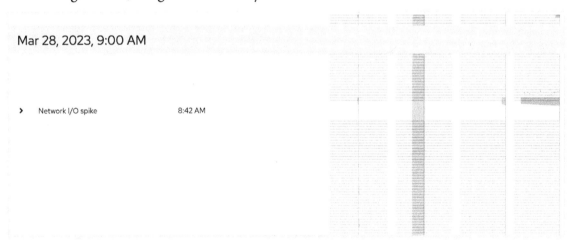

Figure 7-19

7.16 Summary

The Cockpit web interface allows remote system administration tasks to be performed visually from within a web browser without relying on the command prompt and command-line tools. Once installed and enabled, the system administrator opens a web browser, connects to the remote server, and signs into the Cockpit interface. Behind the scenes, Cockpit uses the same command-line tools as those available via the command prompt, allowing both options to be used without the risk of configuration conflicts. In addition, Cockpit uses a modular framework enabling additional extensions to be added and for custom extensions to be developed and integrated. A Cockpit session can be used to administer a single server or configured to access multiple servers simultaneously.

8. Using the Bash Shell on RHEL 9

An essential part of learning to work with RHEL 9 and Linux distributions generally involves gaining proficiency in working in the shell environment. While graphical desktop environments such as GNOME, included with Linux, provide a user-friendly interface to the operating system, the shell environment provides far greater capabilities, flexibility, and automation than can ever be achieved using graphical desktop tools. The shell environment also provides a means for interacting with the operating system when a desktop environment is unavailable, a common occurrence when working with a server-based operating system such as RHEL 9 or a damaged system that will not fully boot.

Therefore, this chapter aims to provide an overview of the default shell environment on RHEL 9 (specifically the Bash shell).

8.1 What is a Shell?

The shell is an interactive command interpreter environment within which commands may be typed at a prompt or entered into a file as a script and executed. The origins of the shell can be traced back to the early days of the UNIX operating system. In fact, in the early days of Linux, before the introduction of graphical desktops, the shell was the only way for a user to interact with the operating system.

A variety of shell environments have been developed over the years. The first widely used shell was the Bourne shell, written by Stephen Bourne at Bell Labs.

Yet another early creation was the C shell which shared some syntax similarities with the C Programming Language and introduced usability enhancements such as command-line editing and history.

The Korn shell (developed by David Korn at Bell Labs) is based on features provided by both the Bourne and C shells.

The default shell on RHEL 9 is the Bash shell (shorthand for Bourne Again SHell). This shell, which began life as an open-source version of the Bourne shell, was developed for the GNU Project by Brian Fox and is based on features provided by both the Bourne shell and the C shell.

8.2 Gaining Access to the Shell

From within the GNOME desktop environment, the shell prompt may be accessed from a Terminal window by selecting the Activities option in the top bar, entering Terminal into the search bar, and clicking the Terminal icon.

When remotely logging into a RHEL 9 server, for example, using SSH, the user is presented with a shell prompt. The chapter entitled *"Configuring SSH Key-based Authentication on RHEL 9"* will cover details on accessing a remote server using SSH. When booting a server-based system in which a desktop environment has not been installed, the shell is entered immediately after the user completes the login procedure at the physical console terminal or remote login session.

8.3 Entering Commands at the Prompt

Commands are entered at the shell command prompt simply by typing the command and pressing the Enter key. While some commands perform tasks silently, most will display some form of output before returning to the prompt. For example, the *ls* command can be used to display the files and directories in the current working directory:

```
$ ls
Desktop  Documents  Downloads  Music  Pictures  Public  Templates  Videos
```

The available commands are either built into the shell itself or reside on the physical file system. The location on the file system of a command may be identified using the *which* command. For example, to find out where the *ls* executable resides on the file system:

```
$ which ls
alias ls='ls --color=auto'
        /usr/bin/ls
```

Clearly, the *ls* command resides in the */usr/bin* directory. Note also that an alias is configured, a topic that will be covered later in this chapter. Using the *which* command to locate the path to commands built into the shell will result in a message indicating the executable cannot be found. For example, attempting to find the location of the *history* command (which is built into the shell rather than existing as an executable on the file system) will result in output similar to the following:

```
$ which history
/usr/bin/which: no history in (/home/demo/.local/bin:/home/demo/bin:/usr/share/
Modules/bin:/usr/local/bin:/usr/bin:/usr/local/sbin:/usr/sbin)
```

8.4 Getting Information about a Command

Many of the commands available to the Linux shell can seem cryptic. To find out detailed information about what a command does and how to use it, use the *man* command specifying the name of the command as an argument. For example, to learn more about the *pwd* command:

```
$ man pwd
```

A detailed description of the *pwd* command will be displayed when the above command is executed. Many commands will also provide additional information when run with the *--help* command-line option:

```
$ wc --help
```

8.5 Bash Command-line Editing

Early shell environments did not provide any form of line editing capabilities. This meant that if you spotted an error at the beginning of a long command-line, you were typing, you had to delete all the following characters, correct the error and then re-enter the remainder of the command. Fortunately, Bash provides a wide range of command-line editing options, as outlined in the following table:

Key Sequence	Action
Ctrl-b or Left Arrow	Move the cursor back one position
Ctrl-f or Right Arrow	Move the cursor forward one position
Delete	Delete the character currently beneath the cursor
Backspace	Delete the character to the left of the cursor
Ctrl-_	Undo previous change (can be repeated to undo all previous changes)
Ctrl-a	Move the cursor to the start of the line
Ctrl-e	Move the cursor to the end of the line
Meta-f or Esc then f	Move cursor forward one word
Meta-b or Esc then b	Move the cursor back one word
Ctrl-l	Clear the screen of everything except the current command
Ctrl-k	Delete to the end of the line from the current cursor position
Meta-d or Esc then d	Delete to end of the current word
Meta-DEL or Esc then DEL	Delete beginning to the current word
Ctrl-w	Delete from the current cursor position to the previous white space

Table 8-1

8.6 Working with the Shell History

In addition to command-line editing features, the Bash shell provides command-line history support. A list of previously executed commands may be viewed using the *history* command:

```
$ history
     1  ps
     2  ls
     3  ls -l /
     4  ls
     5  man pwd
     6  man apropos
```

In addition, Ctrl-p (or up arrow) and Ctrl-n (or down arrow) may be used to scroll back and forth through previously entered commands. Finally, when the desired command from the history is displayed, press the Enter key to execute it.

Another option is to enter the '!' character, followed by the first few characters of the command to be repeated, followed by the Enter key.

8.7 Filename Shorthand

Many shell commands take one or more filenames as arguments. For example, to display the content of a text file named list.txt, the *cat* command would be used as follows:

```
$ cat list.txt
```

Similarly, the content of multiple text files could be displayed by specifying all the file names as arguments:

```
$ cat list.txt list2.txt list3.txt list4.txt
```

Instead of typing in each name, pattern matching can be used to specify all files with names matching certain criteria. For example, the '*' wildcard character can be used to simplify the above example:

```
$ cat *.txt
```

The above command will display the content of all files ending with a *.txt* extension. This could be further restricted to any file names beginning with *list* and ending in *.txt*:

```
$ cat list*.txt
```

Single character matches may be specified using the '?' character:

```
$ cat list?.txt
```

8.8 Filename and Path Completion

Rather than typing in a complete file name or path or using pattern matching to reduce the amount of typing, the shell provides the *filename completion* feature. To use filename completion, enter the first few characters of the file or path name and then press the Esc key twice. The shell will then complete the filename for you with the first file or path name in the directory that matches the characters you entered. To obtain a list of possible matches, press Esc = after entering the first few characters.

8.9 Input and Output Redirection

As previously mentioned, many shell commands output information when executed. By default, this output goes to a device file named *stdout* which is essentially the terminal window or console in which the shell is running. Conversely, the shell takes input from a device file named *stdin*, which by default is the keyboard.

Output from a command can be redirected from stdout to a physical file on the file system using the '>' character. For example, to redirect the output from an ls command to a file named *files.txt*, the following command would be required:

```
$ ls *.txt > files.txt
```

Upon completion, *files.txt* will contain the list of files in the current directory. Similarly, the contents of a file may be fed into a command in place of stdin. For example, to redirect the contents of a file as input to a command:

```
$ wc -l < files.txt
```

The above command will display the number of lines in the *files.txt* file.

It is important to note that the '>' redirection operator creates a new file or truncates an existing file when used. To append to an existing file, use the '>>' operator:

```
$ ls *.dat >> files.txt
```

In addition to standard output, the shell also provides standard error output using *stderr*. While output from a command is directed to stdout, any error messages generated by the command are directed to stderr. This means that if stdout is directed to a file, error messages will still appear in the terminal. This is generally the desired behavior, though stderr may also be redirected if desired using the '2>' operator:

```
$ ls dkjfnvkjdnf 2> errormsg
```

On completion of the command, an error reporting that the file named dkjfnvkjdnf could not be found will be contained in the errormsg file.

Both stderr and stdout may be redirected to the same file using the &> operator:

```
$ ls /etc dkjfnvkjdnf &> alloutput
```

On completion of execution, the *alloutput* file will contain both a listing of the contents of the */etc* directory and the error message associated with the attempt to list a non-existent file.

8.10 Working with Pipes in the Bash Shell

In addition to I/O redirection, the shell also allows output from one command to be piped directly as input to another command. A pipe operation is achieved by placing the '|' character between two or more commands on a command line. For example, to count the number of processes running on a system, the output from the *ps* command can be piped through to the *wc* command:

```
$ ps -ef | wc -l
```

There is no limit to the number of pipe operations that can be performed on a command line. For example, to find the number of lines in a file that contain the name Smith:

```
$ cat namesfile | grep Smith | wc -l
```

8.11 Configuring Aliases

As you gain proficiency with the shell environment, you will likely frequently issue commands with the same arguments. For example, you may often use the *ls* command with the l and t options:

```
$ ls -lt
```

To reduce the amount of typing involved in issuing a command, it is possible to create an alias that maps to the command and arguments. For example, to create an alias such that entering the letter l will cause the *ls -lt* command to be executed, the following statement would be used:

```
$ alias l="ls -lt"
```

Entering l at the command prompt will now execute the original statement.

8.12 Environment Variables

Shell environment variables provide temporary storage of data and configuration settings. The shell itself sets up several environment variables that the user may change to modify the behavior of the shell. A listing of currently defined variables may be obtained using the *env* command:

```
$ env
SSH_CONNECTION=192.168.0.19 61231 192.168.0.28 22
MODULES_RUN_QUARANTINE=LD_LIBRARY_PATH
LANG=en_US.UTF-8
HISTCONTROL=ignoredups
HOSTNAME=RHELdemo-pc.ebookfrenzy.com
XDG_SESSION_ID=15
MODULES_CMD=/usr/share/Modules/libexec/modulecmd.tcl
USER=demo
ENV=/usr/share/Modules/init/profile.sh
SELINUX_ROLE_REQUESTED=
PWD=/home/demo
HOME=/home/demo
SSH_CLIENT=192.168.0.19 61231 22
SELINUX_LEVEL_REQUESTED=
.
.
```

Perhaps the most useful environment variable is PATH. This defines the directories in which the shell will search for commands entered at the command prompt and the order in which it will do so. The PATH environment variable for a user account on a newly installed RHEL 9 system will likely be configured as follows:

```
$ echo $PATH
/home/demo/.local/bin:/home/demo/bin:/usr/share/Modules/bin:/usr/local/bin:/usr/
bin:/usr/local/sbin:/usr/sbin
```

Another useful variable is HOME, which specifies the current user's home directory. If, for example, you wanted the shell to also look for commands in the *scripts* directory located in your home directory, you would modify the PATH variable as follows:

```
$ export PATH=$PATH:$HOME/scripts
```

The current value of an existing environment variable may be displayed using the *echo* command:

```
$ echo $PATH
```

You can create your own environment variables using the *export* command. For example:

```
$ export DATAPATH=/data/files
```

A useful trick to assign the output from a command to an environment variable involves using back quotes (`) around the command. For example, to assign the current date and time to an environment variable called NOW:

```
$ export NOW=`date`
```

```
$ echo $NOW
Wed Mar 29 12:39:20 PM EDT 2023
```

If there are environment variables or alias settings that need to be configured each time you enter the shell environment, they may be added to a file in your home directory named *.bashrc*. For example, the following *.bashrc* file is configured to set up the DATAPATH environment variable and an alias:

```
# .bashrc

# Source global definitions
if [ -f /etc/bashrc ]; then
        . /etc/bashrc
fi

# User specific environment
PATH="$HOME/.local/bin:$HOME/bin:$PATH"
export PATH

# Uncomment the following line if you don't like systemctl's auto-paging feature:
# export SYSTEMD_PAGER=

# User specific aliases and functions
export DATAPATH=/data/files
alias l="ls -lt"
```

8.13 Writing Shell Scripts

So far, we have focused exclusively on the interactive nature of the Bash shell. By interactive, we mean manually entering commands individually and executing them at the prompt. In fact, this is only a small part of what the shell is capable of. Arguably one of the most powerful aspects of the shell involves the ability to create shell scripts. Shell scripts are text files containing statement sequences that can be executed within the shell environment to perform tasks. In addition to the ability to execute commands, the shell provides many programming constructs, such as *for* and *do* loops and *if* statements, that you might reasonably expect to find in a scripting language.

Unfortunately, a detailed overview of shell scripting is beyond the scope of this chapter. However, many books and web resources dedicated to shell scripting do the subject much more justice than we could ever hope to achieve here. In this section, therefore, we will only be providing a very small taste of shell scripting.

The first step in creating a shell script is to create a file (for this example, we will name it *simple. sh*) and add the following as the first line:

```
#!/bin/sh
```

The #! is called the "shebang" and is a special sequence of characters indicating that the path to the interpreter needed to execute the script is the next item on the line (in this case, the *sh* executable located in *bin*). This could equally be, for example, */bin/csh* or */bin/ksh* if either were the interpreter you wanted to use.

The next step is to write a simple script:

```
#!/bin/sh
for i in *
do
     echo $i
done
```

All this script does is iterate through all the files in the current directory and display the name of each file. This script may be executed by passing the name of the script through as an argument to *sh*:

```
$ sh simple.sh
```

To make the file executable (thereby negating the need to pass it through to the *sh* command), the *chmod* command can be used:

```
$ chmod +x simple.sh
```

Once the execute bit has been set on the file's permissions, it may be executed directly. For example:

```
$ ./simple.sh
```

8.14 Summary

We briefly toured the Bash shell environment in this chapter of Red Hat Enterprise Linux 9 Essentials. In the world of graphical desktop environments, it is easy to forget that an operating system's true power and flexibility can often only be utilized by dropping down below the user-friendly desktop interface and using a shell environment. Moreover, familiarity with the shell is necessary to administer and maintain server-based systems that do not have the desktop installed or when attempting to repair a system damaged to the point that the desktop or Cockpit interface will no longer launch.

The shell's capabilities go far beyond the areas covered in this chapter. If you are new to the shell, we strongly encourage you to seek additional resources. Once familiar with the concepts, you will quickly find that it is quicker to perform many tasks using the shell in a terminal window than to wade through menus and dialogs on the desktop.

9. Managing RHEL 9 Users and Groups

During the installation of RHEL 9, the installer created a root or superuser account and required that a password be configured. The installer also provided the opportunity to create a user account for the system. We should remember that RHEL 9 is an enterprise-class, multi-user, and multi-tasking operating system. To use the full power of RHEL 9, therefore, it is likely that more than one user will need to be given access to the system. Each user should have their own user account login, password, home directory, and privileges.

Users are further divided into groups for easier administration, and those groups can have different levels of privileges. For example, you may have a group of users who work in the Accounting department. In such an environment, you can create an accounts group and assign all the Accounting department users to that group.

This chapter will cover the steps to add, remove and manage users and groups on a RHEL 9 system. Users and groups may be managed on RHEL 9 using command-line tools, the Cockpit web interface, and the desktop Settings app. In this chapter, we will look at each of these approaches to user management.

9.1 User Management from the Command-line

New users may be added to a RHEL 9 system via the command line using the *adduser* utility. To create a new user account, enter a command similar to the following:

```
# useradd john
```

By default, this will create a home directory for the user in the */home* directory (in this case, */home/john*). To specify a different home directory, use the -d command-line option when creating the account:

```
# useradd -d /users/johnsmith john
```

Once the account has been created, a password needs to be assigned using the *passwd* tool before the user will be able to log into the system:

```
# passwd john
Changing password for user john.
New password:
Retype new password:
passwd: all authentication tokens updated successfully.
```

An existing user may be deleted via the command line using the *userdel* utility. While this will delete the account, the user's files and data will remain intact on the system:

Managing RHEL 9 Users and Groups

```
# userdel john
```

It is also possible to remove the user's home directory and mail spool as part of the deletion process:

```
# userdel --remove john
```

All users on a RHEL 9 system are members of one or more groups. By default, new users are added to a private group with the same name as the user (in the above example, the account created for user john was a member of a private group also named john). However, as an administrator, it makes sense to organize users into more logical groups. For example, all salespeople might belong to a sales group, and accounting staff might belong to the accounts group, and so on. New groups are added from the command line using the *groupadd* command-line tool, for example:

```
# groupadd accounts
```

Use the *usermod* tool to add an existing user to an existing group from the command line:

```
# usermod -G accounts john
```

To add an existing user to multiple existing groups, run the *usermod* command with the -G option:

```
# usermod -G accounts,sales,support john
```

Note that the above commands remove the user from supplementary groups not listed after the -G but to which the user is currently a member. To retain any current group memberships, use the -a flag to append the new group memberships:

```
# usermod -aG accounts,sales,support john
```

An existing group may be deleted from a system using the *groupdel* utility:

```
# groupdel accounts
```

Note that if the group to be deleted is the primary or initial group for any user, it cannot be deleted. The user must first be deleted or assigned a new primary group using the *usermod* command before the group can be removed. A user can be assigned to a new primary group using the *usermod* -g option:

```
# usermod -g sales john
# groupdel accounts
```

Run the *groups* command to find out the groups to which a user belongs. For example:

```
$ groups john
john : accounts support
```

By default, a user account cannot perform tasks requiring superuser (root) privileges unless they know the root password. It is, however, possible to configure a user account so that privileged tasks can be performed using the *sudo* command. This involves adding the user account as a member of the *wheel* group, for example:

```
# usermod -aG wheel john
```

Once added to the *wheel* group, the user will be able to perform otherwise restricted tasks using sudo as follows:

```
$ sudo dnf update
[sudo] password for demo:
Updating Subscription Management repositories.
 .

 .
```

The sudo capabilities of the wheel group may be modified by editing the */etc/sudoers* file and locating the following section:

```
## Allows people in group wheel to run all commands
%wheel  ALL=(ALL)         ALL


## Same thing without a password
# %wheel        ALL=(ALL)        NOPASSWD: ALL
```

To disable sudo for all wheel group members, comment out the second line as follows:

```
## Allows people in group wheel to run all commands
# %wheel  ALL=(ALL)        ALL
```

To allow wheel group members to use sudo without entering a password (for security reasons, this is not recommended), uncomment the corresponding line in the sudoers file:

```
## Same thing without a password
%wheel        ALL=(ALL)        NOPASSWD: ALL
```

Behind the scenes, all these commands are simply changing the */etc/passwd*, */etc/group*, and */etc/shadow* files on the system.

9.2 User Management with Cockpit

If the Cockpit web interface is installed and enabled on the system (a topic covered in the chapter entitled *"An Overview of the Cockpit Web Interface"*), several user management tasks can be performed within the Accounts screen shown in Figure 9-1 below:

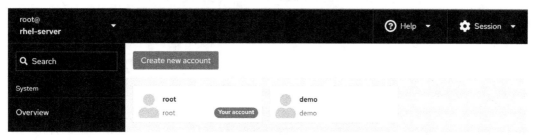

Figure 9-1

The screen will display any existing user accounts on the system and provides a button to add additional accounts. To create a new account, click the Create New Account button and enter the requested information in the resulting dialog (Figure 9-2). Note that the option is also available to create the account but to lock it until later:

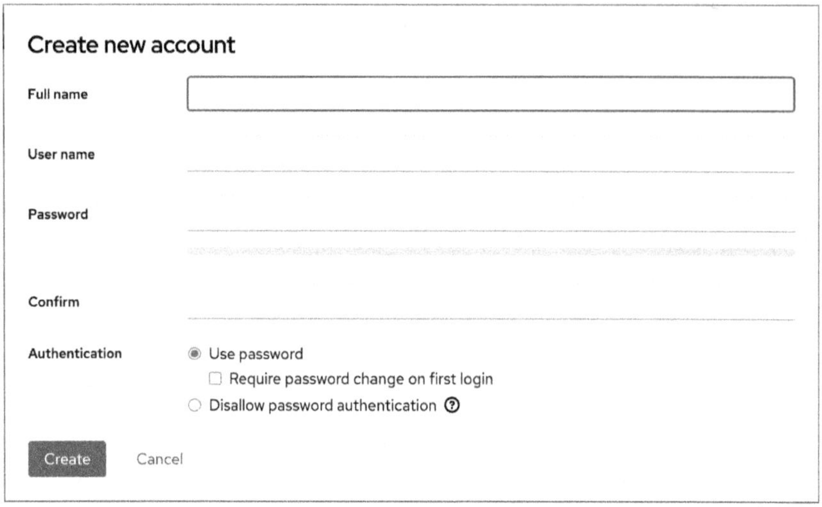

Figure 9-2

To modify a user account, select it from the main screen and make any modifications to the account details:

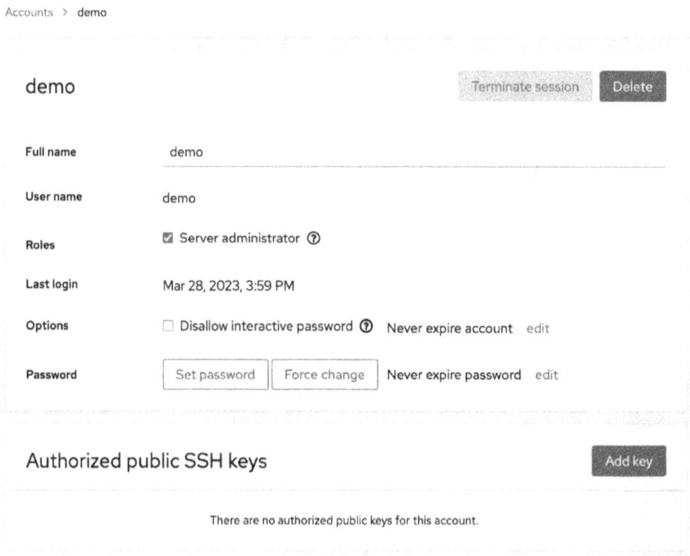

Figure 9-3

This screen allows various tasks, including locking or unlocking the account, changing the password, or forcing the user to configure a new password to be performed. In addition, if the Server Administrator option is selected, the user will be added to the wheel group and permitted to use sudo to perform administrative tasks. A button is also provided to delete the user from the system.

If the user is accessing the system remotely using an SSH connection with key encryption, the user's public key may be added within this screen. SSH access and authentication will be covered later in *"Configuring SSH Key-based Authentication on RHEL 9"*.

9.3 User Management using the Settings App

A third user account management option is available via the GNOME desktop settings app. This app is accessed by clicking on icons in the top right-hand corner of the GNOME desktop and selecting the Settings option, as shown in Figure 9-4:

Figure 9-4

When the main settings screen appears, click the Users option in the left-hand navigation panel. By default, the settings will be locked, and making any changes to the user accounts on the system will not be possible. To unlock the Settings app, click the Unlock button in Figure 9-5 below and enter your password. Note that it will only be possible to unlock the settings if you are logged in as a user with sudo privileges:

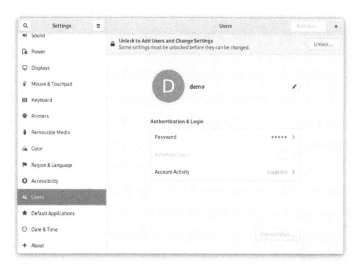

Figure 9-5

Once the app has been unlocked, a button labeled *Add User...* will appear in the title bar. Click this button to display the dialog shown in Figure 9-6 below:

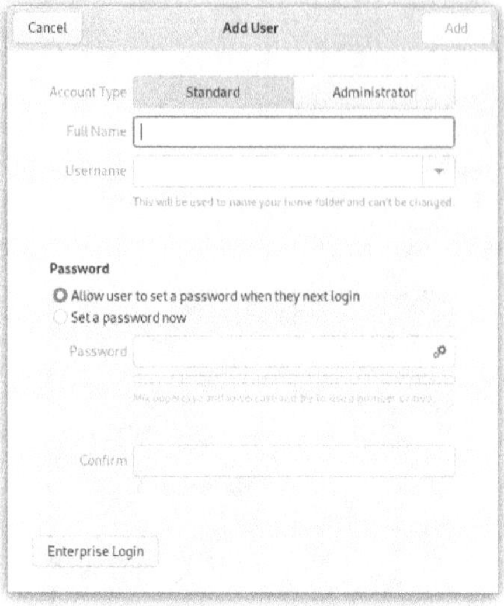

Figure 9-6

Select the Administrator account to assign sudo access to the new user; otherwise, leave Standard selected. Next, enter the user's full name and username and assign a password now, or allow the user to set up the password when they first log into their account. Once the information has been entered, click the Add button to create the account.

The settings for an existing user can be viewed, modified, or the account deleted at any time by selecting the corresponding icon within the Users screen, as shown in Figure 9-7. The option is also available to view the user's login activity. Note that it will be necessary to unlock the Settings app again before any changes can be made to an account:

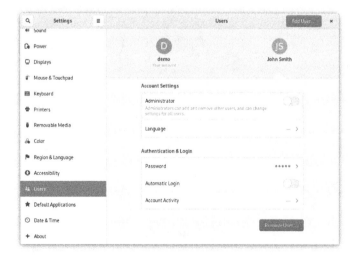

Figure 9-7

9.4 Summary

As a multi-user operating system, RHEL 9 has been designed to support controlled access for multiple users. During installation, the root user account was created and assigned a password, and the option to create a user account was also provided. Additional user accounts may be added to the system using a set of command-line tools via the Cockpit web interface or the GNOME Settings app. In addition to user accounts, Linux also implements the concept of groups. New groups can be added, and users assigned to those groups using command-line tools, and each user must belong to at least one group. By default, a standard, non-root user does not have permission to perform privileged tasks. Users that are members of the special *wheel* group, however, may perform privileged tasks by making use of the sudo command.

10. Understanding RHEL 9 Software Installation and Management

It is doubtful that a newly installed RHEL 9 system will contain all of the software packages to perform the tasks for which it is intended. Even once all the required software has been installed, it is almost certain that newer versions of many of those packages will be released during the system's lifespan. In some cases, you will need to ensure that these latest package releases are installed on the system to ensure that any bugs are fixed. In other cases, however, an older version of a particular software package may need to be kept on the system for compatibility with other software.

This chapter introduces the basic concepts of software management on RHEL 9, explains how these issues are addressed, explains repositories, software packages, and the Red Hat Application Stream (AppStream), and explores how to list, install and remove the software packages that make up a functioning RHEL 9 system.

10.1 Repositories

Linux is essentially comprised of a set of base packages that provide the core functionality of the operating system together with a range of other packages and modules that add functionality and features on top of the base operating system.

Several packages will be installed when RHEL 9 is first installed, depending on the software options selected during the installation phase. Once the system is up and running, however, additional software can be installed as needed. Typically, all software that is part of RHEL 9 (in other words, software that a third-party vendor does not provide) is downloaded and installed on the system using the *dnf* command. As we have seen in earlier chapters, this typically consists of a command similar to the following being issued at the command prompt:

```
# dnf install httpd
```

When such a command is issued, the requested software is downloaded from a remote repository and installed on the local system. By default, RHEL 9 is configured to download software from repositories named BaseOS and AppStream. For example, running the following command will provide a list of the repositories the system is currently configured to use when downloading software:

```
# dnf repolist
Updating Subscription Management repositories.
repo id                              repo name
rhel-9-for-x86_64-appstream-rpms     Red Hat Enterprise Linux 9 for x86_64 -
AppStream (RPMs)
rhel-9-for-x86_64-baseos-rpms        Red Hat Enterprise Linux 9 for x86_64 -
```

```
BaseOS (RPMs)
```

The above example shows that repositories for both AppStream and BaseOS are enabled on the system. Remember that repositories may be added for third-party software.

Additional repositories may be added to the system by placing entries in the */etc/dnf/dnf.conf* file, or by adding *.repo* files to the */etc/yum.repos.d/* directory. Alternatively, the repository may be added using the *dnf config-manager* tool, passing the URL of the *.repo* file for the repository as a command-line argument:

```
# dnf config-manager --add-repo https://url/of/repo/file
```

10.2 The BaseOS Repository

The BaseOS repository contains the packages that make up the core functionality of the operating system. These software elements are downloaded in the form of Red Hat Package Manager (RPM) package files and then installed on the system. A typical RHEL 9 system will have around 1500 RPM packages installed. To see a list of all the RPM packages currently installed on the system, run the *rpm* command as follows:

```
# rpm -qa | more
qemu-kvm-block-rbd-2.12.0-41.el8+2104+3e32e6f8.x86_64
kyotocabinet-libs-1.2.76-17.el8.x86_64
cyrus-sasl-scram-2.1.27-0.3rc7.el8.x86_64
curl-7.61.1-5.el8.x86_64
.
.
```

A list of packages available for installation from the BaseOS repository is available by running the *dnf* command as follows:

```
# dnf list
```

To obtain a list of packages that match a search string, use *dnf* as follows:

```
# dnf search "search string"
```

It is also possible to identify which package contains a specific file:

```
# dnf provides filename
```

For example:

```
Updating Subscription Management repositories.
httpd-2.4.51-7.el9_0.x86_64 : Apache HTTP Server
Repo        : rhel-9-for-x86_64-appstream-rpms
Matched from:
Filename    : /etc/httpd/conf/httpd.conf

httpd-core-2.4.53-7.el9.x86_64 : httpd minimal core
Repo        : rhel-9-for-x86_64-appstream-rpms
Matched from:
Filename    : /etc/httpd/conf/httpd.conf
```

```
httpd-core-2.4.53-7.el9_1.1.x86_64 : httpd minimal core
Repo         : rhel-9-for-x86_64-appstream-rpms
Matched from:
Filename     : /etc/httpd/conf/httpd.conf
```

To install a package, run the following command:

```
# dnf install packagename
```

Similarly, to delete a package:

```
# dnf delete packagename
```

When a newer version of a package is made available, it will be downloaded and installed when the system is next updated, typically via the *dnf* command:

```
# dnf update
```

Any updated packages will replace the older version currently installed on the system. While this is generally the ideal situation when working with base operating system packages, this is not necessarily the desired behavior when dealing with other packages, such as programming environments or development libraries, where upgrading to a new version may cause compatibility issues with other packages installed on the system. This issue is addressed by the AppStream repository.

10.3 The AppStream Repository

The AppStream repository manages software in terms of *packages, modules, streams,* and *profiles.* AppStream packages are, once again, RPM packages, as outlined in the previous section describing BaseOS. AppStream modules, on the other hand, are groups of packages that belong together or for which dependencies exist (for example, the group of packages that would need to be installed together when building a web server). Each module can have multiple streams, where each *module stream* represents a different version of the software module.

Consider, for example, a RHEL 9 system hosting a website that depends on version 7.2 of the PHP scripting language. The server still needs to receive any updates to PHP 7.2 to benefit from patches and bug fixes but is not compatible with the latest version of PHP (version 8.1). Before the introduction of AppStream, it would have been difficult to continue receiving version 7.2 updates when newer versions have been released.

To address this issue, the RHEL software management tools can use the AppStream repository to subscribe only to a specific stream for a specific module (in this case, the version 7.2 stream of the PHP module).

In addition to streams, modules may also be sub-classed by *module profile.* Module profiles provide different configurations of packages that make up a module to be installed, dependent on the requirements of the system. The nodejs JavaScript runtime environment module, for example, is available for installation using either the *development* or *minimal* profiles. On a system where development is taking place using nodejs, the development profile would most likely be used.

Understanding RHEL 9 Software Installation and Management

When the software developed using nodejs is deployed, the minimal system containing just the runtime might be installed instead.

To view the list of modules available for installation, use the *dnf* command as follows:

```
# dnf module list
Updating Subscription Management repositories.
Last metadata expiration check: 1:27:42 ago on Mon 27 Mar 2023 11:02:15 AM EDT.
Red Hat Enterprise Linux 9 for x86_64 - AppStream (RPMs)
Name       Stream     Profiles                              Summary
maven      3.8        common [d]                            Java project
management and project comprehension tool
nodejs     18         common [d], development, minimal, s2i Javascript runtime
php        8.1        common [d], devel, minimal            PHP scripting language
.
.
Hint: [d]efault, [e]nabled, [x]disabled, [i]nstalled
```

The first column in the list is the name of the module, and the second is the stream name (which is typically the version of the module). The letter after the stream name ([d]) indicates whether the stream is the default (i.e., this is the stream that will be used for installation if no specific stream is referenced) or if it has been enabled for use when performing installations. The third column lists the profiles available for the corresponding package together with an indication of whether the profile is the default, has been installed, or is disabled.

The *dnf* command to list information about a specific module is structured as follows:

```
# dnf module list modulename
```

The following output, for example, lists information about the PHP modules available for installation:

```
# dnf module list php
.
.
Name       Stream     Profiles                    Summary
php        8.1 [d]    common [d], devel, minimal  PHP scripting language
```

Clearly, PHP version 8.1 will be installed on the system by default, and the module is available in common, development, and minimal profile configurations.

To install a module using the default stream and profile, the *dnf* command can be used with the following syntax:

```
# dnf install @modulename
```

For example:

```
# dnf install @php
```

Alternatively, a specific stream may be specified from which to perform the installation:

```
# dnf install @modulename:stream
```

For example:

```
# dnf install @php:8.1
```

Finally, a profile may also be declared as follows:

```
# dnf install @modulename:stream/profile
```

For example, to install the minimal set of packages for PHP 8.1:

```
# dnf install @php:8.1/minimal
```

After installing the module using the above command, the PHP modules will now be listed as follows:

```
php        8.1 [e]      common [d], devel, minimal [i]   PHP scripting language
```

The "[e]" indicator in the stream column tells us that the 8.1 stream has been enabled, while the "[i]" in the profile column shows that the module has been installed using the minimal profile.

To enable a stream without installing a module, use *dnf* as follows:

```
# dnf module enable modulename
```

Similarly, a stream may be disabled as follows:

```
# dnf module disable modulename
```

To uninstall a module, use the following syntax:

```
# dnf module remove modulename
```

Additional information about a module may be identified using the following *dnf* command:

```
# dnf module info modulename
```

To find out which RPM packages make up the different profiles of a specific module and stream combination, use *dnf* as follows:

```
# dnf module info --profile modulename:stream
```

For example:

```
# dnf module info --profile php:8.1
Updating Subscription Management repositories.
Last metadata expiration check: 1:44:32 ago on Mon 27 Mar 2023 11:02:15 AM EDT.
Name    : php:8.1:9010020220706080036:9:x86_64
common  : php-cli
        : php-common
        : php-fpm
        : php-mbstring
        : php-xml
devel   : php-cli
        : php-common
        : php-devel
        : php-fpm
        : php-mbstring
```

```
            : php-pecl-zip
            : php-process
            : php-xml
minimal  : php-cli
            : php-common
```

Finally, to switch from one module stream to another, run the installation command referencing the new stream as follows:

```
# dnf install @modulename:otherstream
```

This command will download the packages for the new stream and either upgrade or downgrade the existing packages to the specified version. Once this process is complete, resynchronize module packages for the new stream:

```
# dnf distro-sync
```

10.4 Summary

The RHEL 9 system comprises RPM format software packages that are downloaded and installed from the Red Hat BaseOS and AppStream repositories. Additional repositories can be added to the system for installation packages as needed.

The BaseOS repository contains the packages that implement the base core functionality of the operating system. The AppStream packages, on the other hand, provide additional features and functionality that will be installed selectively depending on the purpose for which the system is being configured. In a complex system of this nature, there can be a significant amount of package interdependency where part of the system may require a specific version of another software package to function correctly. AppStreams allow modules and profiles to be created that contain all of the dependent packages necessary to install a particular feature together at the correct version level. AppStreams also allow installed packages to receive updates to the current version without downloading the next major version, thereby avoiding disrupting the dependencies of other packages.

Chapter 11

11. Managing RHEL 9 systemd Units

To gain proficiency in RHEL 9 system administration, it is essential to understand the concepts of systemd units with a particular emphasis on two specific types known as targets and services. This chapter aims to provide a basic overview of the different systemd units supported by RHEL 9 combined with an overview of how to configure the many services that run in the background of a running Linux system.

11.1 Understanding RHEL 9 systemd Targets

RHEL 9 can be configured to boot into one of several states (referred to as targets), each designed to provide a specific level of operating system functionality. The system administrator configures the target to which a system will boot by default based on the purpose for which the system is being used. A desktop system, for example, will likely be configured to boot using the graphical user interface target. In contrast, a cloud-based server system would be more likely to boot to the multi-user target level.

During the boot sequence, a process named *systemd* looks in the */etc/systemd/system* folder to find the default target setting. Having identified the default target, it proceeds to start the systemd units associated with that target so that the system boots with all the necessary processes running.

For those familiar with older RHEL versions, systemd targets replace the older runlevel system.

11.2 Understanding RHEL 9 systemd Services

A service is a process, typically running in the background, that provides specific functionality. The sshd service, for example, is the background process (also referred to as a *daemon*) that provides secure shell access to the system. Different systemd targets are configured to automatically launch different collections of services, depending on the functionality to be provided by that target.

Targets and services are types of systemd unit, a topic that will be covered later in this chapter.

11.3 RHEL 9 systemd Target Descriptions

As previously outlined, RHEL 9 can be booted into one of several target levels. The default target to which the system is configured to boot will, in turn, dictate which systemd units are started. The targets that relate specifically to system startup and shutdown can be summarized as follows:

• **poweroff.target** - This target shuts down the system. It is unlikely you would want this as your default target.

• **rescue.target** – Causes the system to start up in a single-user mode under which only the root user can log in. The system does not start any networking, graphical user interface, or multi-user services in this mode. This run level is ideal for system administrators to perform system maintenance or repair activities.

• **multi-user.target** - Boots the system into a multi-user mode with text-based console login capability.

• **graphical.target** - Boots the system into a networked, multi-user state with X Window System capability. By default, the graphical desktop environment will start at the end of the boot process. This is the most common run level for desktop or workstation use.

• **reboot.target** - Reboots the system. Another target that, for obvious reasons, you are unlikely to want as your default.

In addition to the above targets, the system includes about 70 other targets, many of which are sub-targets used by the above main targets. Behind the scenes, for example, *multi-user.target* will also start a target named *basic.target* which will, in turn, start the *sockets.target* unit, which is required for communication between different processes. This ensures that all the services on which the multi-user target depends are also started during the boot process.

A list of the targets and services on which a specified target is dependent can be viewed by running the following command in a terminal window:

```
# systemctl list-dependencies <target>
```

Figure 11-1, for example, shows a partial listing of the systemd unit dependencies for the graphical target (the complete listing contains over 140 targets and services required for a fully functional multi-user system):

```
[demo@rhel-server ~]$ systemctl list-dependencies graphical.target
graphical.target
●  ├─accounts-daemon.service
●  ├─gdm.service
○  ├─nvmefc-boot-connections.service
●  ├─power-profiles-daemon.service
●  ├─rtkit-daemon.service
●  ├─switcheroo-control.service
○  ├─systemd-update-utmp-runlevel.service
●  ├─udisks2.service
●  ├─upower.service
●  └─multi-user.target
●    ├─atd.service
●    ├─auditd.service
●    ├─avahi-daemon.service
●    ├─chronyd.service
```

Figure 11-1

The listing is presented as a hierarchical tree illustrating how some dependencies have sub-dependencies of their own. Scrolling to the bottom of the list, for example, would reveal that the graphical target depends on two network filesystem related targets (namely *nfs-client.target* and *remote-fs.target*), each with its own service and target sub-dependencies:

```
[●  ├─nfs-client.target
[○  │  ├─auth-rpcgss-module.service
[●  │  ├─rpc-statd-notify.service
[●  │  └─remote-fs-pre.target
[●  └─remote-fs.target
[○     ├─iscsi.service
[○     ├─var-lib-machines.mount
[●     └─nfs-client.target
[○        ├─auth-rpcgss-module.service
[●        ├─rpc-statd-notify.service
[●        └─remote-fs-pre.target
```

Figure 11-2

The colored dots to the left of each entry in the list indicate the current status of that service or target as follows:

- **Green** - The service or target is active and running.

- **White** - The service or target is inactive (dead). Typically because the service or target has yet to be enabled, has been stopped for some reason, or a condition on which the service or target depends has not been met.

- **Red** - The service or target failed to start due to a fatal error.

To find out more details about the status of a systemd unit, use the *systemctl status* command followed by the unit name as follows:

```
# systemctl status systemd-machine-id-commit.service
○ systemd-machine-id-commit.service - Commit a transient machine-id on disk
     Loaded: loaded (/usr/lib/systemd/system/systemd-machine-id-commit.service;
static)
     Active: inactive (dead)
  Condition: start condition failed at Thu 2023-03-30 08:41:05 EDT; 16min ago
           └ ConditionPathIsMountPoint=/etc/machine-id was not met
       Docs: man:systemd-machine-id-commit.service(8)
```

11.4 Identifying and Configuring the Default Target

The current default target for a RHEL 9 system can be identified using the *systemctl* command as follows:

```
# systemctl get-default
multi-user.target
```

The system is configured to boot using the multi-user target by default in the above case. The default setting can be changed anytime using the *systemctl* command with the *set-default* option. The following example changes the default target to start the graphical user interface the next time the system boots:

```
# systemctl set-default graphical.target
Removed /etc/systemd/system/default.target.
Created symlink /etc/systemd/system/default.target → /usr/lib/systemd/system/
graphical.target.
```

The output from the default change operation reveals the steps performed in the background by the *systemctl* command to implement the change. The current default is configured by establishing a symbolic link from the *default.target* file located in */etc/systemd/system* to point to the corresponding target file located in the */usr/lib/systemd/system* folder (in this case the *graphical.target* file).

11.5 Understanding systemd Units and Unit Types

As previously mentioned, targets and services are both types of systemd unit. All the files within the */usr/lib/systemd/system* folder are referred to as systemd unit configuration files, each representing a systemd unit. Each unit is, in turn, categorized as being of a particular unit type. RHEL 9 supports 12 different unit types, including the target and service unit types already covered in this chapter.

The type of a unit file is represented by the filename extension as outlined in Table 11-1 below:

Unit Type	Filename Extension	Type Description
Service	.service	System service.
Target	.target	Group of systemd units.
Automount	.automount	File system auto-mount point.
Device	.device	Device file recognized by the kernel.
Mount	.mount	File system mount point.
Path	.path	File or directory in a file system.
Scope	.scope	Externally created process.
Slice	.slice	Group of hierarchically organized units that manage system processes.
Snapshot	.snapshot	Saved state of the systemd manager.
Socket	.socket	Inter-process communication socket.
Swap	.swap	Swap device or a swap file.
Timer	.timer	Systemd timer.

Table 11-1

Note that the target unit type differs from other types in that it comprises a group of systemd units such as services or other targets.

11.6 Dynamically Changing the Current Target

The *systemctl set-default* command outlined previously specifies the target that will be used the next time the system starts but does not change the current system's state. To change to a different target dynamically, use the *systemctl* command again, using the *isolate* option followed by the destination target. To switch the current system to the graphical target without rebooting, for example, the following command would be used:

```
# systemctl isolate graphical.target
```

Once executed, the system will start the graphical desktop environment.

11.7 Enabling, Disabling, and Masking systemd Units

A newly installed RHEL 9 system will include the base systemd service units but is unlikely to include all the services the system will eventually need once it goes into a production environment. A basic RHEL 9 installation, for example, will typically not include the packages necessary to run an Apache web server, a key element of which is the *httpd.service* unit.

The system administrator will resolve this problem by installing the necessary httpd packages using the following command:

```
# dnf install httpd
```

Having configured the web server, the next task will be to check the status of the httpd service unit to identify whether it was activated as part of the installation process:

```
# systemctl status httpd.service
 httpd.service - The Apache HTTP Server
   Loaded: loaded (/usr/lib/systemd/system/httpd.service; disabled; vendor
preset: disabled)
   Active: inactive (dead)
     Docs: man:httpd.service(8)
```

Note that the service has loaded but is inactive because it is preset by the vendor to be disabled when first installed. To start the service, the following command can be used:

```
# systemctl start httpd.service
```

A status check will now indicate that the service is active:

```
# systemctl status httpd.service
 httpd.service - The Apache HTTP Server
   Loaded: loaded (/usr/lib/systemd/system/httpd.service; disabled; vendor
preset: disabled)
   Active: active (running) since Fri 2019-02-15 11:13:26 EST; 8s ago
     Docs: man:httpd.service(8)
 Main PID: 10721 (httpd)
   Status: "Started, listening on: port 80"
    Tasks: 213 (limit: 13923)
   Memory: 24.1M
```

.

.

.

Note, however, that the status indicates that the service is still disabled. This means that the next time the system reboots, the httpd service will not start automatically and will need to be started manually by the system administrator.

To configure the httpd service to start automatically each time the system starts, it must be enabled as follows:

```
# systemctl enable httpd.service
```

Once the service has been enabled, the Loaded section of the status output will read as follows:

```
Loaded: loaded (/usr/lib/systemd/system/httpd.service; enabled; vendor preset:
disabled)
# systemctl status httpd.service
● httpd.service - The Apache HTTP Server
     Loaded: loaded (/usr/lib/systemd/system/httpd.service; enabled; vendor
preset: disabled)
     Active: active (running) since Thu 2023-03-30 09:04:21 EDT; 2min 17s ago
       Docs: man:httpd.service(8)
   Main PID: 4500 (httpd)
     Status: "Total requests: 0; Idle/Busy workers 100/0;Requests/sec: 0; Bytes
served/sec:   0 B/sec"
      Tasks: 213 (limit: 22087)
     Memory: 35.4M
```

.

.

A currently running service may be stopped at any time as follows:

```
# systemctl stop httpd.service
```

Now that it has been enabled, the next time the system reboots to the current target, the httpd service will start automatically. Assuming, for example, that the service was enabled while the system was running the multi-user target, the httpd service will have been added as another dependency to the *multi-user.target* systemd unit.

Behind the scenes, *systemctl* adds dependencies to targets by creating symbolic links in the *.wants* folder for the target within the */etc/systemd/system* folder. For example, the *multi-user.target* unit has a folder named *multi-user.target.wants* in */etc/systemd/system* containing symbolic links to all of the systemd units located in */usr/lib/systemd/system* on which it is dependent. A review of this folder will show a correlation with the dependencies listed by the *systemctl list-dependencies* command outlined earlier in the chapter.

To configure a service so that it no longer starts automatically as a target dependency, disable it as follows:

```
# systemctl disable httpd.service
```

This command will remove the symbolic link to the *httpd.service* unit file from the *.wants* directory so that it is no longer a dependency and, as such, will not be started the next time the system boots.

The *.wants* folder contains dependencies that, if not available, will not prevent the unit from starting and functioning. Mandatory dependencies (in other words, dependencies that will cause the unit to fail if not available) should be placed in the *.requires* folder (for example, *multi-user. target.requires*).

In addition to enabling and disabling, it is also possible to mask a systemd unit as follows:

```
# systemctl mask httpd.service
```

A masked systemd unit cannot be enabled, disabled, or started under any circumstances, even if it is listed as a dependency for another unit. As far as the system is concerned, it is as though a masked systemd unit no longer exists. This can be useful for ensuring that a unit is never started, regardless of the system conditions. The only way to regain access to the service is to unmask it:

```
# systemctl unmask httpd.service
```

11.8 Working with systemd Units in Cockpit

In addition to the command-line techniques outlined in this chapter, it is also possible to review and manage systemd units from within the Cockpit web-based interface. For example, assuming that Cockpit has been installed and set up as outlined in the chapter entitled *"An Overview of the Cockpit Web Interface"*, access to the list of systemd units on the system can be accessed by logging into Cockpit and selecting the Services option in the left-hand navigation panel marked A in Figure 11-3:

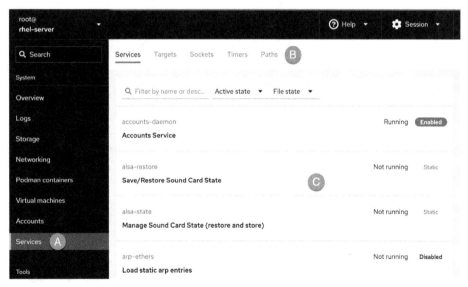

Figure 11-3

The row of options marked B displays units of specific types in the main area marked C where the current status of each unit is listed in the State column.

Managing RHEL 9 systemd Units

Selecting a unit from the list will display detailed information. Figure 11-4, for example, shows the detail screen for an httpd instance, including service logs (A) and a switch and menu (B) for performing tasks such as starting, stopping, enabling/disabling, and masking/unmasking the unit:

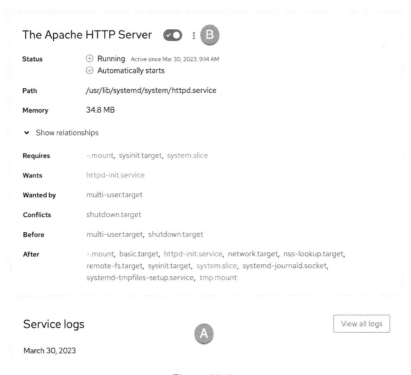

Figure 11-4

11.9 Summary

A newly installed RHEL 9 system includes a base set of systemd units, many of which run in the background to provide much of the system's functionality. These units are categorized by type, the most common being targets and services. A target unit is a group of other units to be started collectively. The system has a default target unit that defines the other units to be started up each time the system boots. The most common targets are those which boot the system to either multi-user or graphical mode. In addition, the *systemctl* command-line tool provides a range of options for performing systemd unit configuration tasks, many of which are also available through the Cockpit web-based interface.

Chapter 12

12. RHEL 9 Network Management

It is difficult to envisage a RHEL 9 system that does not have at least one network connection and harder still to imagine how such an isolated system could be of much practical use. The simple fact is that RHEL 9 is designed to provide enterprise-level services over network and internet connections. Therefore, a crucial part of learning how to administer a RHEL 9 system involves learning how to configure and manage the network interfaces installed on the system.

This chapter provides an overview of network management on RHEL 9, including the NetworkManager service and tools and some other useful utilities.

12.1 An Introduction to NetworkManager

NetworkManager is a service and set of tools designed specifically to make it easier to manage the networking configuration on Linux systems and is the default network management service on RHEL 9.

In addition to a service that runs in the background, NetworkManager also includes the following tools:

- **nmcli** - A tool for working with NetworkManager via the command line. This tool is useful when access to a graphical environment is unavailable and can also be used within scripts to make network configuration changes.

- **nmtui** - A basic text-based user interface for managing NetworkManager. This tool can be run within any terminal window and allows changes to be made by making menu selections and entering data. While helpful in performing basic tasks, *nmtui* lacks many of the features provided by the *nmcli* tool.

- **nm-connection-editor** - A complete graphical management tool providing access to most NetworkManager configuration options.

- **GNOME Settings** - The Network screen of the GNOME desktop Settings application allows basic network management tasks to be performed.

- **Cockpit Network Settings** - The Network screen of the Cockpit web interface allows a range of network management tasks to be performed.

Although there are several ways to manage the network environment on a RHEL 9 system, this chapter will focus on the *nmcli* command. While the graphical tools are certainly helpful when you have access to a desktop environment or Cockpit has been enabled, understanding the command-line interface is essential for situations where a command prompt is all that is available. Also, the graphical tools (Cockpit included) only include some of the capabilities of the *nmcli* tool. Finally, once you are familiar with NetworkManager and *nmcli*, those skills will translate easily when using the more intuitive tool options. The same cannot be said of the graphical tool options. It is harder to use *nmcli* if, for example, you have only ever used *nm-connection-editor*.

12.2 Installing and Enabling NetworkManager

NetworkManager should be installed by default for most RHEL 9 installations. Use the *rpm* command to find out if it needs to be installed:

```
# rpm -q NetworkManager
NetworkManager-1.14.0-14.el8.x86_64
```

If necessary, install the package as follows:

```
# dnf install NetworkManager
```

Once the package is installed, the NetworkManager daemon will need to be enabled so that it starts each time the system boots:

```
# systemctl enable NetworkManager
```

Finally, start the service running and check the status to verify that the launch was successful:

```
# systemctl start NetworkManager
# systemctl status NetworkManager
● NetworkManager.service - Network Manager
   Loaded: loaded (/usr/lib/systemd/system/NetworkManager.service; enabled;
vendor >
   Drop-In: /usr/lib/systemd/system/NetworkManager.service.d
            └─NetworkManager-ovs.conf
   Active: active (running) since Tue 2019-04-09 10:07:22 EDT; 2h 48min ago
 .
 .
```

12.3 Basic nmcli Commands

The *nmcli* tool will have been installed as part of the NetworkManager package and can be executed from the command line using the following syntax:

```
# nmcli [Options] Object {Command | help}
```

In the above syntax, Object will be one of general, networking, radio, connection, monitor, device, or agent, which can be abbreviated to a few letters of the word (for example, con, or even just the letter c, for connection). For example, all of the following commands will output help information relating to the device object:

```
# nmcli device help
# nmcli dev help
# nmcli d help
```

To check the overall status of NetworkManager on the system, use the following command:

```
# nmcli general status
STATE       CONNECTIVITY  WIFI-HW  WIFI     WWAN-HW  WWAN
connected   full          enabled  enabled  enabled  enabled
```

To check the status of the devices installed on a system, the following command can be used:

```
# nmcli dev status
DEVICE          TYPE       STATE       CONNECTION
eno1            ethernet   connected   eno1
wlp0s26u1u2     wifi       connected   zoneone
virbr0          bridge     connected   virbr0
lo              loopback   unmanaged   --
virbr0-nic      tun        unmanaged   --
```

The output may also be modified by using the -p (pretty) option to make the output more human-friendly:

```
# nmcli -p dev status
=====================
  Status of devices
=====================
DEVICE          TYPE       STATE       CONNECTION
---------------------------------------------------------------
eno1            ethernet   connected   eno1
wlp0s26u1u2     wifi       connected   zoneone
virbr0          bridge     connected   virbr0
lo              loopback   unmanaged   --
virbr0-nic      tun        unmanaged   --
```

Conversely, the -t option may be used to make the output more terse and suitable for automated processing:

```
# nmcli -t dev status
eno1:ethernet:connected:eno1
wlp0s26u1u2:wifi:connected:emilyzone
virbr0:bridge:connected:virbr0
lo:loopback:unmanaged:
virbr0-nic:tun:unmanaged:
```

The status output shows that the system has two physical devices installed, one Ethernet and the other a WiFi device.

The bridge (virbr) entries are virtual devices used to provide networking for virtual machines (the topic of virtualization will be covered starting with the chapter entitled *"An Overview of Virtualization Techniques"*). Finally, the loopback interface is a special virtual device that allows the system to communicate with itself and is typically used to perform network diagnostics.

When working with NetworkManager, it is important to understand the difference between a device and a connection. As described above, a device is either a physical or virtual network device, while a connection is a network configuration that the device connects to.

The following command displays information about the connections configured on the system:

```
# nmcli con show
```

RHEL 9 Network Management

```
NAME           UUID                                     TYPE      DEVICE
zoneone        2abecafa-4ea2-47f6-b20f-4fb0c0fd5e94     wifi      wlp0s26u1u2
eno1           99d40009-6bb1-4182-baad-a103941c90ff     ethernet  eno1
virbr0         e13e9552-1765-42d1-b739-ff981668fbee     bridge    virbr0
zonetwo        f940a2d1-8c18-4a9e-bf29-817702429b8a     wifi      --
zonethree      fd65c5e5-3e92-4e9e-b924-1b0b07b70032     wifi      --
```

The above output shows that the WiFi device (wlp0s26u1u2) is connected to a wireless network named zoneone while the Ethernet device (eno1) is connected to a connection named eno1. In addition to zoneone, NetworkManager has also listed two other WiFi connections named zonetwo and zonethree, neither of which currently has a device connected.

To find out the IP address allocated to a connection, the *ip* tool can be used with the address option:

```
# ip address
```

The above command can also be abbreviated:

```
# ip a
.
.
.
3: wlp0s26u1u2: <BROADCAST,MULTICAST,UP,LOWER_UP> mtu 1500 qdisc mq state UP
group default qlen 1000
    link/ether 74:da:38:ee:be:50 brd ff:ff:ff:ff:ff:ff
    inet 192.168.1.121/24 brd 192.168.1.255 scope global dynamic noprefixroute
wlp0s26u1u2
        valid_lft 57584sec preferred_lft 57584sec
.
.
.
```

The *ip* command will output information for all the devices detected on the system. For example, the above output shows that the WiFi device has been assigned an IP address of 192.168.1.121.

If we only wanted to list active connections, the *nmcli* command could have been used with the -a option:

```
# nmcli con show -a
NAME           UUID                                     TYPE      DEVICE
zoneone        2abecafa-4ea2-47f6-b20f-4fb0c0fd5e94     wifi      wlp0s26u1u2
eno1           99d40009-6bb1-4182-baad-a103941c90ff     ethernet  eno1
virbr0         e13e9552-1765-42d1-b739-ff981668fbee     bridge    virbr0
```

To switch the WiFi device connection from zoneone to zonetwo, we can run the following command:

```
# nmcli device wifi connect zonetwo -ask
Password:
```

The -ask flag causes *nmcli* to prompt the user to enter the password for the WiFi network. To include the WiFi password on the command line (particularly useful if the command is being executed in a script), use the password option:

```
# nmcli device wifi connect zonetwo password <password here>
```

The *nmcli* tool may also be used to scan for available WiFi networks as follows:

```
# nmcli device wifi list
IN-USE  SSID        MODE   CHAN  RATE         SIGNAL  BARS  SECURITY
        zoneone     Infra  6     195 Mbit/s   80            WPA2
*       zonetwo     Infra  11    130 Mbit/s   74            WPA1 WPA2
```

A currently active connection can be deactivated as follows:

```
# nmcli con down <connection name>
```

Similarly, an inactive connection can be brought back up at any time:

```
# nmcli con up <connection name>
```

When a connection is brought down, NetworkManager automatically searches for another connection, activates it, and assigns it to the device to which the previous connection was established. To prevent a connection from being used in this situation, disable the autoconnect option as follows:

```
# nmcli con mod <connection name> connection.autoconnect no
```

The following command may be used to obtain additional information about a specific connection. This includes the current values for all the connection properties:

```
# nmcli con show eno1
connection.id:                      eno1
connection.uuid:                    99d40009-6bb1-4182-baad-a103941c90ff
connection.stable-id:               --
connection.type:                    802-3-ethernet
connection.interface-name:          eno1
connection.autoconnect:             yes
connection.autoconnect-priority:    0
connection.autoconnect-retries:     -1 (default)
connection.multi-connect:           0 (default)
connection.auth-retries:            -1
connection.timestamp:               1554833695
connection.read-only:               no
connection.permissions:             --
connection.zone:                    --
connection.master:                  --
connection.slave-type:              --
connection.autoconnect-slaves:      -1 (default)
 .
 .
```

All of these properties can be modified using *nmcli* with the modify option using the following syntax:

```
# nmcli con mod <connection name> connection.<property name> <setting>
```

12.4 Working with Connection Profiles

So far, we have explored using connections without explaining how a connection is configured. The configuration of a connection is referred to as a connection profile and is stored in a file located in the */etc/NetworkManager/system-connections* directory, the contents of which might read as follows:

```
# ls /etc/NetworkManager/system-connections
zoneone.nmconnection     eno1.nmconnection
zonethree.nmconnection   zonetwo.nmconnection
Consider, for example, the contents of the eno1.nmconnection file:
id=eno1
uuid=efc69a99-17a3-3636-b68f-bfcc56a73844
type=ethernet
autoconnect-priority=-999
interface-name=eno1
timestamp=1679678184


[ethernet]

[ipv4]
method=auto

[ipv6]
addr-gen-mode=eui64
method=auto


[proxy]
```

The file contains basic information about the connection, including the type (Ethernet) of the device to which it is currently assigned (eno1) and the fact that the connection is to be automatically activated on system boot with an IP address obtained using DHCP (auto). Changes to the connection profile can be implemented by modifying this file and instructing *nmcli* to reload the connection configuration files:

```
# nmcli con reload
```

New connection profiles can also be created manually or generated automatically by *nmcli*. For example, assume a new network device has been installed on the system. When this happens, the NetworkManager service will detect the new hardware and create a device for it. In the example below, the new device has been assigned the name eno2:

```
# nmcli dev status
DEVICE      TYPE      STATE      CONNECTION
en01        ethernet  connected  eno1
eno2        ethernet  connected  Wired connection 1
```

NetworkManager automatically detected the device, activated it, and assigned it to a connection named "Wired connection 1". This is a default connection over which we have no configuration control because there is no interface configuration file for it in */etc/NetworkManager/system-connections*. Therefore, the next steps are to delete the "Wired connection 1" connection and use *nmcli* to create a new connection and assign it to the device. The command to delete a connection is as follows:

```
# nmcli con delete "Wired connection 1"
```

Next, *nmcli* can be used to create a new connection profile configured either with a static IP address or a dynamic IP address obtained from a DHCP server. To create a dynamic connection profile named *dyn_ip*, the following command would be used:

```
# nmcli connection add type ethernet con-name dyn_ip ifname eno2
Connection 'dyn_ip' (160d9e10-bbc8-439a-9c47-a2ec52990472) successfully added.
```

To create a new connection profile without locking it to a specific device, simply omit the ifname option in the command:

```
# nmcli connection add type ethernet con-name dyn_ip
```

After creating the connection, a file named *dyn_ip.nmconnection* will be added to the */etc/NetworkManager/system-connections* directory.

Alternatively, to create a connection named *static_ip* assigned a static IP address (in this case 192.168.1.200) the following command would be used:

```
# nmcli con add type ethernet con-name static_ip ifname eno0 ip4 192.168.1.200/24
gw4 192.168.1.1
Connection 'static_ip' (3fccafb3-e761-4271-b310-ad0f28ee8606) successfully added.
```

The corresponding *static_ip.nmconnection* file will read as follows:

```
[connection]
id=static_ip
uuid=41eca181-381c-4d12-b6c9-30446d4e29d1
type=ethernet
interface-name=eno0

[ethernet]

[ipv4]
address1=192.168.1.200/24,192.168.1.1
method=manual

[ipv6]
addr-gen-mode=default
method=auto

[proxy]
```

The command to add a new connection may be altered slightly to assign both IPv4 and IPv6 static addresses:

```
# nmcli con add type ethernet con-name static_ip ifname eno0 ip4 192.168.1.200/24
gw4 192.168.1.1  gw4 192.168.1.1 ip6 cabf::4532 gw6 2010:dfa::1
```

12.5 Interactive Editing

In addition to using *nmcli* with command-line options, the tool also includes an interactive mode that can be used to create and modify connection profiles. The following transcript, for example, shows interactive mode being used to create a new Ethernet connection named *demo_con*:

```
# nmcli con edit
Valid connection types: 6lowpan, 802-11-olpc-mesh (olpc-mesh), 802-11-wireless
(wifi), 802-3-ethernet (ethernet), adsl, bluetooth, bond, bridge, cdma, dummy,
generic, gsm, infiniband, ip-tunnel, macsec, macvlan, ovs-bridge, ovs-interface,
ovs-port, pppoe, team, tun, vlan, vpn, vxlan, wimax, wpan, bond-slave, bridge-
slave, team-slave
Enter connection type: ethernet


===| nmcli interactive connection editor |===


Adding a new '802-3-ethernet' connection


Type 'help' or '?' for available commands.
Type 'print' to show all the connection properties.
Type 'describe [<setting>.<prop>]' for detailed property description.


You may edit the following settings: connection, 802-3-ethernet (ethernet), 802-
1x, dcb, sriov, ethtool, match, ipv4, ipv6, tc, proxy
nmcli> set connection.id demo_con
nmcli> set connection.interface eno1
nmcli> set connection.autoconnect yes
nmcli> set ipv4.method auto
nmcli> set 802-3-ethernet.mtu auto
nmcli> set ipv6.method auto
nmcli> save
Saving the connection with 'autoconnect=yes'. That might result in an immediate
activation of the connection.
Do you still want to save? (yes/no) [yes] yes
Connection 'demo_con' (cb837408-6c6f-4572-9548-4932f88b9275) successfully saved.
nmcli> quit
```

The following transcript, on the other hand, modifies the previously created *static_ip* connection profile to use a different static IP address than the one originally specified:

```
# nmcli con edit static_ip


===| nmcli interactive connection editor |===
```

```
Editing existing '802-3-ethernet' connection: 'static_ip'

Type 'help' or '?' for available commands.
Type 'print' to show all the connection properties.
Type 'describe [<setting>.<prop>]' for detailed property description.

You may edit the following settings: connection, 802-3-ethernet (ethernet), 802-
1x, dcb, sriov, ethtool, match, ipv4, ipv6, tc, proxy
nmcli> print ipv4.addresses
ipv4.addresses: 192.168.1.200/24
nmcli> set ipv4.addresses 192.168.1.201/24
nmcli> save
Connection 'static_ip' (3fccafb3-e761-4271-b310-ad0f28ee8606) successfully
updated.
nmcli> quit
```

After modifying an existing connection, remember to instruct NetworkManager to reload the configuration profiles:

```
# nmcli con reload
```

When using interactive mode, it is useful to know that an extensive built-in help system is available to learn how to use the tool. The help topics can be accessed by typing help or ? at the *nmcli >* prompt:

```
nmcli> ?
-------------------------------------------------------------------------------
---[ Main menu ]---
goto      [<setting> | <prop>]          :: go to a setting or property
remove    <setting>[.<prop>] | <prop>   :: remove setting or reset property value
set       [<setting>.<prop> <value>]    :: set property value
describe  [<setting>.<prop>]            :: describe property
print     [all | <setting>[.<prop>]]    :: print the connection
verify    [all | fix]                   :: verify the connection
save      [persistent|temporary]        :: save the connection
activate  [<ifname>] [/<ap>|<nsp>]      :: activate the connection
back                                    :: go one level up (back)
help/?    [<command>]                   :: print this help
nmcli     <conf-option> <value>         :: nmcli configuration
quit                                    :: exit nmcli
-------------------------------------------------------------------------------
```

12.6 Configuring NetworkManager Permissions

In addition to making it easier to manage networks on RHEL 9, NetworkManager also allows permissions to be specified for connections. The following command, for example, restricts a connection profile to root and user accounts named john and caitlyn:

```
# nmcli con mod static_ip connection.permissions user:root,john,caitlyn
```

Once NetworkManager has reloaded the connection profiles, the *static_ip* connection will only be active and accessible to other users when at least one designated user is logged in to an active session on the system. As soon as the last of these users logs out, the connection will go down and remain inactive until one of the users signs back in.

In addition, only users with permission can change the connection status or configuration.

12.7 Summary

The NetworkManager service handles network management on RHEL 9. NetworkManager views a network as consisting of network interface devices and connections. A network device can be a physical Ethernet or WiFi device or a virtual device used by a virtual machine guest. Connections represent the network to which the devices connect and are configured by connection profiles. A configuration profile will, among other settings, define whether the connection has a static or dynamic IP address, the IP address of any gateway used by the network, and whether or not the connection should be established automatically each time the system starts up.

NetworkManager can be administered using several tools, including the *nmcli* and *nmtui* command-line tools, the *nm-connection-editor* graphical tool, and the network settings section of the Cockpit web interface. In general, the nmcli command-line tool provides the most features and flexibility.

Chapter 13

13. RHEL 9 Firewall Basics

A firewall is a vital component in protecting an individual computer system or network of computers from external attacks (typically from an internet connection). Any computer connected directly to an internet connection should ideally run a firewall to protect against malicious activity. Similarly, any internal network must have some form of firewall between it and an external internet connection.

RHEL 9 is supplied with powerful firewall technology known as *iptables* built-in. Entire books can, and indeed have, been written about configuring iptables. If you would like to learn about iptables, we recommend the following:

https://www.linuxtopia.org/Linux_Firewall_iptables/index.html

This chapter will cover some basic concepts of firewalls, TCP/IP ports, and services. Firewall configuration on RHEL 9 will be covered in the chapter entitled *"RHEL 9 Firewall Configuration with firewalld"*.

13.1 Understanding Ports and Services

The predominant network communications protocol in use these days is TCP/IP. It is the protocol used by the internet and, as such, has swept away most of the formerly popular protocols used for local area networks (LANs).

TCP/IP defines a total of 65,535 ports, of which 1023 are considered *well-known ports*. It is essential to understand that these are not physical ports into which network cables are connected but rather virtual ports on each network connection which can be used by applications and services to communicate over a TCP/IP network connection. In reality, the number of ports used by popular network clients and services comprises an even smaller subset of the well-known group of ports.

An operating system can provide several different TCP/IP services. A comprehensive list of such services is provided in the table at the end of this chapter. Still, such services include HTTPS for running a secure web server, FTP for allowing file transfers, SSH for providing secure remote login access and file transfer, and SMTP for transporting email messages. Each service is, in turn, assigned to a standard TCP/IP port. For example, HTTPS is assigned to port 443, while SSH communication occurs on port 22.

13.2 Securing Ports and Services

A large part of securing servers involves defining roles and, based on the roles, defining which services and ports should be enabled. For example, a server that acts solely as a web server should only run the HTTPS service (in addition to perhaps SSH for remote administration access). All other services should be disabled and, ideally, removed entirely from the operating system (thereby making it harder for an intruder to re-enable the service).

Securing a system involves removing any unnecessary services from the operating system and ensuring that the ports associated with the non-essential services are blocked using a firewall. The rules that define which ports are accessible and under what circumstances are determined using iptables.

Many operating systems are installed with several services installed and activated by default. Before installing a new operating system, the installation must be carefully planned. This planning involves deciding which services are not required and identifying which services have been installed and enabled by default. Deployment of new operating system installations should never be rushed. The fewer services and open ports available on a system, the smaller the surface area and opportunities for attackers.

13.3 RHEL 9 Services and iptables Rules

By default, a newly installed RHEL 9 system has no iptables rules defined to restrict access to ports. The following command may be executed in a terminal window to view the current iptables settings:

```
# iptables -L
Chain INPUT (policy ACCEPT)
target     prot opt source               destination

Chain FORWARD (policy ACCEPT)
target     prot opt source               destination

Chain OUTPUT (policy ACCEPT)
target     prot opt source               destination
```

As illustrated in the above output, no rules are currently defined. While this may appear to be an unsafe configuration, it is essential to remember that a newly installed RHEL 9 system also has few services running by default, making the ports useless to a potential attacker. For example, accessing a web server on a newly installed RHEL 9 system is impossible because no web server services are installed or running by default. Once services begin to be activated on the system, it will be important to establish a firewall strategy by defining iptables rules.

Several methods are available for defining iptables rules, including using command line tools and configuration files. For example, to block access to port 25 (used by the SMTP mail transfer protocol) from IP address 192.168.2.76, the following command could be issued in a terminal window:

```
# iptables -A INPUT -s 192.168.2.76 -p tcp --destination-port 25 -j DROP
```

If we now check the current rules, we will see that this one is currently listed:

```
# iptables -L
Chain INPUT (policy ACCEPT)
target     prot opt source               destination
```

```
DROP        tcp  --  192.168.2.76        anywhere            tcp dpt:smtp

Chain FORWARD (policy ACCEPT)
target     prot opt source              destination

Chain OUTPUT (policy ACCEPT)
target     prot opt source              destination
```

The rule may subsequently be removed as follows:

```
# iptables -D INPUT -s 192.168.2.76 -p tcp --destination-port 25 -j DROP
```

Given the complexity of iptables it is unsurprising that several user-friendly configuration tools have been created to ease the rule creation process. One such tool is the *firewall-cmd* command-line tool which will be covered in the chapter *"RHEL 9 Firewall Configuration with firewalld"*.

13.4 Well-Known Ports and Services

Before moving on to cover more complex firewall rules, it is first worth taking time to outline some of the key services that can be provided by an RHEL 9 system, together with the corresponding port numbers:

Port	Assignment	Description
20	FTP	**File Transfer Protocol (Data)** - The File Transfer protocol provides a mechanism for transferring specific files between network-connected computer systems. The transfer is typically performed using the ftp client. Most modern web browsers can also browse and download files on a remote FTP server. FTP uses TCP (rather than UDP) to transfer files, which is considered a highly reliable transport mechanism. FTP does not encrypt data and is not considered a secure file transfer protocol. Secure Copy Protocol (SCP) and Secure File Transfer Protocol (SFTP) are strongly recommended in place of FTP.
21	FTP	**File Transfer (Control)** - Traditionally, FTP has two ports assigned (port 20 and port 21). Port 20 was initially considered the data transfer port, while port 21 was assigned to communicate control information. However, in modern implementations, port 20 is rarely used, with all communication taking place on port 21.

22	SSH	**Secure Shell** - The Secure Shell provides a safe, encrypted, remote login session to a host over a TCP/IP network. The original mechanism for remote access was the Telnet protocol. However, because Telnet transmits data in plain text, its use is strongly discouraged in favor of the secure shell, which encrypts all communications, including login and password credentials. SSH also provides the mechanism by which files can be securely transferred using the Secure Copy Protocol (SCP) and is also the basis for the Secure File Transfer Protocol (SFTP). SSH also replaces both the rsh and rlogin clients.
23	Telnet	**Telnet** - Telnet is a terminal emulation protocol that can log into a remote system over a TCP/IP connection. The access is text-based, allowing the user to type into a command prompt on the remote host, and text displayed by the remote host is displayed on the local Telnet client. Telnet encrypts neither the password nor the text communicated between the client and server. As such, the use of telnet is strongly discouraged. Most modern systems will have port 23 closed and the telnet service disabled to prevent its use. SSH should be used in place of Telnet.
25	SMTP	**Simple Mail Transfer Protocol** - SMTP defines the mechanism by which email messages are sent from one network host to another. SMTP is a straightforward protocol requiring the mail service to always be available at the receiving host. Typically the receiving host will store incoming messages in a spool for subsequent access by the recipient using the POP3 or IMAP protocols. In addition, SMTP uses the TCP transport protocol to ensure error-free message delivery.
53	DNS	**Domain Name Server** - The service used by TCP/IP networks to translate host names and Fully Qualified Domain Names (FQDN) to IP addresses.
69	TFTP	**Trivial File Transfer Protocol** - TFTP is a stripped-down version of the File Transfer Protocol (FTP). It has a reduced command set and lacks authentication. The most significant feature of TFTP is that it uses UDP to transfer data. This results in high-speed transfer speeds but, consequently, lacks data reliability. TFTP is typically used in network-based booting for diskless workstations.

80	HTTP	**Hypertext Text Transfer Protocol** - HTTP is used to download text, graphics, and multimedia from a web server to a web browser. It defines the command and control mechanism between the browser and server, defining client requests and server responses. HTTP is based on the TCP transport protocol and, as such, is a connection-oriented protocol.
110	POP3	**Post Office Protocol** - The POP3 protocol is a mechanism for storing and retrieving incoming email messages from a server. In most corporate environments, incoming email is stored on an email server and then downloaded to an email client running on the user's desktop or laptop when the user checks email. However, POP3 downloads all new messages to the client and does not allow the user to choose which messages to download, view headers, or download only parts of messages. For this reason, the IMAP protocol is increasingly being used in place of POP3.
119	NNTP	**Network News Transfer Protocol** - The protocol responsible for posting and retrieving messages to and from Usenet News Servers (i.e., newsgroups and discussion forums hosted on remote servers). NNTP operates at the Application layer of the OSI stack and uses TCP to ensure error-free message retrieval and transmission.
123	NTP	**Network Time Protocol** - A protocol designed to synchronize computer clocks with an external time source. Using this protocol, an operating system or application can request the current time from a remote NTP server. The remote NTP server is usually based on the time provided by a nuclear clock. NTP is useful for ensuring that all systems in a network are set to the same, accurate time of day. This is of particular importance in security situations when, for example, the time a file was accessed or modified on a client or server is in question.
143	IMAP4	**Internet Message Access Protocol, Version 4** - IMAP4 is an advanced and secure email retrieval protocol. IMAP is similar to POP3, allowing users to access email messages stored on an email server. However, IMAP includes many additional features, such as the ability to selectively download messages, view message headers, search messages, and download part of a message. In addition, IMAP4 uses authentication and fully supports Kerberos authentication.

161	SNMP	**Simple Network Management Protocol** - Provides a mechanism whereby network administrators can collect information about network devices (such as hubs, bridges, routers, and switches). The SNMP protocol enables agents running on network devices to communicate their status to a central manager and, in turn, allows the manager to send new configuration parameters to the device agent. The agents can further be configured to notify the manager when certain events, known as traps, occur. SNMP uses UDP to send and receive data.
443	HTTPS	**Hypertext Transfer Protocol Secure** - The standard HTTP (non-secure) protocol transfers data in clear text (i.e., with no encryption and visible to anyone who might intercept the traffic). While this is acceptable for most web browsing purposes, it poses a severe security risk when confidential information such as credit card details needs to be transmitted from the browser to the web server. HTTPS addresses this using the Secure Sockets Layer (SSL) to send encrypted data between the client and server.
2049	NFS	**Network File System** - Originally developed by Sun Microsystems and subsequently widely adopted throughout the industry, NFS allows a file system on a remote system to be accessed over the network by another system as if the file system were on a local disk drive. NFS is widely used on UNIX and LINUX-based systems. Later versions of Microsoft Windows can also access NFS-shared file systems on UNIX and LINUX-based systems.

Table 13-1

13.5 Summary

A newly installed RHEL 9 system is generally considered secure due to the absence of services running on the system ports. Once the system begins to be configured for use, however, it is important to ensure that it is protected from attack through the implementation of a firewall. When configuring firewalls, it is important to understand the various ports and the corresponding services.

Several firewall options are available, the most basic being the command-line configuration of the iptables firewall interface. More intuitive and advanced options are available via firewalld, which will be covered in the next chapter.

14. RHEL 9 Firewall Configuration with firewalld

A firewall is vital in protecting a computer system or network of computers from external attack (typically from an external source via an internet connection). For example, any computer connected directly to an internet connection must run a firewall to protect against malicious activity. Similarly, any internal network must have some form of firewall between it and an external internet connection.

All Linux distributions are provided with a firewall solution of some form. In the case of RHEL 9, this takes the form of a service named *firewalld*.

While the subject of firewall configuration can be complex, fortunately, RHEL 9 provides command-line, web-based, and graphical tools that ease the firewall configuration process. This chapter will introduce the basic concepts of firewalld and cover the steps necessary to configure a firewall using the tools provided with the operating system.

14.1 An Introduction to firewalld

The firewalld service uses a set of rules to control incoming network traffic and define which traffic is to be blocked and which is to be allowed to pass through to the system and is built on top of a more complex firewall tool named *iptables*.

The firewalld system provides a flexible way to manage incoming traffic. The firewall could, for example, be configured to block traffic from arriving from a specific external IP address or to prevent all traffic arriving on a particular TCP/IP port. Rules may also be defined to forward incoming traffic to different systems or to act as an internet gateway to protect other computers on a network.

In keeping with standard security practices, a default firewalld installation is configured to block all access except SSH remote login and the DHCP service used by the system to obtain a dynamic IP address (both of which are essential if the system administrator is to be able to gain access to the system after completing the installation).

The critical elements of firewall configuration on RHEL 9 are *zones*, *interfaces*, *services*, and *ports*.

14.1.1 Zones

By default, firewalld is installed with a range of pre-configured zones. A zone is a pre-configured set of rules that can be applied to the system at any time to implement firewall configurations for specific scenarios quickly. The block zone, for example, blocks all incoming traffic, while the home zone imposes less strict rules on the assumption that the system is running in a safer environment where a greater level of trust is expected. New zones may be added to the system, and existing zones modified to add or remove rules. Zones may also be deleted entirely from the system. Table 14-1 lists the set of zones available by default on a RHEL 9 system:

Zone	Description
drop	The most secure zone. Only outgoing connections are permitted, and all incoming connections are dropped without any notification to the connecting client.
block	Similar to the drop zone, with the exception that incoming connections are rejected with an icmp-host-prohibited or icmp6-adm-prohibited notification.
public	Intended for use when connected to public networks or the internet where other computers are not known to be trustworthy. Allows select incoming connections.
external	When a system acts as the internet gateway for a network of computers, the external zone is applied to the interface connected to the internet. This zone is used with the *internal* zone when implementing masquerading or network address translation (NAT), as outlined later in this chapter. Allows select incoming connections.
internal	Used with the *external* zone and applied to the interface connected to the internal network. Assumes that the computers on the internal network are trusted. Allows select incoming connections.
dmz	For use when the system is running in the demilitarized zone (DMZ). These are generally computers that are publicly accessible but isolated from other parts of your internal network. Allows select incoming connections.
work	For use when running a system on a network in a work environment where other computers are trusted. Allows select incoming connections.
home	For use when running a system on a home network where other computers are trusted. Allows select incoming connections.
trusted	The least secure zone. All incoming connections are accepted.
nm-shared	This zone is used internally by NetworkManager when implementing connection sharing.
libvirt	Used by virtual networks, typically when the server is hosting virtual machines.

Table 14-1

To review specific settings for a zone, refer to the corresponding XML configuration file located on the system in the */usr/lib/firewalld/zones* directory. The following, for example, lists the content of the *public.xml* zone configuration file:

```xml
<?xml version="1.0" encoding="utf-8"?>
<zone>
  <short>Public</short>
  <description>For use in public areas. You do not trust the other computers
on networks to not harm your computer. Only selected incoming connections are
accepted.</description>
  <service name="ssh"/>
  <service name="dhcpv6-client"/>
  <service name="cockpit"/>
  <forward/>
</zone>
```

14.1.2 Interfaces

Any RHEL 9 system connected to the internet or a network (or both) will contain at least one *interface* in the form of either a physical or virtual network device. When firewalld is active, each of these interfaces is assigned to a zone allowing different levels of firewall security to be assigned to different interfaces. For example, consider a server containing two interfaces; one connected externally to the internet and the other to an internal network. In such a scenario, the external facing interface would most likely be assigned to the more restrictive *external* zone, while the internal interface might use the *internal* zone.

14.1.3 Services

TCP/IP defines a set of services that communicate on standard ports. Secure HTTPS web connections, for example, use port 443, while the SMTP email service uses port 25. To selectively enable incoming traffic for specific services, firewalld rules can be added to zones. The *home* zone, for example, does not permit incoming HTTPS connections by default. This traffic can be enabled by adding rules to a zone to allow incoming HTTPS connections without having to reference the specific port number.

14.1.4 Ports

Although common TCP/IP services can be referenced when adding firewalld rules, situations will arise where incoming connections need to be allowed on a specific port that is not allocated to a service. This can be achieved by adding rules that reference specific ports instead of services. This technique was used in the chapter *"An Overview of the Cockpit Web Interface"* when port 9090 was opened to allow access to the Cockpit web interface.

14.2 Checking firewalld Status

The firewalld service is installed and enabled by default on all RHEL 9 installations. The status of the service can be checked via the following command:

```
# systemctl status firewalld
 firewalld.service - firewalld - dynamic firewall daemon
    Loaded: loaded (/usr/lib/systemd/system/firewalld.service; enabled; vendor
preset: enabled)
```

```
  Active: active (running) since Thu 2019-02-14 14:24:31 EST; 3 days ago
    Docs: man:firewalld(1)
Main PID: 816 (firewalld)
   Tasks: 2 (limit: 25026)
  Memory: 30.6M
  CGroup: /system.slice/firewalld.service
          816 /usr/libexec/platform-python -s /usr/sbin/firewalld --nofork
--nopid
```

If necessary, the firewalld service may be installed as follows:

```
# dnf install firewalld
```

The firewalld service is enabled by default and will start automatically after installation and each time the system boots.

14.3 Configuring Firewall Rules with firewall-cmd

The *firewall-cmd* command-line utility allows information about the firewalld configuration to be viewed and changes to be made to zones and rules from within a terminal window.

When making changes to the firewall settings, it is important to be aware of the concepts of *runtime* and *permanent* configurations. By default, any rule changes are considered to be runtime configuration changes. This means that while the changes will take effect immediately, they will be lost next time the system restarts or the firewalld service reloads, for example, by issuing the following command:

```
# firewall-cmd --reload
```

The *--permanent* command-line option must be used to make a change permanent. Permanent changes do not occur until the firewalld service reloads but will remain in place until manually changed.

14.3.1 Identifying and Changing the Default Zone

To identify the default zone (in other words, the zone to which all interfaces will be assigned unless a different zone is specifically selected), use the *firewall-cmd* tool as follows:

```
# firewall-cmd --get-default-zone
public
```

To change the default to a different zone:

```
# firewall-cmd --set-default-zone=home
success
```

14.3.2 Displaying Zone Information

To list all of the zones available on the system:

```
# firewall-cmd --get-zones
block dmz drop external home internal libvirt nm-shared public trusted work
```

Obtain a list of zones currently active together with the interfaces to which they are assigned as follows:

```
# firewall-cmd --get-active-zones
external
  interfaces: eth0
internal
 interfaces: eth1
```

All of the rules currently configured for a specific zone may be listed as follows:

```
# firewall-cmd --zone=home --list-all
home (active)
  target: default
  icmp-block-inversion: no
  interfaces: eth0
  sources:
  services: cockpit dhcpv6-client mdns samba-client ssh
  ports:
  protocols:
  masquerade: no
  forward-ports:
  source-ports:
  icmp-blocks:
  rich rules:
```

Use the following command to list the services currently available for inclusion in a firewalld rule:

```
# firewall-cmd --get-services
RH-Satellite-6 amanda-client amanda-k5-client amqp amqps apcupsd audit bacula
bacula-client bgp bitcoin bitcoin-rpc bitcoin-testnet bitcoin-testnet-rpc ceph
ceph-mon cfengine cockpit ...
```

To list the services currently enabled for a zone:

```
# firewall-cmd --zone=public --list-services
cockpit dhcpv6-client ssh
```

A list of port rules can be obtained as follows:

```
# firewall-cmd --zone=public --list-ports
9090/tcp
```

14.3.3 Adding and Removing Zone Services

To add a service to a zone, in this case, adding HTTPS to the public zone, the following command would be used:

```
# firewall-cmd --zone=public --add-service=https
success
```

By default, this is a *runtime* change, so the added rule will be lost after a system reboot. To add a service permanently so that it remains in effect next time the system restarts, use the *--permanent* flag:

```
# firewall-cmd --zone=public --permanent --add-service=https
```

```
success
```

To verify that a service has been added permanently, be sure to include the *--permanent* flag when requesting the service list:

```
# firewall-cmd --zone=public --permanent --list-services
cockpit dhcpv6-client http https ssh
```

Note that as a permanent change, this new rule will not take effect until the system restarts or firewalld reloads:

```
# firewall-cmd --reload
```

Remove a service from a zone using the *--remove-service* option. Since this is a runtime change, the rule will be re-instated the next time the system restarts:

```
# firewall-cmd --zone=public --remove-service=https
```

To remove a service permanently, use the *--permanent* flag, remembering to reload firewalld if the change is required to take immediate effect:

```
# firewall-cmd --zone=public --permanent --remove-service=https
```

14.3.4 Working with Port-based Rules

To enable a specific port, use the *--add-port* option. Note that when manually defining the port, both the port number and protocol (TCP or UDP) will need to be provided:

```
# firewall-cmd --zone=public --permanent --add-port=5000/tcp
```

It is also possible to specify a range of ports when adding a rule to a zone:

```
# firewall-cmd --zone=public --permanent --add-port=5900-5999/udp
```

14.3.5 Creating a New Zone

An entirely new zone may be created by running the following command. Once created, the zone may be managed in the same way as any of the pre-defined zones:

```
# firewall-cmd --permanent --new-zone=myoffice
success
```

After adding a new zone, firewalld will need to be restarted before the zone becomes available:

```
# firewall-cmd --reload
success
```

14.3.6 Changing Zone/Interface Assignments

As previously discussed, each interface on the system must be assigned to a zone. The zone to which an interface is assigned can also be changed using the *firewall-cmd* tool. In the following example, the eth0 interface is assigned to the *public* zone:

```
# firewall-cmd --zone=public --change-interface=eth0
success
```

14.3.7 Masquerading

Masquerading is better known in networking administration circles as Network Address Translation (NAT). When using a RHEL 9 system as a gateway to the internet for a network of computers, masquerading allows all of the internal systems to use the IP address of that RHEL 9 system when communicating over the internet. This has the advantage of hiding the internal IP addresses of any systems from malicious external entities and also avoids the necessity to allocate a public IP address to every computer on the network.

Use the following command to check whether masquerading is already enabled on the firewall:

```
# firewall-cmd --zone=external --query-masquerade
```

Use the following command to enable masquerading (remembering to use the *--permanent* flag if the change is to be permanent):

```
# firewall-cmd --zone=external --add-masquerade
```

14.3.8 Adding ICMP Rules

The Internet Control Message Protocol (ICMP) is used by client systems on networks to send information, such as error messages, to each other. It is also the foundation of the ping command, which is used by network administrators and users alike to detect whether a particular client is alive on a network. The ICMP category allows for the blocking of specific ICMP message types. For example, an administrator might choose to block incoming ping (Echo Request) ICMP messages to prevent the possibility of a ping-based denial of service (DoS) attack (where a server is maliciously bombarded with so many ping messages that it becomes unable to respond to legitimate requests).

To view the ICMP types available for inclusion in firewalld rules, run the following command:

```
# firewall-cmd --get-icmptypes
address-unreachable bad-header beyond-scope communication-prohibited destination-
unreachable echo-reply ...
```

The following command, for example, permanently adds a rule to block echo-reply (ping request) messages for the public zone:

```
# firewall-cmd --zone=public --permanent --add-icmp-block=echo-reply
```

14.3.9 Implementing Port Forwarding

Port forwarding is used in conjunction with masquerading when the RHEL 9 system is acting as a gateway to the internet for an internal network of computer systems. Port forwarding allows traffic arriving at the firewall via the internet on a specific port to be forwarded to a particular system on the internal network. This is perhaps best described by way of an example.

Suppose that a RHEL 9 system is acting as the firewall for an internal network of computers, and one of the systems on the network is configured as a web server. Let's assume the web server system has an IP address of 192.168.2.20. The domain record for the website hosted on this system is configured with the public IP address behind which the RHEL 9 firewall system sits. When an HTTP web page request arrives on port 80 the RHEL 9 system acting as the firewall needs to know what to do with it. By configuring port forwarding, it is possible to direct all web traffic to the internal system hosting the web server (in this case, IP address 192.168.2.20), either continuing to use port 80, or diverting the traffic to a different port on the destination server. In fact, port forwarding can even be configured to forward the traffic to a different port on the same system as the firewall (a concept known as local forwarding).

To use port forwarding, begin by enabling masquerading as follows (in this case, the assumption is made that the interface connected to the internet has been assigned to the *external* zone):

```
# firewall-cmd --zone=external --add-masquerade
```

To forward from a port to a different local port, a command similar to the following would be used:

```
# firewall-cmd --zone=external --add-forward-port=port=22:proto=tcp:toport=2750
```

In the above example, any TCP traffic on port 22 will be forwarded to port 2750 on the local system. The following command, on the other hand, forwards port 20 on the local system to port 22 on the system with the IP address 192.168.0.19:

```
# firewall-cmd --zone=external \
        --add-forward-port=port=20:proto=tcp:toport=22:toaddr=192.168.0.19
```

Similarly, the following command forwards local port 20 to port 2750 on the system with IP address 192.168.0.18:

```
# firewall-cmd --zone=external --add-forward-port=port=20:proto=tcp:toport=2750:to
addr=192.168.0.18
```

14.4 Managing firewalld from the Cockpit Interface

So far, this chapter has provided an overview of firewalld and explored using the *firewall-cmd* command-line tool to manage firewall zones and interfaces. While *firewall-cmd* provides the most flexible way to manage the firewalld configuration, it is also possible to view and manage the services for the default zone within the Cockpit web console.

To access the firewalld settings, sign into the Cockpit interface and select *Networking* from the navigation panel. On the networking page, locate the *Firewall* section as shown in Figure 14-1 below and click on the *Edit rules and zones* button:

Figure 14-1

The Firewall page displays the current service rules configured for the default zone (and allows services to be removed), new services to be added to the zone, and for the firewall to be turned on and off:

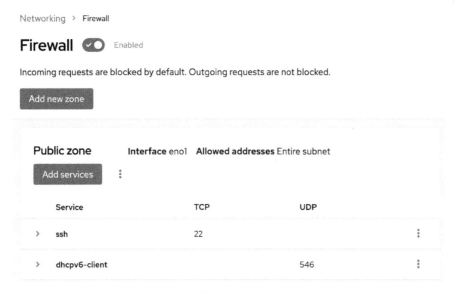

Figure 14-2

14.5 Managing firewalld using firewall-config

If you have access to the graphical desktop environment, the firewall may also be configured using the *firewall-config* tool. Though not installed by default, *firewall-config* may be installed as follows:

```
# dnf install firewall-config
```

When launched, the main *firewall-config* screen appears as illustrated in Figure 14-3:

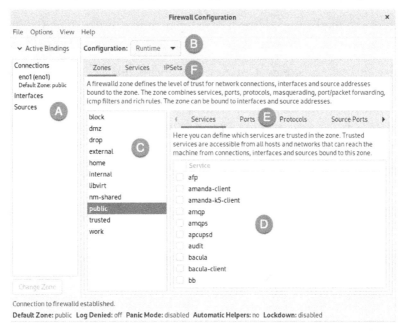

Figure 14-3

The key areas of the tool can be summarized as follows:

A - Displays all of the currently active interfaces and the zones to which they are assigned. To assign an interface to a different zone, select it from this panel, click the *Change Zone* button and select the required zone from the resulting dialog.

B - Controls whether the information displayed and any changes made within the tool apply to the runtime or permanent rules.

C - The list of zones, services, or IPSets configured on the system. The information in this panel depends on the selection made from toolbar F. Selecting an item from the list in this panel updates the main panel marked D.

D - The main panel contains information about the current category selection in toolbar E. In this example, the panel displays services for the *public* zone. The checkboxes next to each service control whether the service is enabled within the firewall. Within these category panels, new rules can be added or existing rules configured or removed.

E - Controls the content displayed in panel D. Selecting items from this bar shows the current rule for the chosen category.

F - Controls the list displayed in panel C.

The *firewall-config* tool is straightforward and intuitive to use and allows many of the tasks available with *firewall-cmd* to be performed in a visual environment.

14.6 Summary

A carefully planned and implemented firewall is vital to any secure system. In the case of RHEL 9, the firewalld service provides a firewall system that is both flexible and easy to administer.

The firewalld service uses the concept of zones to group sets of firewall rules and includes a suite of pre-defined zones designed to meet a range of firewall protection requirements. These zones may be modified to add or remove rules, or entirely new zones created and configured. The network devices on the system that connect to networks or the internet are referred to as interfaces. Each interface, in turn, is assigned to a zone. The primary tools for working with firewalld are the *firewall-cmd* command-line tool and the *firewall-config* graphical utility. Minimal firewall management options are also available via the Cockpit web interface.

Chapter 15

15. Configuring SSH Key-based Authentication on RHEL 9

When a RHEL 9 system is first installed, it is configured by default to allow remote command-line access via Secure Shell (SSH) connections. SSH provides password-protected and encrypted access to the system for the root account and any other users added during the installation phase. However, this level of security is inadequate and should be upgraded to SSH key-based authentication as soon as possible.

This chapter will outline the steps to increase the security of a RHEL 9 system by implementing key-based SSH authentication.

15.1 An Overview of Secure Shell (SSH)

SSH is designed to allow secure remote access to systems to gain shell access and transfer files and data. As will be covered in *"RHEL 9 Remote Desktop Access with VNC"*, SSH can also provide a secure tunnel through which remote access to the GNOME desktop can be achieved over a network connection.

A basic SSH configuration consists of a client (used on the computer establishing the connection) and a server (running on the system to which the connection is to be established). A user might, for example, use an SSH client running on a Linux, Windows, or macOS system to connect to the SSH server running on a RHEL 9 system to gain access to a shell command-line prompt or to perform file transfers. All communications between the client and server, including the password entered to gain access, are encrypted to prevent outside parties from intercepting the data.

The inherent weakness in a basic SSH implementation is that it depends entirely on the strength of the passwords assigned to the accounts on the system. If a malicious party is able to identify the password for an account (either through guesswork, deception, or a brute force attack), the system becomes vulnerable. This weakness can be addressed by implementing SSH key-based authentication.

15.2 SSH Key-based Authentication

SSH key-based authentication uses asymmetric public key encryption to add an extra layer of security to remote system access. The concept of public key encryption was devised in 1975 by Whitfield Diffie and Martin Hellman and is based on using a pair of private and public keys.

In a public key encryption system, the public key is used to encrypt data that can only be decrypted by the owner of the private key.

In the case of SSH key-based authentication, the host holds the private key on which the SSH client is located, while the corresponding public key resides on the system on which the SSH server is running. Therefore, it is vital to protect the private key since ownership of the key will allow anyone to log into the remote system. As an added layer of protection, the private key may also be encrypted and protected by a password which must be entered each time a connection is established to the server.

15.3 Setting Up Key-based Authentication

There are four steps to setting up key-based SSH authentication, which can be summarized as follows:

1. Generate the public and private keys.

2. Install the public key on the server.

3. Test authentication.

4. Disable password-based authentication on the server.

The remainder of this chapter will outline these steps in greater detail for Linux, macOS, and Windows-based client operating systems.

15.4 Installing and Starting the SSH Service

If the SSH server is not already installed and running on the system, it can be added using the following commands:

```
# dnf install openssh-server
# systemctl start sshd.service
# systemctl enable sshd.service
```

15.5 SSH Key-based Authentication from Linux and macOS Clients

The first step in setting up SSH key-based authentication is to generate the key pairs on the client system. If the client system is running Linux or macOS, this is achieved using the *ssh-keygen* utility:

```
# ssh-keygen
```

This command will result in output similar to the following:

```
Generating public/private rsa key pair.
Enter file in which to save the key (/home/<username>/.ssh/id_rsa):
```

Press the Enter key to accept the default location for the key files. This will place two files in the *.ssh* sub-directory of the current user's home directory. The private key will be stored in a file named *id_rsa* while the public key will reside in the file named *id_rsa.pub*.

Next, *ssh-keygen* will prompt for a passphrase with which to protect the private key. If a passphrase is provided, the private key will be encrypted on the local disk, and the passphrase will be required to access the remote system. Therefore, for better security, the use of a passphrase is recommended.

```
Enter passphrase (empty for no passphrase):
```

Finally, the *ssh-keygen* tool will generate the following output indicating that the keys have been generated:

```
Your identification has been saved in /home/neil/.ssh/id_rsa.
Your public key has been saved in /home/neil/.ssh/id_rsa.pub.
The key fingerprint is:
SHA256:FOLGWEEGFIjWnCT5wtTOv5VK4hdimzWghZizUEMYbfo <username>@<hostname>
The key's randomart image is:
+---[RSA 2048]----+
|.BB+=+*..        |
|o+B= *  . .      |
|===.. + .        |
|*+ *  . .        |
|.++ o   S        |
|..E+ * o         |
|  o B *          |
|   + +           |
|    .            |
+----[SHA256]-----+
```

The next step is to install the public key onto the remote server system. This can be achieved using the *ssh-copy-id* utility as follows:

```
$ ssh-copy-id username@remote_hostname
```

For example:

```
$ ssh-copy-id neil@192.168.1.100
/usr/bin/ssh-copy-id: INFO: Source of key(s) to be installed: "/home/neil/.ssh/
id_rsa.pub"
/usr/bin/ssh-copy-id: INFO: attempting to log in with the new key(s), to filter
out any that are already installed
/usr/bin/ssh-copy-id: INFO: 1 key(s) remain to be installed -- if you are
prompted now it is to install the new keys
neil@192.168.1.100's password:

Number of key(s) added: 1

Now try logging into the machine, with:   "ssh 'neil@192.168.1.100'"
and check to make sure that only the key(s) you wanted were added.
```

Once the key is installed, test that the authentication works by attempting a remote login using the *ssh* client:

```
$ ssh -l <username> <hostname>
```

If the private key is encrypted and protected with a passphrase, enter the phrase when prompted to complete the authentication and establish remote access to the RHEL 9 system:

```
Enter passphrase for key '/home/neil/.ssh/id_rsa':
Last login: Fri Mar 31 14:29:28 2023 from 192.168.86.21
```

Configuring SSH Key-based Authentication on RHEL 9

```
[neil@demosystem02 ~]$
```

Repeat these steps for any other accounts on the server for which remote access is required. If access is also required from other client systems, copy the *id_rsa* private key file to the *.ssh* sub-directory of your home folder on the other systems.

As currently configured, access to the remote system can still be achieved using less secure password authentication. Once you have verified that key-based authentication works, password authentication will need to be disabled on the system. To understand how to change this setting, begin by opening the */etc/ssh/sshd_config* file and locating the following line:

```
Include /etc/ssh/sshd_config.d/*.conf
```

This tells us that sshd configuration settings are controlled by files in the */etc/ssh/sshd_config.d* directory. These filenames must be prefixed with a number and have a *.conf* filename extension, for example:

```
01-permitrootlogin.conf
50-redhat.conf
```

The number prefix designates the priority assigned to the file relative to the other files in the folder, with 01 being the highest priority. This ensures that if a configuration file contains a setting conflicting with another file, the one with the highest priority will always take precedence.

Within the */etc/ssh/sshd_config.d* folder, create a new file named *02-nopasswordlogin.conf* with content that reads as follows:

```
PasswordAuthentication no
```

Save the file and restart the sshd service to implement the change:

```
# systemctl restart sshd.service
```

From this point on, it will only be possible to remotely access the system using SSH key-based authentication, and when doing so, you won't be required to enter a password.

15.6 Managing Multiple Keys

It is common for multiple private keys to reside on a client system, each providing access to a different server. As a result, several options exist for selecting a specific key when establishing a connection. It is possible, for example, to specify the private key file to be used when launching the ssh client as follows:

```
$ ssh -l neilsmyth -i ~/.ssh/id_work 35.194.18.119
```

Alternatively, the SSH client user configuration file may associate key files with servers. The configuration file is named config, must reside in the *.ssh* directory of the user's home directory, and can be used to configure a wide range of options, including the private key file, the default port to use when connecting, the default user name, and an abbreviated nickname via which to reference the server. The following example config file defines different key files for two servers and allows them to be referenced by the nicknames home and work. In the case of the work system, the file also specifies the user name to be used when authenticating:

```
Host work
  HostName 35.194.18.119
  IdentityFile ~/.ssh/id_work
  User neilsmyth

Host home
  HostName 192.168.0.21
  IdentityFile ~/.ssh/id_home
```

Before setting up the configuration file, the user would have used the following command to connect to the work system:

```
$ ssh -l neilsmyth -i ~/.ssh/id_work 35.194.18.119
```

Now, however, the command can be shortened as follows:

```
$ ssh work
```

A full listing of configuration file options can be found by running the following command:

```
$ man ssh_config
```

15.7 SSH Key-based Authentication from Windows Clients

Recent releases of Windows include a subset of the OpenSSH implementation used by most Linux and macOS systems as part of Windows PowerShell. This allows SSH key-based authentication to be set up from a Windows client using similar steps to those outlined above for Linux and macOS.

On Windows, search for Windows PowerShell and select it from the results. Once running, the PowerShell window will appear as shown in Figure 15-1:

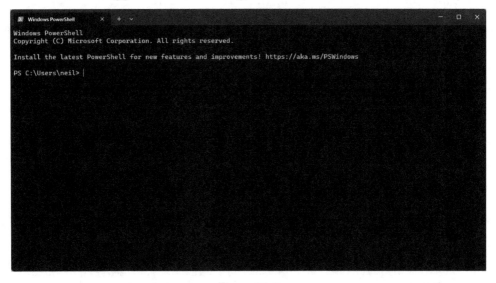

Figure 15-1

If you already have a private key from another client system, copy the *id_rsa* file to a folder named *.ssh* on the Windows system. Once the file is in place, test the authentication within the PowerShell

Configuring SSH Key-based Authentication on RHEL 9

window as follows:

```
$ ssh -l <username>@<hostname>
```

For example:

```
PS C:\Users\neil> ssh -l neil 192.168.1.101
Enter passphrase for key 'C:\Users\neil\.ssh\id_rsa':
```

Enter the passphrase when prompted and complete the authentication process.

If the private key does not yet exist, generate a new private and public key pair within the PowerShell window using the *ssh-keygen* utility using the same steps outlined for Linux and macOS. Once the keys have been generated, they will again be located in the *.ssh* directory of the current user's home folder, and the public key file *id_rsa.pub* will need to be installed on the remote RHEL 9 system. Unfortunately, Windows PowerShell does not include the *ssh-copy-id* utility, so this task must be performed manually.

Within the PowerShell window, change directory into the *.ssh* sub-directory and display the content of the public key *id_rsa.pub* file:

```
PS C:\Users\neil> cd .ssh
PS C:\Users\neil\.ssh> type id_rsa.pub
ssh-rsa AAAAB3NzaC1yc2EAAAADAQABAAABAQDFgx1vzu591l16/uQw7FbmKVsQ3fzLz9MW1fgo4sdsx
Xp81wCHNAlqcjx1Pgr9BJPXWUMInQOi7BQ5I+vc2xQ2AS0kMq3ZH9ybWuQe/U2GjueXZd0FKrEXrT55wM
36Rm6Ii3roUCoGCzGR8mn95JvRB3VtCyDdzTWSi8JBpK5gV5oOxNTNPsewlLzouBlCT1qW3CKwEiIwu8S
9MTL7m3nrcaNeLewTTHevvHw4QDwzFQ+B0PDg96fzsYoTXVhzyHSWyo6H0gqrft7aK+gILBtEIhWTkSVE
MAzy1piKtCr1IYTmVK6engv0aoGtMUq6FnOeGp5FjvKkF4aQkh1QR28r neil@DESKTOP-S8P8D3N
```

Highlight the file's content and copy it using the Ctrl-C keyboard shortcut.

Remaining within the PowerShell window, log into the remote system using password authentication:

```
PS C:\Users\neil\.ssh> ssh -l <username> <hostname>
```

Once signed in, check if the *.ssh* sub-directory exists. If it does not, create it as follows:

```
$ mkdir .ssh
```

Change directory into *.ssh* and check whether a file named *authorized_keys* already exists. If it does not, create it and paste the content of the public key file from the Windows system into it.

If the *authorized_keys* file already exists, it likely contains other keys. If this is the case, edit the file and paste the new public key at the end of the file. The following file, for example, contains two keys:

```
ssh-rsa AAAAB3NzaC1yc2EAAAADAQABAAABAQCzRWH27Xs8ZA5rIbZXKgxFY5XXauMv+6F5PljBLJ6j
+9nkmykVe3GjZTp3oD+KMRbT2kTEPbDpFD67DNL0eiX2ZuEEiYsxZfGCRCPBGYmQttFRHEAFnlS1Jx/
G4W5UNKvhAXWyMwDEKiWvqTVy6syB2Ritoak+D/Sc8nJflQ6dtw0jBs+S7Aim8TPfgpi4p5XJGruXNRS
camk68NgnPfTL3vT726EuABCk6C934KARd+/AXa8/5rNOh4ETPstjBRfFJ0tpmsWWhhNEnwJRqS2LD0
ug7E3yFI2qsNKGEzvAYUC8Up45MRP7liR3aMlCBilltsy9R+IB7oMEycZAe/qj neil@localhost.
localdomain
ssh-rsa AAAAB3NzaC1yc2EAAAADAQABAAABAQDFgx1vzu591l16/uQw7FbmKVsQ3fzLz9MW1fgo4sdsx
Xp81wCHNAlqcjx1Pgr9BJPXWUMInQOi7BQ5I+vc2xQ2AS0kMq3ZH9ybWuQe/U2GjueXZd0FKrEXrT55wM
```

```
36Rm6Ii3roUCoGCzGR8mn95JvRB3VtCyDdzTWSi8JBpK5gV5oOxNTNPsewlLzouBlCT1qW3CKwEiIwu8S
9MTL7m3nrcaNeLewTTHevvHw4QDwzFQ+B0PDg96fzsYoTXVhzyHSWyo6H0gqrft7aK+gILBtEIhWTkSVE
MAzy1piKtCr1IYTmVK6engv0aoGtMUq6FnOeGp5FjvKkF4aQkh1QR28r neil@DESKTOP-S8P8D3N
```

Once the public key is installed on the server, test the authentication by logging in to the server from within the PowerShell window, for example:

```
PS C:\Users\neil\.ssh> ssh -l neil 192.168.1.100
Enter passphrase for key 'C:\Users\neil\.ssh\id_rsa':
```

When key-based authentication has been set up for all the accounts and verified, disable password authentication on the RHEL 9 system as outlined at the end of the previous section.

15.8 SSH Key-based Authentication using PuTTY

For Windows systems that do not have OpenSSH available or as a more flexible alternative to using PowerShell, the PuTTY tool is a widely used alternative. The first step in using PuTTY is downloading and installing it on any Windows system that needs an SSH client. PuTTY is a free utility and can be downloaded using the following link:

https://www.chiark.greenend.org.uk/~sgtatham/putty/latest.html

Download the Windows installer executable that matches your Windows system (32-bit and 64-bit versions are available), then execute the installer to complete the installation.

If a private key already exists on another system, create the *.ssh* folder in the current user's home folder and copy the private *id_rsa* key into it.

Next, the private key file needs to be converted to a PuTTY private key format file using the PuTTYgen tool. Locate this utility by typing "PuTTY Key Generator" into the search bar of the Windows Start menu and launch it:

Figure 15-2

Once launched, click on the Load button located in the Actions section and navigate to the private key file previously copied to the *.ssh* folder (note that it may be necessary to change the file type filter to All Files (*.*) for the key file to be visible). Once located, select the file and load it into PuttyGen. When prompted, enter the passphrase used initially to encrypt the file. Once the private key has been imported, save it as a PuTTY key file by clicking the Save Private Key button. For consistency, save the key file to the *.ssh* folder but give it a different name to differentiate it from the original key file.

Launch PuTTY from the Start menu and enter the IP address or hostname of the remote server into the main screen before selecting the *Connection -> SSH -> Auth -> Credentials* category in the left-hand panel, as highlighted in Figure 15-3:

Figure 15-3

Click the Browse button next to the *Private key for authentication* field and navigate to and select the previously saved PuTTY private key file. Then, optionally, scroll to the top of the left-hand panel, select the Session entry, and enter a name for the session in the Saved Sessions field before clicking on the Save button. This will save the session configuration for future use without re-entering the settings each time.

Finally, click on the Open button to establish the connection to the remote server, entering the user name and passphrase when prompted to do so to complete the authentication.

15.9 Generating a Private Key with PuTTYgen

The previous section explored using existing private and public keys when working with PuTTY. If keys do not exist, they can be created using the PuTTYgen tool, which is included in the main PuTTY installation.

To create new keys, launch PuttyGen and click on the Generate button highlighted in Figure 15-4:

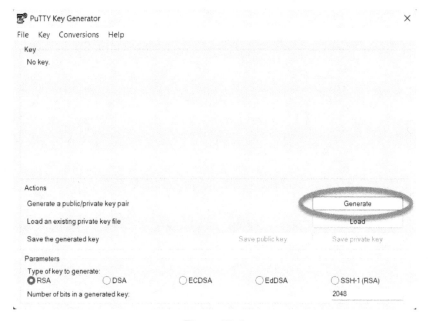

Figure 15-4

Move the mouse pointer to generate random data as instructed, then enter an optional passphrase to encrypt the private key. Once the keys have been generated, save the files to suitable locations using the Save public key and Save private key buttons. As outlined in the previous section, the private key can be used with PuTTY. To install the public key on the remote server, use the steps covered in the earlier section on SSH within PowerShell on Windows.

15.10 Summary

Any remote access to a RHEL 9 system must be implemented in a way that provides a high level of security. By default, SSH allows remote system access using password-based authentication. However, this leaves the system vulnerable to anyone who can guess a password or find out the password through other means. For this reason, key-based authentication is recommended to protect system access. Key-based authentication uses public key encryption involving public and private keys. When implemented, users can only connect to a server if they are using a client with a private key that matches a public key on the server. As an added layer of security, the private key may also be encrypted and password protected. Once key-based encryption has been implemented, the server system is configured to disable support for the less secure password-based authentication.

This chapter has provided an overview of SSH key-based authentication and outlined the steps involved in generating keys and configuring clients on macOS, Linux, and Windows, as well as installing and managing public keys on a RHEL 9 server.

16. RHEL 9 Remote Desktop Access with VNC

RHEL 9 can be configured to provide remote access to the graphical desktop environment over a network or internet connection. Although not enabled by default, displaying and accessing a RHEL 9 desktop from a system anywhere else on a network or the internet is relatively straightforward. This can be achieved regardless of whether that system runs Linux, Windows, or macOS. There are even apps available for Android and iOS that will allow you to access your RHEL 9 desktop from just about anywhere that a data signal is available.

Remote desktop access can be helpful in many scenarios. For example, it enables you or another person to view and interact with your RHEL 9 desktop environment from another computer system on the same network or over the internet. This is useful if you need to work on your computer when you are away from your desk, such as while traveling. It is also helpful when a co-worker or IT support technician needs access to your desktop to resolve a problem.

When the RHEL 9 system runs on a cloud-based server, it also allows access to the desktop environment as an alternative to performing administrative tasks using the command-line prompt or Cockpit web console.

The RHEL 9 remote desktop functionality is based on a technology known as Virtual Network Computing (VNC). This chapter will cover the key aspects of configuring and using remote desktops within RHEL 9.

16.1 Secure and Insecure Remote Desktop Access

In this chapter, we will cover both secure and insecure remote desktop access methods. Assuming you are accessing one system from another within a secure internal network, using the insecure access method is generally safe. If, on the other hand, you plan to access your desktop remotely over any public network, you must use the secure method of access to avoid your system and data being compromised.

16.2 Installing the GNOME Desktop Environment

It is, of course, only possible to access the desktop environment if the desktop itself has been installed. If, for example, the system was initially configured as a server, it is unlikely that the desktop packages were installed. The easiest way to install the packages necessary to run the GNOME desktop is to perform a group install. The key to installing groups of packages to enable a specific feature is knowing the group's name. At the time of writing, there are two groups for installing the desktop environment on RHEL 9: "Server with GUI" and "Workstation". As the group names tend to change from one RHEL release to another, it is helpful to know that the list of groups that are either installed or available to be installed can be obtained using the *dnf* utility as follows:

```
# dnf grouplist
Updating Subscription Management repositories.
Available Environment Groups:
    Server with GUI
    Minimal Install
    Workstation
    Custom Operating System
    Virtualization Host
Installed Environment Groups:
    Server
Installed Groups:
    Container Management
    Headless Management
Available Groups:
    Legacy UNIX Compatibility
    Graphical Administration Tools
    Smart Card Support
    RPM Development Tools
    .NET Development
    System Tools
    Development Tools
    Console Internet Tools
    Security Tools
    Network Servers
    Scientific Support
```

The Workstation environment group is listed as available (and therefore not already installed) in the above example. To find out more information about the contents of a group before installation, use the following command:

```
# dnf groupinfo workstation
Updating Subscription Management repositories.
Environment Group: Workstation
 Description: Workstation is a user-friendly desktop system for laptops and PCs.
 Mandatory Groups:
    Common NetworkManager submodules
    Core
    Fonts
    GNOME
    Guest Desktop Agents
    Hardware Support
    Internet Browser
    Multimedia
```

```
    Printing Client
    Standard
    Workstation product core
    base-x
  Optional Groups:
    Backup Client
    GNOME Applications
    Headless Management
    Internet Applications
    Office Suite and Productivity
    Remote Desktop Clients
    Smart Card Support
```

Having confirmed that this is the correct group, it can be installed as follows:

```
# dnf groupinstall workstation
```

Once installed, and assuming that the system has a display added, the desktop can be launched using the following *startx* command:

```
$ startx
```

If, on the other hand, the system is a server with no directly connected display, the only way to run and access the desktop will be to configure VNC support on the system.

16.3 Installing VNC on RHEL 9

Access to a remote desktop requires a VNC server installed on the remote system, a VNC viewer on the system from which access is being established, and, optionally, a secure SSH connection. While several VNC server and viewer implementations are available, Red Hat has standardized on TigerVNC, which provides both server and viewer components for Linux-based operating systems. VNC viewer clients for non-Linux platforms include RealVNC and TightVNC.

To install the TigerVNC server package on RHEL 9, run the following command:

```
# dnf install tigervnc-server
```

If required, the TigerVNC viewer may also be installed as follows:

```
# dnf install tigervnc
```

Once the server has been installed, the system must be configured to run one or more VNC services and open the appropriate ports on the firewall.

16.4 Configuring the VNC Server

With the VNC server packages installed, the next step is configuring the server. The first step is to specify a password for the remote desktop environment user. While logged in as root, execute the *vncpasswd* command (where the user name is assumed to be demo):

```
# su - demo
[demo@demoserver ~]$ vncpasswd
Password:
```

RHEL 9 Remote Desktop Access with VNC

```
Verify:
Would you like to enter a view-only password (y/n)? n
A view-only password is not used
[demo@demoserver ~]$ exit
#
```

Next, a VNC server configuration file named *vncserver@.service* needs to be created in the */etc/systemd/system* directory. The content of this file should read as follows, where all instances of <USER> are replaced with the username referenced when the VNC password was set:

```
[Unit]
Description=Remote desktop service (VNC)
After=syslog.target network.target

[Service]
Type=forking
WorkingDirectory=/home/<USER>
User=<USER>
Group=<USER>

ExecStartPre=/bin/sh -c '/usr/bin/vncserver -kill %i > /dev/null 2>&1 || :'
ExecStart=/usr/bin/vncserver -autokill %i
ExecStop=/usr/bin/vncserver -kill %i

Restart=on-success
RestartSec=15
[Install]
WantedBy=multi-user.target
```

Next, the firewall needs to be configured to provide external access to the VNC server for remote VNC viewer instances, for example:

```
# firewall-cmd --permanent --zone=public --add-port=5901/tcp
# firewall-cmd --reload
```

With the service configuration file created, the service needs to be enabled and started as follows:

```
# systemctl daemon-reload
# systemctl start  vncserver@:1.service
# systemctl enable  vncserver@:1.service
```

Note that :1 is included in the service name to indicate that this is the service for VNC server display number 1. This matches port 5901, which was previously opened in the firewall.

Check that the service has started successfully as follows:

```
# systemctl status vncserver@:1.service
```

If the service fails to start, run the *journalctl* command to check for error messages:

```
# journalctl -xe
```

Also, try again after rebooting the system. If the service continues to fail, the VNC server can be started manually by logging in as the designated user and running the vncserver command:

```
$ vncserver :1
```

16.5 Connecting to a VNC Server

VNC viewer implementations are available for a wide range of operating systems. Therefore, a quick internet search will likely provide numerous links containing details on obtaining and installing this tool on your chosen platform.

From the desktop of a Linux system on which a VNC viewer such as TigerVNC is installed, a remote desktop connection can be established as follows from a Terminal window:

```
$ vncviewer <hostname>:<display number>
```

In the above example, <hostname> is either the hostname or IP address of the remote system, and <display number> is the display number of the VNC server desktop, for example:

```
$ vncviewer 192.168.1.115:1
```

Alternatively, run the command without any options to be prompted for the details of the remote server:

Figure 16-1

Enter the hostname or IP address followed by the display number (for example, 192.168.1.115:1) into the VNC server field and click on the Connect button. The viewer will prompt for the user's VNC password to complete the connection, at which point a new window containing the remote desktop will appear.

This section assumed that the remote desktop was accessed from a Linux or UNIX system; the same steps apply to most other operating systems.

Connecting to a remote VNC server using the steps in this section results in an insecure, unencrypted connection between the client and server. This means the data transmitted during the remote session is vulnerable to interception. Therefore, a few extra steps are necessary to establish a secure and encrypted connection.

16.6 Establishing a Secure Remote Desktop Session

The remote desktop configurations explored in this chapter are considered insecure because no encryption is used. This is acceptable when the remote connection does not extend outside an internal network protected by a firewall. However, a more secure option is needed when a remote session is required over an internet connection. This is achieved by tunneling the remote desktop through a secure shell (SSH) connection. This section will cover how to do this on Linux, UNIX, and macOS client systems.

The SSH server is typically installed and activated by default on RHEL 9 systems. If this is not the case on your system, refer to the chapter *"Configuring SSH Key-based Authentication on RHEL 9"*.

Assuming the SSH server is installed and active, it is time to move to the other system. At the other system, log in to the remote system using the following command, which will establish the secure tunnel between the two systems:

```
$ ssh -l <username> -L 5901:localhost:5901 <remotehost>
```

In the above example, <username> references the user account on the remote system for which VNC access has been configured, and <remotehost> is either the hostname or IP address of the remote system, for example:

```
$ ssh -l neilsmyth -L 5901:localhost:5901 192.168.1.115
```

When prompted, log in using the account password. With the secure connection established, it is time to launch *vncviewer* to use the secure tunnel. Leaving the SSH session running in the other terminal window, launch another terminal and enter the following command:

```
$ vncviewer localhost:5901
```

The *vncviewer* session will prompt for a password if one is required, and then launch the VNC viewer providing secure access to your desktop environment.

Although the connection is now secure and encrypted, the VNC viewer will most likely still report that the connection is insecure. Figure 16-2, for example, shows the warning dialog displayed by the RealVNC viewer running on a macOS system:

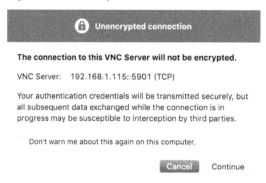

Figure 16-2

Unfortunately, although the connection is now secure, the VNC viewer software has no way of knowing this and consequently continues to issue warnings. However, rest assured that as long as the SSH tunnel is being used, the connection is indeed secure.

In the above example, we left the SSH tunnel session running in a terminal window. If you would prefer to run the session in the background, this can be achieved by using the –f and –N flags when initiating the connection:

```
$ ssh -l <username> -f -N -L 5901:localhost:5901 <remotehost>
```

The above command will prompt for a password for the remote server and then establish the connection in the background, leaving the terminal window available for other tasks.

If you are connecting to the remote desktop from outside the firewall, keep in mind that the IP address for the SSH connection will be the external IP address provided by your ISP or cloud hosting provider, not the LAN IP address of the remote system (since this IP address is not visible to those outside the firewall). Therefore, you will also need to configure your firewall to forward port 22 (for the SSH connection) to the IP address of the system running the desktop. It is not necessary to forward port 5900. Steps to perform port forwarding differ between firewalls, so refer to the documentation for your firewall, router, or wireless base station for details specific to your configuration.

16.7 Establishing a Secure Tunnel on Windows using PuTTY

A similar approach is taken to establishing a secure desktop session from a Windows system to a RHEL 9 server. Assuming you already have a VNC client such as TightVNC installed, the remaining requirement is a Windows SSH client (in this case, PuTTY).

Once PuTTY is downloaded and installed, the first step is establishing a secure connection between the Windows system and the remote RHEL 9 system with appropriate tunneling configured. When launched, PuTTY displays the following screen:

Figure 16-3

Enter the IP address or hostname of the remote host (or the external IP address of the gateway if you are connecting from outside the firewall). The next step is to set up the tunnel. Click on the + next to SSH in the Category tree on the left-hand side of the dialog and select Tunnels. The screen should subsequently appear as follows:

Figure 16-4

Enter 5901 as the Source port and localhost:5901 as the Destination, and click the Add button. Finally, return to the main screen by clicking on the Session category. Enter a name for the session in the Saved Sessions text field and press Save. Click on Open to establish the connection. A terminal window will appear with the login prompt from the remote system. Enter the appropriate user login and password credentials.

The SSH connection is now established. Launch the TightVNC viewer, enter localhost:5901 in the VNC Server text field, and click Connect. The viewer will establish the connection, prompt for the password, and then display the desktop. You are now accessing the remote desktop of a Linux system from Windows over a secure SSH tunnel connection.

16.8 Shutting Down a Desktop Session

To shut down a VNC Server hosted desktop session, use the –kill command-line option and the number of the desktop to be terminated. For example, to kill desktop :1:

```
# vncserver -kill :1
```

16.9 Troubleshooting a VNC Connection

With so much happening in the background, VNC can sometimes seem opaque, particularly when problems arise and the server fails to start or connect, resulting in error messages. There are, however, some techniques for tracking down and resolving VNC problems:

If the VNC service fails to start, check the *systemctl* status of the service and check for error messages:

```
# systemctl status vncserver@:1.service
```

For more detailed information, check the systemd journal by running the *journalctl* command:

```
# journalctl -xe
```

Additional information may be available in the log file located at:

```
/home/<username>/.vnc/<hostname>.<domain>:<display number>.log
```

For example:

```
/home/neilsmyth/.vnc/rhelserver01.localdomain:1.log
```

If the systemd VNC service is still unable to start the VNC server, try starting it manually using the following command:

```
# vncserver :<display number>
```

For example:

```
# vncserver :1
```

Check the output and log file for errors that may help identify the problem. Then, if the server starts successfully, try connecting again with a VNC viewer.

If the VNC server appears to be running, but attempts to connect from a viewer fail, it may be worth checking that the correct firewall ports are open. Begin by identifying the default zone as follows:

```
# firewall-cmd --get-default-zone
public
```

Having obtained the default zone, check that the necessary ports are open:

```
# firewall-cmd --permanent --zone=public --list-ports
5901/tcp 5900/tcp
```

If a port used by VNC is not open, add the port as follows:

```
# firewall-cmd --permanent --zone=public --add-port=<port number>/tcp
```

16.10 Summary

Remote access to the GNOME desktop environment of a RHEL 9 system can be enabled by using Virtual Network Computing (VNC). Comprising the VNC server running on the remote server and a corresponding client on the local host, VNC allows remote access to multiple desktop instances running on the server.

When the VNC connection is being used over a public connection, SSH tunneling is recommended to ensure that the communication between the client and server is encrypted and secure.

Chapter 17

17. Displaying RHEL 9 Applications Remotely (X11 Forwarding)

In the previous chapter, we looked at how to display the entire RHEL 9 desktop on a remote computer. While this works well if you need to display the entire desktop remotely, it could be considered overkill if you only want to display a single application. Therefore, this chapter will look at displaying individual applications on a remote system.

17.1 Requirements for Remotely Displaying RHEL 9 Applications

There are a couple of prerequisites to running an application on one RHEL 9 system and displaying it on another. First, the system on which the application is to be displayed must be running an X server. If the system is a Linux or UNIX-based system with a desktop environment running, then this is no problem. However, if the system is running Windows or macOS, you must install an X server on it before you can display applications from a remote system. Several commercial and free Windows-based X servers are available for this purpose, and a web search should provide you with a list of options.

Second, the system on which the application is being run (as opposed to the system on which the application is to be displayed) must be configured to allow SSH access. Details on configuring SSH on a RHEL 9 system can be found in the chapter *"Configuring SSH Key-based Authentication on RHEL 9"*. This system must also run the X Window System from X.org instead of Wayland. To enable the X.org system, edit the */etc/gdm/custom.conf* file and uncomment the WaylandEnable line as follows and restart the system:

```
# Uncomment the line below to force the login screen to use Xorg
WaylandEnable=false
```

Finally, SSH must be configured to allow X11 forwarding. This is achieved by adding the following directive to the SSH configuration on the system from which forwarding is to occur. By default on RHEL 9, the */etc/sshd_config* file contains a directive to include all of the configuration files contained in the */etc/ssh/sshd_config.d* directory:

```
Include /etc/ssh/sshd_config.d/*.conf
```

A file named *50-redhat.conf* will have been created on a newly installed system in the */etc/ssh/sshd_config.d* folder. Edit this file and ensure that the X11Forwarding property is enabled as follows:

```
X11Forwarding yes
```

After making the change, save the file and restart the SSH service:

```
# systemctl restart sshd
```

Once the above requirements are met, it should be possible to display an X-based desktop application remotely.

17.2 Displaying a RHEL 9 Application Remotely

The first step in remotely displaying an application is to move to the system where the application is to be displayed. At this system, establish an SSH connection to the remote system so that you have a command prompt. This can be achieved using the ssh command. When using the *ssh* command, we need to use the -X flag to tell it that we plan to tunnel X11 traffic through the connection:

```
$ ssh -X user@hostname
```

In the above example, *user* is the user name to use to log into the remote system, and *hostname* is the hostname or IP address of the remote system. Enter your password at the login prompt and, once logged in, run the following command to see the DISPLAY setting:

```
$ echo $DISPLAY
```

The command should output something similar to the following:

```
localhost:10.0
```

To display an application, run it from the command prompt. For example:

```
$ gedit
```

When executed, the above command should run the *gedit* tool on the remote system but display the user interface on the local system.

17.3 Trusted X11 Forwarding

If the */etc/ssh/sshd_config.d/50-redhat.conf* file on the remote system contains the following line, then it is possible to use trusted X11 forwarding:

```
ForwardX11Trusted yes
```

Trusted X11 forwarding is slightly faster than untrusted forwarding but is less secure since it does not engage the X11 security controls. The -Y flag is needed when using trusted X11 forwarding:

```
$ ssh -Y user@hostname
```

17.4 Compressed X11 Forwarding

When using slower connections, the X11 data can be compressed using the *ssh* -C flag to improve performance:

```
$ ssh -X -C user@hostname
```

17.5 Displaying Remote RHEL 9 Apps on Windows

To display RHEL 9-based apps on Windows, an SSH client and an X server must be installed on the Windows system. The subject of installing and using the PuTTY client on Windows was covered earlier in the book in the *"Configuring SSH Key-based Authentication on RHEL 9"* chapter. Refer to this chapter if you have not already installed PuTTY on your Windows system.

In terms of the X server, several options are available, though a popular choice appears to be VcXsrv which is available for free from the following URL:

https://sourceforge.net/projects/vcxsrv/

Once the VcXsrv X server has been installed, an application named XLaunch will appear on the desktop and in the start menu. Start XLaunch and select a display option (the most flexible being the Multiple windows option which allows each client app to appear in its own window):

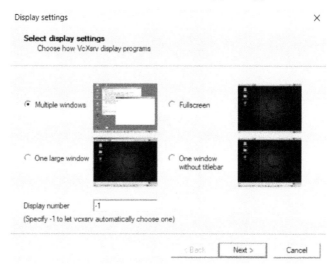

Figure 17-1

Click the Next button to proceed through the remaining screens, accepting the default configuration settings. On the final screen, click the Finish button to start the X server. If the Windows Defender dialog appears, click the button to allow access to your chosen networks.

Once running, XLaunch will appear in the taskbar and can be exited by right-clicking on the icon and selecting the Exit... menu option:

Figure 17-2

With the X server installed and running, launch PuTTY and either enter the connection

139

information for the remote host or load a previously saved session profile. Before establishing the connection, however, X11 forwarding needs to be enabled. Therefore, within the PuTTY main window, scroll down the options in the left-hand panel, unfold the SSH section, and select the X11 option, as shown in Figure 17-3:

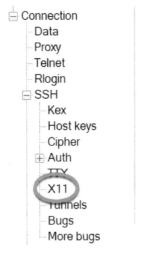

Figure 17-3

Turn on the Enable X11 forwarding checkbox highlighted in Figure 17-4, return to the sessions screen, and open the connection (saving the session beforehand if you plan to use it again):

Figure 17-4

Log into the RHEL 9 system within the PuTTY session window and run a desktop app. After a short delay, the app will appear on the Windows desktop in its own window. Any dialogs that the app opens will also appear in separate windows, just as they would on the RHEL 9 GNOME desktop. Figure 17-5, for example, shows the RHEL 9 *nm-connection-editor* tool displayed on a Windows 11 system:

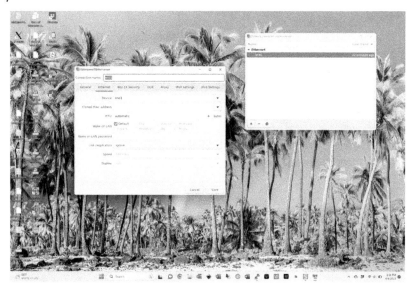

Figure 17-5

17.6 Summary

For situations where remote access to individual RHEL 9 desktop applications is required as opposed to the entire GNOME desktop, X11 forwarding provides a lightweight solution to remotely displaying graphical applications. The system on which the applications are to appear must be running an X Window System-based desktop environment (such as GNOME) or have an X server installed and running. Once X11 forwarding has been enabled on the remote server and a secure SSH connection established from the local system using the X11 forwarding option, most applications can be displayed remotely on the local X server.

18. Using NFS on RHEL 9 to Share Files with Remote Systems

RHEL 9 provides two mechanisms for sharing files and folders with other systems on a network. One approach is to use a technology called Samba. Samba is based on Microsoft Windows Folder Sharing and allows Linux systems to make folders accessible to Windows systems and access Windows-based folder shares from Linux. This approach can also be used to share folders between other Linux and UNIX-based systems as long as they have Samba support installed and configured. This is the most popular approach to sharing folders in heterogeneous network environments. Folder sharing using Samba is covered in *"Sharing Files between RHEL 9 and Windows Systems with Samba"*.

Another option, explicitly targeted at sharing folders between Linux and UNIX-based systems, uses Network File System (NFS). NFS allows the file system on one Linux computer to be accessed over a network connection by another Linux or UNIX system. NFS was originally developed by Sun Microsystems (now part of Oracle Corporation) in the 1980s and remains the standard mechanism for sharing remote Linux/UNIX file systems.

NFS is very different from the Windows SMB resource-sharing technology used by Samba. This chapter will look at the network-based sharing of folders between RHEL 9 and other UNIX/Linux-based systems using NFS.

18.1 Ensuring NFS Services are running on RHEL 9

The first task is to verify that the NFS services are installed and running on your RHEL 9 system. This can be achieved from the command line or the Cockpit interface.

Behind the scenes, NFS makes use of Remote Procedure Calls (RPC) to share filesystems over a network between different computers in the form of the rpcbind service. Begin by installing both rpcbind and the NFS service by running the following command from a terminal window:

```
# dnf install rpcbind nfs-utils
```

Next, configure these services so that they automatically start at boot time:

```
# systemctl enable rpcbind
# systemctl enable nfs-server
```

Once the services have been enabled, start them as follows:

```
# systemctl start rpcbind
# systemctl start nfs-server
```

18.2 Configuring the RHEL 9 Firewall to Allow NFS Traffic

Next, the firewall needs to be configured to allow NFS traffic. To achieve this, run the following *firewall-cmd* commands where <zone> is replaced by the appropriate zone for your firewall and system configuration:

```
# firewall-cmd --zone=<zone> --permanent --add-service=mountd
# firewall-cmd --zone=<zone> --permanent --add-service=nfs
# firewall-cmd --zone=<zone> --permanent --add-service=rpc-bind
# firewall-cmd --reload
```

18.3 Specifying the Folders to be Shared

Now that NFS is running and the firewall has been configured, we need to specify which parts of the RHEL 9 file system may be accessed by remote Linux or UNIX systems. These settings can be declared in the */etc/exports* file, which must be modified to export the directories for remote access via NFS. The syntax for an export line in this file is as follows:

```
<export> <host1>(<options>) <host2>(<options>)...
```

In the above line, <export> is replaced by the directory to be exported, <host1> is the name or IP address of the system to which access is being granted, and <options> represents the restrictions that are to be imposed on that access (read-only, read-write, etc.). Multiple host and options entries may be placed on the same line if required. For example, the following line grants read-only permission to the */datafiles* directory to a host with the IP address 192.168.2.38:

```
/datafiles 192.168.2.38(ro)
```

The use of wildcards is permitted to apply an export to multiple hosts. For example, the following line permits read-write access to */home/demo* to all external hosts:

```
/home/demo *(rw)
```

A complete list of options supported by the exports file may be found by reading the exports man page:

```
# man exports
```

For this chapter, we will configure the */etc/exports* file as follows:

```
/tmp        *(rw,sync)
/vol1       192.168.86.42(ro,sync)
```

Once configured, the table of exported file systems maintained by the NFS server needs to be updated with the latest */etc/exports* settings using the *exportfs* command as follows:

```
# exportfs -a
```

It is also possible to view the current share settings from the command line using the *exportfs* tool:

```
# exportfs
```

The above command will generate the following output:

```
/vol1               192.168.86.42
/tmp                <world>
```

18.4 Accessing Shared Folders

The shared folders may be accessed from a client system by mounting them manually from the command line. However, before attempting to mount a remote NFS folder, the *nfs-utils* package must first be installed on the client system:

```
# dnf install nfs-utils
```

To mount a remote folder from the command line, open a terminal window and create a directory where you would like the remote shared folder to be mounted:

```
$ mkdir /home/demo/tmp
```

Next, enter the command to mount the remote folder using either the IP address or hostname of the remote NFS server, for example:

```
$ sudo mount -t nfs 192.168.86.24:/tmp /home/demo/tmp
```

The remote /tmp folder will then be mounted on the local system. Once mounted, the */home/demo/tmp* folder will contain the remote folder and all its contents.

Options may also be specified when mounting a remote NFS filesystem. The following command, for example, mounts the same folder but configures it to be read-only:

```
$ sudo mount -t nfs -o ro 192.168.86.24:/tmp /home/demo/tmp
```

18.5 Mounting an NFS Filesystem on System Startup

It is also possible to configure a RHEL 9 system to automatically mount a remote file system each time it starts up by editing the */etc/fstab* file. When loaded into an editor, it will likely resemble the following:

```
/dev/mapper/rhel-root    /                       xfs     defaults         0 0
UUID=c4ba0b0f-777a-42a8 /boot                    xfs     defaults         0 0
UUID=052D-19D8           /boot/efi               vfat    umask=0077,shortname=winnt
0 2
/dev/mapper/rhel-swap    none                    swap    defaults         0 0
```

To mount, for example, a folder with the path */tmp*, which resides on a system with the IP address 192.168.86.24 in the local folder with the path */home/demo/tmp* (note that this folder must already exist) add the following line to the */etc/fstab* file:

```
192.168.86.24:/tmp      /home/demo/tmp          nfs     rw               0 0
```

Next time the system reboots, the */tmp* folder on the remote system will be mounted on the local */home/demo/tmp* mount point. All the files in the remote folder can then be accessed as if they reside on the local hard disk drive.

18.6 Unmounting an NFS Mount Point

Once a remote file system is mounted using NFS, it can be unmounted using the *umount* command with the local mount point as the command-line argument. The following command, for example, will unmount our example filesystem mount point:

```
$ sudo umount /home/demo/tmp
```

18.7 Accessing NFS Filesystems in Cockpit

In addition to mounting a remote NFS file system on a client using the command line, it is also possible to perform mount operations from within the Cockpit web interface. Assuming that Cockpit has been installed and configured on the client system, log into the Cockpit interface from within a web browser and select the Storage option from the left-hand navigation panel. If the Storage option is not listed, the *cockpit-storaged* package will need to be installed:

```
# dnf install cockpit-storaged
# systemctl restart cockpit.socket
```

Once the Cockpit service has restarted, log back into the Cockpit interface, at which point the Storage option should now be visible.

Once selected, the main storage page will include a section listing any currently mounted NFS file systems, as illustrated in Figure 18-1:

Figure 18-1

To mount a remote filesystem, click on the '+' button highlighted above and enter information about the remote NFS server and file system share together with the local mount point and any necessary options into the resulting dialog before clicking on the Add button:

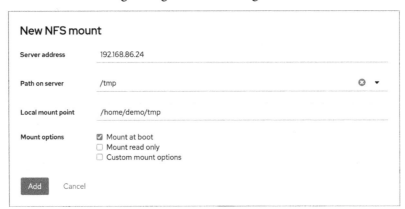

Figure 18-2

To modify, unmount or remove an NFS filesystem share, select the corresponding mount in the NFS Mounts list (Figure 18-1 above) to display the page shown in Figure 18-3 below:

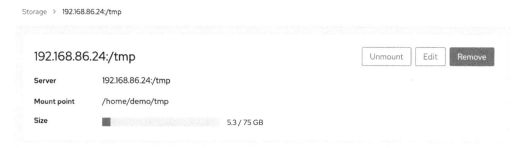

Figure 18-3

Within this screen, perform tasks such as changing the server or mount points or unmounting the file system. For example, the Remove option unmounts the file system and deletes the entry from the */etc/fstab* file so that it does not re-mount the next time the system reboots.

18.8 Summary

The Network File System (NFS) is a client/server-based system, originally developed by Sun Microsystems, which provides a way for Linux and Unix systems to share filesystems over a network. NFS allows a client system to access and (subject to permissions) modify files located on a remote server as though those files are stored on a local filesystem. This chapter has provided an overview of NFS and outlined the options for configuring client and server systems using the command line or the Cockpit web interface.

19. Sharing Files between RHEL 9 and Windows Systems with Samba

Although Linux has made some inroads into the desktop market, its origins and future are very much server based. It is unsurprising, therefore, that RHEL 9 can act as a file server. It is also common for RHEL and Windows systems to be used side by side in networked environments. Therefore, it is a common requirement that files on a RHEL 9 system be accessible to Linux, UNIX, and Windows-based systems over network connections. Similarly, shared folders and printers residing on Windows systems may also need to be accessible from RHEL 9-based systems.

Windows systems share resources such as file systems and printers using a protocol known as Server Message Block (SMB). For a RHEL 9 system to serve such resources over a network to a Windows system and vice versa, it must support SMB. This is achieved using a technology called Samba. In addition to providing integration between Linux and Windows systems, Samba may also provide folder sharing between Linux systems (as an alternative to NFS covered in the previous chapter).

In this chapter, we will look at the steps necessary to share file system resources and printers on a RHEL 9 system with remote Windows and Linux systems and to access Windows resources from RHEL 9.

19.1 Accessing Windows Resources from the GNOME Desktop

Before getting into more details of Samba sharing, it is worth noting that if all you want to do is access Windows shared folders from within the GNOME desktop, then support is already provided within the GNOME Files application. The Files application is located in the dash as highlighted in Figure 19-1:

Figure 19-1

Once launched, select the *Other Locations* option in the left-hand navigation panel, followed by the Windows Network icon in the main panel to browse available Windows resources:

Figure 19-2

19.2 Samba and Samba Client

Samba allows both RHEL 9 resources to be shared with Windows systems and Windows resources to be shared with RHEL 9 systems. RHEL accesses Windows resources using the Samba client. RHEL resources, on the other hand, are shared with Windows systems by installing and configuring the Samba service.

19.3 Installing Samba on RHEL 9

The default settings used during the RHEL 9 installation process do not typically install the necessary Samba packages. Unless you specifically requested that Samba be installed, it is unlikely that you have Samba installed on your system. To check whether Samba is installed, open a terminal window and run the following command:

```
# rpm -q samba samba-common samba-client
```

Any missing packages can be installed using the *dnf* command-line tool:

```
# dnf install samba samba-common samba-client
```

19.4 Configuring the RHEL 9 Firewall to Enable Samba

Next, the firewall protecting the RHEL 9 system must be configured to allow Samba traffic. This can be achieved using the *firewall-cmd* command as follows:

```
# firewall-cmd --permanent --add-port={139/tcp,445/tcp}
# firewall-cmd --reload
```

Before starting the Samba service, some configuration steps are necessary to define how the RHEL system will appear to Windows systems and the resources to be shared with remote clients. Most configuration tasks occur within the */etc/samba/smb.conf* file.

19.5 Configuring the smb.conf File

Samba is a highly flexible and configurable system that provides many options for controlling how resources are shared on Windows networks. Unfortunately, this flexibility can lead to the sense that Samba is overly complex. In reality, however, the typical installation does not need many configuration options, and the learning curve to set up a basic configuration is relatively short.

For this chapter, we will look at joining a RHEL 9 system to a Windows workgroup and setting up a directory as a shared resource that a specific user can access. This is a configuration known as a *standalone Samba server*. More advanced configurations, such as integrating Samba within an Active Directory environment, are also available, though these are outside the scope of this book.

The first step in configuring Samba is to edit the */etc/samba/smb.conf* file.

19.5.1 Configuring the [global] Section

The *smb.conf* file is divided into sections. The first section is the [global] section, where settings that apply to the entire Samba configuration can be specified. While these settings are global, each option may be overridden within other configuration file sections.

The first task is defining the Windows workgroup name on which the RHEL 9 resources will be shared. This is controlled via the *workgroup =* directive of the [global] section, which by default is configured as follows:

```
workgroup = SAMBA
```

Begin by changing this to the actual name of the workgroup if necessary.

In addition to the workgroup setting, the other settings indicate that this is a standalone server on which user passwords will protect the shared resources. Before moving on to configuring the resources to be shared, other parameters also need to be added to the [global] section as follows:

```
[global]
.

.

        netbios name = LinuxServer
```

The "netbios name" property specifies the name by which the server will be visible to other systems on the network.

19.5.2 Configuring a Shared Resource

The next step is configuring the shared resources (in other words, the resources that will be accessible from other systems on the Windows network). To achieve this, the section is given a name by which it will be referred when shared. For example, if we plan to share the */sampleshare* directory of our RHEL 9 system, we might entitle the section [sampleshare]. In this section, a variety of configuration options are possible. For this example, however, we will simply define the directory that is to be shared, indicate that the directory is both browsable and writable, and declare the resource public so that guest users can gain access:

```
[sampleshare]
```

```
        comment = Example Samba share
        path = /sampleshare
        browseable = Yes
        public = yes
        writable = yes
```

To restrict access to specific users, the "valid users" property may be used, for example:

```
valid users = demo, bobyoung, marcewing
```

19.5.3 Removing Unnecessary Shares

The *smb.conf* file is pre-configured with sections for sharing printers and the home folders of the users on the system. If these resources do not need to be shared, the corresponding sections can be commented out so that Samba ignores them. In the following example, the [homes] section has been commented out:

```
.
.
# [homes]
#         comment = Home Directories
#         valid users = %S, %D%w%S
#         browseable = No
#         read only = No
#         inherit acls = Yes
.
.
```

19.6 Configuring SELinux for Samba

SELinux is a system integrated by default into the Linux kernel on all RHEL 9 systems, providing an extra layer of security and protection to the operating system and user files.

Traditionally, Linux security has been based on allowing users to decide who has access to their files and other resources they own. Consider, for example, a file located in the home directory of, and owned by, a particular user. That user can control the access permissions of that file in terms of whether other users on the system can read and write to or, in the case of a script or binary, execute the file. This type of security is called *discretionary access control* since resource access is left to the user's discretion.

With SELinux, however, access is controlled by the system administrator and cannot be overridden by the user. This is called *mandatory access control* and is defined by the administrator using the SELinux *policy*. To continue the previous example, the owner of a file can only perform tasks on that file if the SELinux policy, defined either by default by the system or by the administrator, permits it.

The current status of SELinux on a RHEL 9 system may be identified using the *sestatus* tool as follows:

```
SELinux status:                 enabled
```

```
SELinuxfs mount:                /sys/fs/selinux
SELinux root directory:         /etc/selinux
Loaded policy name:             targeted
Current mode:                   enforcing
Mode from config file:          enforcing
Policy MLS status:              enabled
Policy deny_unknown status:     allowed
Memory protection checking:     actual (secure)
Max kernel policy version:      33
```

SELinux can be run in either *enforcing* or *permissive* mode. When enabled, enforcing mode denies all actions that are not permitted by SELinux policy. On the other hand, permissive mode allows actions that would generally have been denied to proceed but records the violation in a log file.

SELinux security is based on the concept of context labels. All resources on a system (including processes and files) are assigned SELinux *context labels* consisting of user, role, type, and optional security level. The SELinux context of files or folders, for example, may be viewed as follows:

```
$ ls -Z /home/demo
 unconfined_u:object_r:user_home_t:s0 Desktop
 unconfined_u:object_r:user_home_t:s0 Documents
```

Similarly, the *ps* command may be used to identify the context of a running process, in this case, the *ls* command:

```
$ ps -eZ | grep ls
unconfined_u:unconfined_r:unconfined_t:s0-s0:c0.c1023 14311 tty1 00:00:18 ls
```

When a process (such as the above *ls* command) attempts to access a file or folder, the SELinux system will check the policy to identify whether or not access is permitted. Now consider the context of the Samba service:

```
$ ps -eZ | grep smb
system_u:system_r:smbd_t:s0     14129 ?         00:00:00 smbd
system_u:system_r:smbd_t:s0     14132 ?         00:00:00 smbd-notifyd
```

SELinux implements security in several ways, the most common of which is called *type enforcement*. In basic terms, when a process attempts to perform a task on an object (for example, writing to a file), SELinux checks the context types of both the process and the object and verifies that the security policy allows the action to be taken. Suppose a process of type A, for example, attempts to write to a file of type B. In that case, it will only be permitted if SELinux policy states explicitly that a process of type A may perform a write operation to a file of type B. In SELinux enforcement, all actions are denied by default unless a rule specifically allows the action to be performed.

The issue with SELinux and Samba is that SELinux policy is not configured to allow processes of type *smb_t* to perform actions on files of any type other than *samba_share_t*. For example, the */home/demo* directory listed above will be inaccessible to the Samba service because it has a type of *user_home_t*. To make files or folders on the system accessible to the Samba service, the enforcement type of those specific resources must be changed to *samba_share_t*.

153

Sharing Files between RHEL 9 and Windows Systems with Samba

For this example, we will create the */sampleshare* directory referenced previously in the *smb.conf* file and change the enforcement type to make it accessible to the Samba service. Begin by creating the directory as follows:

```
# mkdir /sampleshare
```

Next, check the current SELinux context on the directory:

```
$ ls -aZ /sampleshare/
unconfined_u:object_r:root_t:s0 .
```

In this instance, the context label of the folder has been assigned a type of *root_t*. To make the folder sharable by Samba, the enforcement type needs to be set to *samba_share_t* using the *semanage* tool as follows:

```
# semanage fcontext -a -t samba_share_t "/sampleshare(/.*)?"
```

Note the use of a wildcard in the *semanage* command to ensure that the type is applied to any sub-directories and files contained within the */sampleshare* directory. Once added, the change needs to be applied using the *restorecon* command, making use of the -R flag to apply the change recursively through any sub-directories:

```
# restorecon -R -v /sampleshare
Relabeled /sampleshare from unconfined_u:object_r:default_t:s0 to
unconfined_u:object_r:samba_share_t:s0
```

Once these changes have been made, the folder is configured to comply with SELinux policy for the smb process and is ready to be shared by Samba.

19.7 Creating a Samba User

Any user that requires access to a Samba shared resource must be configured as a Samba User and assigned a password. This task is achieved using the *smbpasswd* command-line tool. Consider, for example, that a user named demo is required to be able to access the */sampleshare* directory of our RHEL 9 system from a Windows system. To fulfill this requirement, we must add demo as a Samba user as follows:

```
# smbpasswd -a demo
New SMB password:
Retype new SMB password:
Added user demo.
```

Now that we have completed the configuration of an elementary Samba server, it is time to test our configuration file and then start the Samba services.

19.8 Testing the smb.conf File

The settings in the *smb.conf* file may be checked for errors using the *testparm* command-line tool as follows:

```
# testparm
Load smb config files from /etc/samba/smb.conf
Loaded services file OK.
```

```
Weak crypto is allowed

Server role: ROLE_STANDALONE
Press enter to see a dump of your service definitions

# Global parameters
[global]
        log file = /var/log/samba/%m.log
        netbios name = LINUXSERVER
        printcap name = cups
        security = USER
        wins support = Yes
        idmap config * : backend = tdb
        cups options = raw

[sampleshare]
        comment = Example Samba share
        guest ok = Yes
        path = /sampleshare
        read only = No

[homes]
        browseable = No
        comment = Home Directories
        inherit acls = Yes
        read only = No
        valid users = %S %D%w%S

[printers]
        browseable = No
        comment = All Printers
        create mask = 0600
        path = /var/tmp
        printable = Yes
.

.
```

19.9 Starting the Samba and NetBIOS Name Services

For a RHEL 9 server to operate within a Windows network, the Samba (SMB) and NetBIOS nameservice (NMB) services must be started. Optionally, also enable the services so that they start each time the system boots:

```
# systemctl enable smb nmb
# systemctl start smb nmb
```

Before attempting to connect from a Windows system, use the *smbclient* utility to verify that the

Sharing Files between RHEL 9 and Windows Systems with Samba

share is configured:

```
# smbclient -U demo -L localhost
Enter WORKGROUP\demo's password:


        Sharename       Type       Comment
        ---------       ----       -------
        sampleshare     Disk       Example Samba share
        print$          Disk       Printer Drivers
        IPC$            IPC        IPC Service (Samba 4.9.1)
        demo            Disk       Home Directories
```

19.10 Accessing Samba Shares

Now that the Samba resources are configured, and the services are running, it is time to access the shared resource from a Windows system. On a suitable Windows system on the same workgroup as the RHEL 9 system, open Windows Explorer and navigate to the Network panel. At this point, explorer should search the network and list any systems using the SMB protocol that it finds. The following figure illustrates a RHEL 9 system named LINUXSERVER located using Windows Explorer on a Windows system:

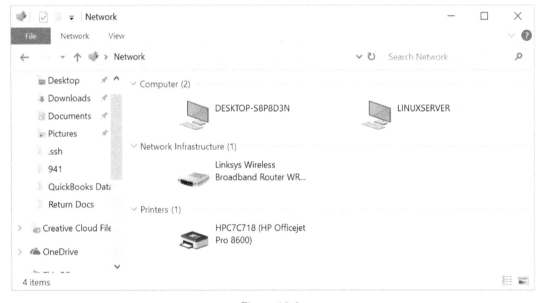

Figure 19-3

Double-clicking on the LINUXSERVER host will prompt for the name and password of a user with access privileges. In this case, it is the demo account that we configured using the *smbpasswd* tool:

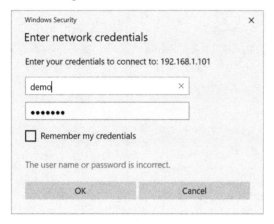

Figure 19-4

Entering the username and password will result in the shared resources configured for that user appearing in the explorer window, including the previously configured */sampleshare* resource:

Figure 19-5

Double-clicking on the */sampleshare* shared resource will display a listing of the files and directories contained therein.

If you are unable to see the Linux system or have problems accessing the shared folder, try mapping the Samba share to a local Windows drive as follows:

1. Open Windows File Explorer, right-click on the Network entry in the left-hand panel, and select *Map network drive...* from the resulting menu.

2. Select a drive letter from the Map Network Drive dialog before entering the path to the shared folder. For example:

```
\\LinuxServer\sampleshare
```

Enable the checkbox next to *Connect using different credentials*. For example, if you do not want the drive to be mapped each time you log into the Windows system, turn off the corresponding check box:

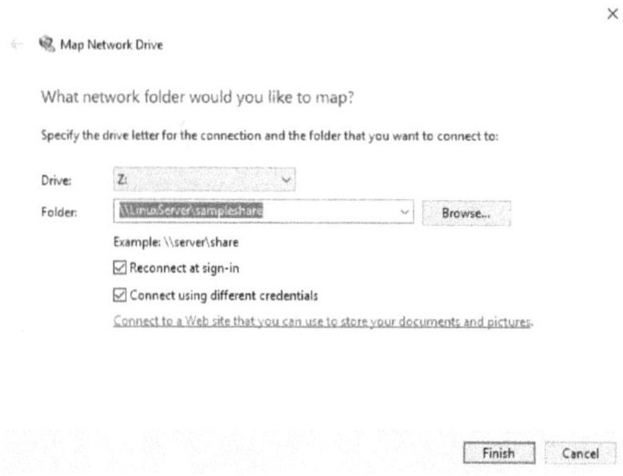

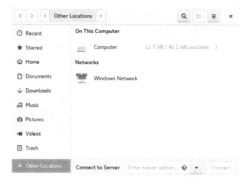

Figure 19-6

With the settings entered, click the Finish button to map the drive, entering the username and password for the Samba user configured earlier in the chapter when prompted. After a short delay, the content of the Samba share will appear in a new File Explorer window.

19.11 Accessing Windows Shares from RHEL 9

As previously mentioned, Samba is a two-way street, allowing not only Windows systems to access files and printers hosted on a RHEL 9 system but also allowing the RHEL 9 system to access shared resources on Windows systems. This is achieved using the samba-client package, installed at this chapter's start. If it is not currently installed, install it from a terminal window as follows:

```
# dnf install samba-client
```

Shared resources on a Windows system can be accessed from the RHEL desktop using the Files application or from the command-line prompt using the *smbclient* and *mount* tools. The steps in this section assume that the Windows system has enabled appropriate network-sharing settings.

To access any shared resources on a Windows system using the GNOME desktop, launch the Files application and select the Other Locations option. This will display the screen shown in Figure 19-7 below, including an icon for the Windows Network (if one is detected):

Figure 19-7

Selecting the Windows Network option will display the Windows systems detected on the network and allow access to any shared resources.

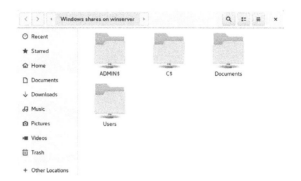

Figure 19-8

Alternatively, the Connect to Server option may be used to connect to a specific system. Note that the name or IP address of the remote system must be prefixed by *smb://* and may be followed by the path to a specific shared resource, for example:

```
smb://WinServer/Documents
```

Without a desktop environment, a remote Windows share may be mounted from the command line using the mount command and specifying the cifs filesystem type. The following command, for example, mounts a share named Documents located on a Windows system named WinServer at a local mount point named */winfiles*:

```
# mount -t cifs //WinServer/Documents /winfiles -o user=demo
```

19.12 Summary

In this chapter, we have looked at how to configure a RHEL 9 system to act as both a Samba client and server, allowing the sharing of resources with Windows systems. Topics covered included the installation of Samba client and server packages and configuring Samba as a standalone server. In addition, the basic concepts of SELinux were introduced together with the steps to provide Samba access to a shared resource.

20. An Overview of Virtualization Techniques

Virtualization is the ability to run multiple operating systems simultaneously on a single computer system. While not necessarily a new concept, Virtualization has come to prominence in recent years because it provides a way to fully utilize the CPU and resource capacity of a server system while providing stability (in that if one virtualized guest system crashes, the host and any other guest systems continue to run).

Virtualization is also helpful in trying out different operating systems without configuring dual boot environments. For example, you can run Windows in a virtual machine without re-partitioning the disk, shut down RHEL 9, and boot from Windows. Instead, you start up a virtualized version of Windows as a guest operating system. Similarly, virtualization allows you to run other Linux distributions within a RHEL 9 system, providing concurrent access to both operating systems.

When deciding on the best approach to implementing virtualization, clearly understanding the different virtualization solutions currently available is essential. Therefore, this chapter's purpose is to describe in general terms the virtualization techniques in common use today.

20.1 Guest Operating System Virtualization

Guest OS virtualization, also called application-based virtualization, is the most straightforward concept to understand. In this scenario, the physical host computer runs a standard unmodified operating system such as Windows, Linux, UNIX, or macOS. Running on this operating system is a virtualization application that executes in much the same way as any other application, such as a word processor or spreadsheet, would run on the system. Within this virtualization application, one or more virtual machines are created to run the guest operating systems on the host computer.

The virtualization application is responsible for starting, stopping, and managing each virtual machine and essentially controlling access to physical hardware resources on behalf of the individual virtual machines. The virtualization application also engages in a process known as binary rewriting, which involves scanning the instruction stream of the executing guest system and replacing any privileged instructions with safe emulations. This makes the guest system think it is running directly on the system hardware rather than in a virtual machine within an application.

The following figure illustrates guest OS-based virtualization:

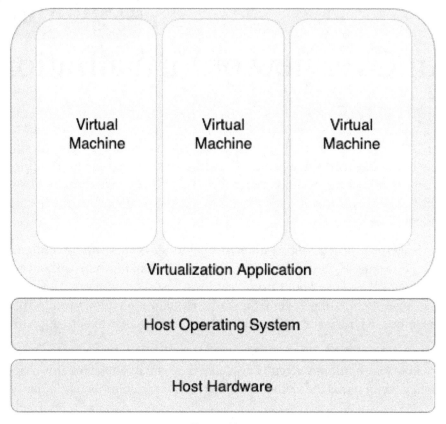

Figure 20-1

As outlined in the above diagram, the guest operating systems operate in virtual machines within the virtualization application, which, in turn, runs on top of the host operating system in the same way as any other application. The multiple layers of abstraction between the guest operating systems and the underlying host hardware are not conducive to high levels of virtual machine performance. However, this technique has the advantage that no changes are necessary to host or guest operating systems, and no special CPU hardware virtualization support is required.

20.2 Hypervisor Virtualization

In hypervisor virtualization, the task of a hypervisor is to handle resource and memory allocation for the virtual machines and provide interfaces for higher-level administration and monitoring tools. Hypervisor-based solutions are categorized as being either Type-1 or Type-2.

Type-2 hypervisors (sometimes called hosted hypervisors) are installed as software applications that run on top of the host operating system, providing virtualization capabilities by coordinating access to resources such as the CPU, memory, and network for guest virtual machines. Figure 21-2 illustrates the typical architecture of a system using Type-2 hypervisor virtualization:

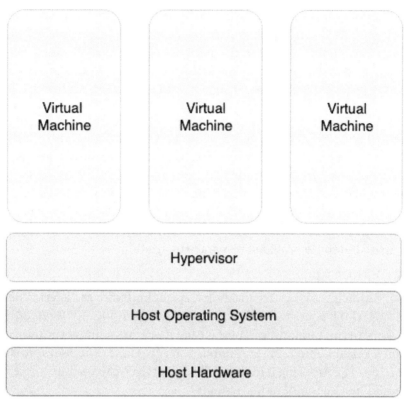

Figure 20-2

To understand how Type-1 hypervisors work, it helps to understand Intel x86 processor architecture. The x86 family of CPUs provides a range of protection levels known as rings in which code can execute. Ring 0 has the highest level privilege, and it is in this ring that the operating system kernel normally runs. Code executing in ring 0 is said to be running in system space, kernel mode, or supervisor mode. All other code, such as applications running on the operating system, operate in less privileged rings, typically ring 3.

In contrast to Type-2 hypervisors, Type-1 hypervisors (also referred to as metal or native hypervisors) run directly on the hardware of the host system in ring 0. With the hypervisor occupying ring 0 of the CPU, the kernels for any guest operating systems running on the system must run in less privileged CPU rings. Unfortunately, most operating system kernels are written explicitly to run in ring 0 because they need to perform tasks only available in that ring, such as the ability to execute privileged CPU instructions and directly manipulate memory. Several different solutions to this problem have been devised in recent years, each of which is described below:

20.2.1 Paravirtualization

Under paravirtualization, the kernel of the guest operating system is modified specifically to run on the hypervisor. This typically involves replacing privileged operations that only run in ring 0 of the CPU with calls to the hypervisor (known as hypercalls). The hypervisor, in turn, performs

An Overview of Virtualization Techniques

the task on behalf of the guest kernel. Unfortunately, this typically limits support to open-source operating systems such as Linux, which may be freely altered, and proprietary operating systems where the owners have agreed to make the necessary code modifications to target a specific hypervisor. These issues notwithstanding, the ability of the guest kernel to communicate directly with the hypervisor results in greater performance levels than other virtualization approaches.

20.2.2 Full Virtualization

Full virtualization provides support for unmodified guest operating systems. The term unmodified refers to operating system kernels that have not been altered to run on a hypervisor and, therefore, still execute privileged operations as though running in ring 0 of the CPU. In this scenario, the hypervisor provides CPU emulation to handle and modify privileged and protected CPU operations made by unmodified guest operating system kernels. Unfortunately, this emulation process requires both time and system resources to operate, resulting in inferior performance levels when compared to those provided by paravirtualization.

20.2.3 Hardware Virtualization

Hardware virtualization leverages virtualization features built into the latest generations of CPUs from both Intel and AMD. These technologies, called Intel VT and AMD-V, respectively, provide extensions necessary to run unmodified guest virtual machines without the overheads inherent in full virtualization CPU emulation. In very simplistic terms, these processors provide an additional privilege mode (ring -1) above ring 0 in which the hypervisor can operate, thereby leaving ring 0 available for unmodified guest operating systems.

The following figure illustrates the Type-1 hypervisor approach to virtualization:

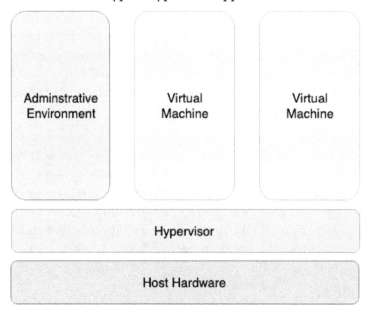

Figure 20-3

As outlined in the above illustration, in addition to the virtual machines, an administrative operating system or management console also runs on top of the hypervisor allowing the virtual machines to be managed by a system administrator.

20.3 Virtual Machine Networking

Virtual machines will invariably need to be connected to a network to be of any practical use. One option is for the guest to be connected to a virtual network running within the host computer's operating system. In this configuration, any virtual machines on the virtual network can see each other, but Network Address Translation (NAT) provides access to the external network. When using the virtual network and NAT, each virtual machine is represented on the external network (the network to which the host is connected) using the IP address of the host system. This is the default behavior for KVM virtualization on RHEL 9 and generally requires no additional configuration. Typically, a single virtual network is created by default, represented by the name *default* and the device *virbr0*.

For guests to appear as individual and independent systems on the external network (i.e., with their own IP addresses), they must be configured to share a physical network interface on the host. The quickest way to achieve this is to configure the virtual machine to use the "direct connection" network configuration option (also called MacVTap), which will provide the guest system with an IP address on the same network as the host. Unfortunately, while this gives the virtual machine access to other systems on the network, it is not possible to establish a connection between the guest and the host when using the MacVTap driver.

A better option is to configure a network bridge interface on the host system to which the guests can connect. This provides the guest with an IP address on the external network while also allowing the guest and host to communicate, a topic covered in the chapter entitled *"Creating a RHEL 9 KVM Networked Bridge Interface"*.

20.4 Summary

Virtualization is the ability to run multiple guest operating systems within a single host operating system. Several approaches to virtualization have been developed, including a guest operating system and hypervisor virtualization. Hypervisor virtualization falls into two categories known as Type-1 and Type-2. Type-2 virtualization solutions are categorized as paravirtualization, full virtualization, and hardware virtualization, the latter using special virtualization features of some Intel and AMD processor models.

Virtual machine guest operating systems have several options in terms of networking, including NAT, direct connection (MacVTap), and network bridge configurations.

Chapter 21

21. Installing KVM Virtualization on RHEL 9

Earlier versions of RHEL provided two virtualization platforms: Kernel-based Virtual Machine (KVM) and Xen. In recent releases, support for Xen has been removed, leaving KVM as the only bundled virtualization option supplied with RHEL 9. In addition to KVM, third-party solutions are available in products such as VMware and Oracle VirtualBox. Since KVM is supplied with RHEL 9, however, this virtualization solution will be covered in this and subsequent chapters.

Before plunging into installing and running KVM, it is worth discussing how it fits into the various types of virtualization outlined in the previous chapter.

21.1 An Overview of KVM

KVM is categorized as a Type-1 hypervisor virtualization solution that implements full virtualization with support for unmodified guest operating systems using Intel VT and AMD-V hardware virtualization support.

KVM differs from many other Type-1 solutions in that it turns the host Linux operating system into the hypervisor, allowing bare metal virtualization to be implemented while running a complete, enterprise-level host operating system.

21.2 KVM Hardware Requirements

Before proceeding with this chapter, we must discuss the hardware requirements for running virtual machines within a KVM environment. First and foremost, KVM virtualization is only available on certain processor types. As previously discussed, these processors must include either Intel VT or AMD-V technology.

To check for virtualization support, run the *lscpu* command in a terminal window:

```
# lscpu | grep Virtualization:
```

If the system contains a CPU with Intel VT support, the above command will provide the following output:

```
Virtualization:        VT-x
```

Alternatively, the following output will be displayed when a CPU with AMD-V support is detected:

```
Virtualization:        AMD-V
```

If the CPU does not support virtualization, no output will be displayed by the above *lscpu* command.

Note that while the above commands only report whether the processor supports the respective feature, it does not indicate whether it is currently enabled in the BIOS. This is because, in practice, virtualization support is typically disabled by default in the BIOS of most systems. Therefore, you should check your BIOS settings to ensure the appropriate virtualization technology is enabled before proceeding with this tutorial.

Unlike a dual-booting environment, a virtualized environment involves running two or more complete operating systems concurrently on a single computer system. This means the system must have enough physical memory, disk space, and CPU processing power to comfortably accommodate all these systems in parallel. Therefore, before beginning the configuration and installation process, check on the minimum system requirements for both RHEL 9 and your chosen guest operating systems and verify that your host system has sufficient resources to handle the requirements of both systems.

21.3 Preparing RHEL 9 for KVM Virtualization

Unlike Xen, it is not necessary to run a special version of the kernel in order to support KVM. As a result, KVM support is already available for use with the standard kernel via installing a KVM kernel module, thereby negating the need to install and boot from a special kernel.

To avoid conflicts, however, if a Xen-enabled kernel is currently running on the system, reboot the system and select a non-Xen kernel from the boot menu before proceeding with the remainder of this chapter.

The tools required to set up and maintain a KVM-based virtualized system are only installed by default if selected explicitly during the RHEL 9 operating system installation process. To install the KVM tools from the command prompt, execute the following command in a terminal window:

```
# dnf install qemu-kvm qemu-img libvirt virt-install libvirt-client
```

If you have access to a graphical desktop environment, the *virt-manager* package is also recommended:

```
# dnf install virt-manager
```

21.4 Verifying the KVM Installation

It is worthwhile checking that the KVM installation worked correctly before moving forward. When KVM is installed and running, two modules will have been loaded into the kernel. The presence or otherwise of these modules can be verified in a terminal window by running the *lsmod* command:

```
# lsmod | grep kvm
```

Assuming that the installation was successful, the above command should generate output similar to the following:

```
kvm_intel            237568  0
kvm                  737280  1 kvm_intel
irqbypass             16384  1 kvm
```

Note that if the system contains an AMD processor, the kvm module will likely read *kvm_amd* rather than *kvm_intel*.

The installation process should also have configured the libvirtd daemon to run in the background. Once again, using a terminal window, run the following command to ensure libvirtd is running:

```
# systemctl status libvirtd
 libvirtd.service - Virtualization daemon
   Loaded: loaded (/usr/lib/systemd/system/libvirtd.service; enabled; vendor
preset: enabled)
   Active: active (running) since Wed 2019-03-06 14:41:22 EST; 3min 54s ago
```

If the process is not running, it may be started as follows:

```
# systemctl enable --now libvirtd
# systemctl start libvirtd
```

If the desktop environment is available, run the *virt-manager* tool by selecting Activities and entering "virt" into the search box. When the Virtual Machine Manager icon appears, click it to launch it. When loaded, the manager should appear as illustrated in the following figure:

Figure 21-1

If the QEMU/KVM entry is not listed, select the *File -> Add Connection* menu option and, in the resulting dialog, select the QEMU/KVM Hypervisor before clicking on the Connect button:

Figure 21-2

If the manager is not currently connected to the virtualization processes, right-click on the entry listed and select Connect from the popup menu.

21.5 Summary

KVM is a Type-1 hypervisor virtualization solution that implements full virtualization with support for unmodified guest operating systems using Intel VT and AMD-V hardware virtualization support. It is the default virtualization solution bundled with RHEL 9 and can be installed quickly and easily on any RHEL 9 system with appropriate processor support. With KVM support installed and enabled, the following chapters will outline some options for installing and managing virtual machines on a RHEL 9 host.

22. Creating KVM Virtual Machines on RHEL 9 using Cockpit

KVM-based virtual machines can easily be configured on RHEL 9 using the *virt-install* command-line tool, the *virt-manager* GUI tool, or the Virtual Machines module of the Cockpit web console. This chapter will use Cockpit to install an operating system as a KVM guest on a RHEL 9 host. The chapter titled *"Creating KVM Virtual Machines on RHEL 9 using virt-manager"* will cover using the *virt-manager* tool to create new virtual machines.

The next chapter, *"Creating KVM Virtual Machines with virt-install and virsh"* will cover the command-line approach to virtual machine creation.

22.1 Installing the Cockpit Virtual Machines Module

The virtual machines module may not be included in a standard Cockpit installation by default. Assuming that Cockpit is installed and configured, the virtual machines module may be installed as follows:

```
# dnf install cockpit-machines
```

Once installed, the Virtual Machines option (marked A in Figure 22-1) will appear in the navigation panel the next time you log into the Cockpit interface:

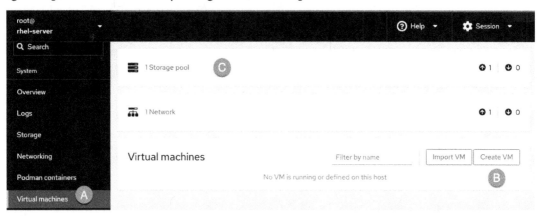

Figure 22-1

22.2 Creating a Virtual Machine in Cockpit

To create a virtual machine in Cockpit, click the Create VM button marked B in Figure 22-1 to display the creation dialog.

Within the dialog, enter a name for the machine and choose whether the installation media is in the form of an ISO accessible via a URL or a local filesystem path, or select the vendor and

Creating KVM Virtual Machines on RHEL 9 using Cockpit

operating system type information for the guest request and choose the *Download an OS* option to have the installation image downloaded automatically during the installation process. If you intend to install RHEL as the guest using the OS download option, you must first generate an RHSM token and copy and paste it into the Offline token field of the VM creation screen. You can obtain a token by opening the following link in a browser, logging into your Red Hat account, and selecting the token generation button:

https://access.redhat.com/management/api

Also, specify the size of the virtual disk drive to be used for the operating system installation and the amount of memory to be allocated to the virtual machine:

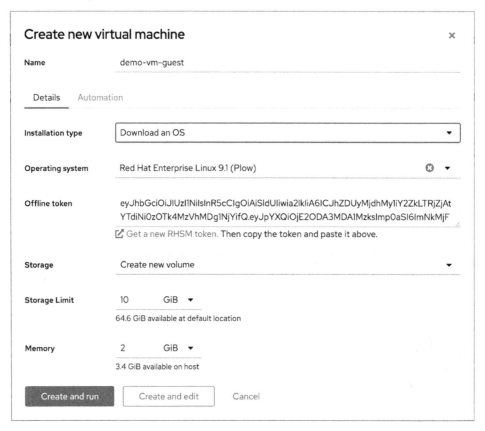

Figure 22-2

Click on the *Create and edit* button to build the virtual machine. After the creation process is complete, details of the new VM will appear in Cockpit, as shown in Figure 22-3:

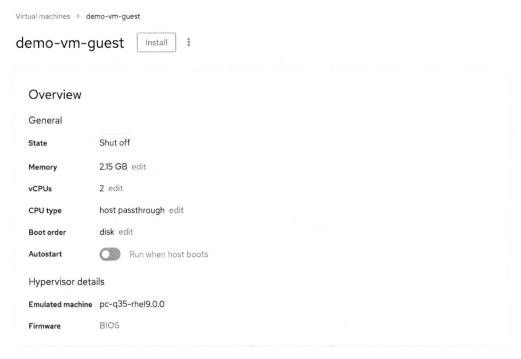

Figure 22-3

As described in *"An Overview of Virtualization Techniques"* KVM provides virtual machines with several options in terms of network configuration. To view and change the network settings of a virtual machine, scroll down to the Network interfaces section of the VM Overview screen and click the Edit button:

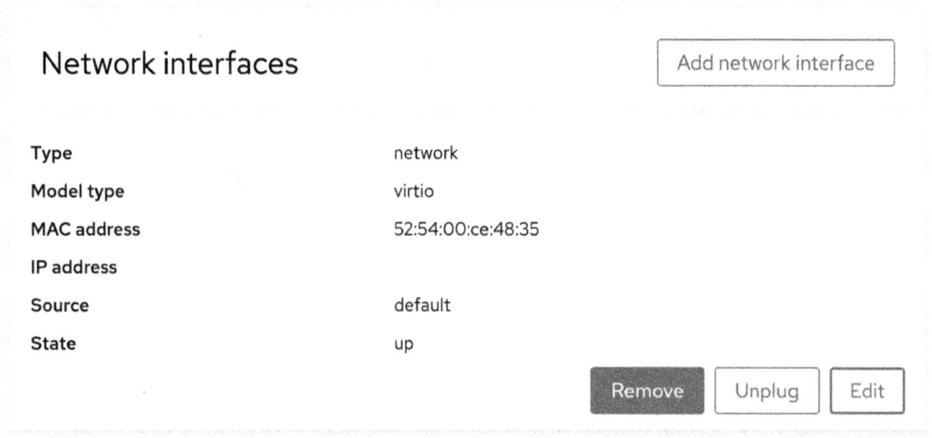

Figure 22-4

In the resulting dialog, the Network Type menu may be used to change the type of network connection, for example, from Virtual network (NAT) to direct attachment (MacVTap) or Bridge to LAN.

22.3 Starting the Installation

To start the new virtual machine and install the guest operating system from the designated installation media, click the Install button at the top of the overview page. Cockpit will start the virtual machine and scroll down to the Console view where the guest OS screen will appear:

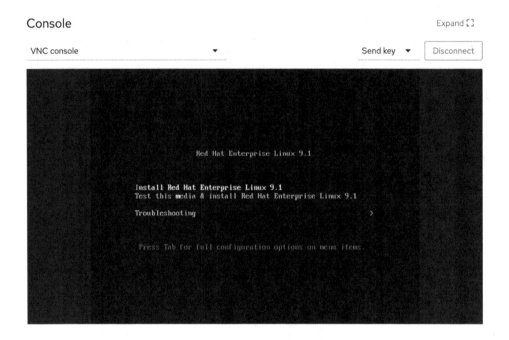

Figure 22-5

If the installation fails, check the message to see if an error occurred when opening the installation image. This usually occurs because the QEMU emulator runs as a user named qemu, which does not have access to the directory in which the ISO installation image is located. To resolve this issue, open a terminal window (or connect with SSH if the system is remote), change directory to the location of the ISO image file, and add the qemu user to the access control list (ACL) of the parent directory as follows:

```
# cd /path/to/iso/directory
# setfacl --modify u:qemu:x ..
```

After making this change, check the setting as follows:

```
# getfacl ..
# file: ..
# owner: demo
# group: demo
user::rwx
user:qemu:--x
group::---
```

```
mask::--x
other::---
```

Once these changes have been made, click the Install button again to complete the installation.

To complete the installation, interact with the screen in the Consoles view just as you would if you were installing the operating system on physical hardware. If the console is too small to accommodate the entire guest operating system screen, click the Expand button in the top right-hand corner.

It is also possible to connect with and display the graphical console for the VM from outside the Cockpit browser session using the *virt-viewer* tool. To install *virt-viewer* on a RHEL 9 system, run the following command:

```
# dnf install virt-viewer
```

The *virt-viewer* tool is also available for Windows systems and can be downloaded from the following URL:

```
https://virt-manager.org/download/
```

To connect with a virtual machine running on the local host, run *virt-viewer* and select the virtual machine to which you wish to connect from the resulting dialog:

Figure 22-6

The above command will list system-based virtual machines. To list and access session-based guests, launch *virt-viewer* as follows:

```
$ virt-viewer --connect qemu:///session
```

Alternatively, it is also possible to specify the virtual machine name and bypass the selection dialog entirely, for example:

```
# virt-viewer demo-vm-guest
```

To connect a *virt-viewer* instance to a virtual machine running on a remote host using SSH, the following command can be used:

```
$ virt-viewer --connect qemu+ssh://<user>@<host>/system <guest name>
```

Creating KVM Virtual Machines on RHEL 9 using Cockpit

For example:

```
$ virt-viewer --connect qemu+ssh://root@192.168.1.122/system demo_vm_guest
```

When using this technique, it is important to note that you will be prompted twice for the user password before the connection is fully established.

Once the virtual machine has been created, the Cockpit interface can monitor the machine and perform tasks such as rebooting, shutting down, or deleting the guest system. An option is also included on the Disks panel to add disks to the virtual machine configuration.

22.4 Working with Storage Volumes and Storage Pools

When a virtual machine is created, it will usually have at least one virtual disk drive. The images that represent these virtual disk drives are stored in *storage pools*. A storage pool can be an existing directory on a local filesystem, a filesystem partition, a physical disk device, Logical Volume Management (LVM) volume group, or even a remote network file system (NFS).

Each storage pool is divided into one or more storage volumes. Storage volumes are typically individual image files, each representing a single virtual disk drive, but they can also take the form of physical disk partitions, entire disk drives, or LVM volume groups.

When a virtual machine was created using the previous steps, a default storage pool was created to store virtual machine images. This default storage pool occupies space on the root filesystem and can be reviewed from within the Cockpit Virtual Machine interface by selecting the Storage Pools option at the top of the panel marked C in Figure 22-1 above.

When selected, the screen shown in Figure 22-7 below will appear containing a list of storage pools currently configured on the system:

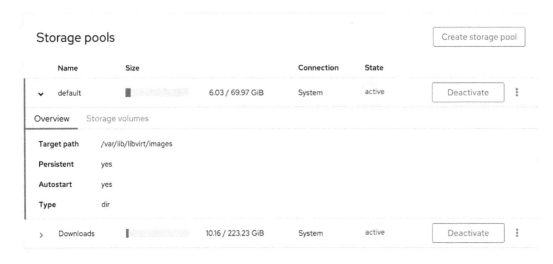

Figure 22-7

In the above example, the default storage pool is located on the root filesystem and stores the virtual machine image in the */var/lib/libvirtd/images* directory. To view the storage volumes contained within the pool, select the Storage Volumes tab highlighted in Figure 22-8:

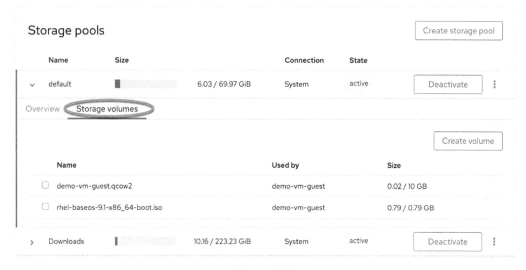

Figure 22-8

In the case of the demo guest, the storage volume takes the form of an image file named *demo-vm-guest.qcow2*. In addition, the pool also includes a storage volume containing the installation ISO image. To find out which storage volume a particular virtual machine uses, return to the main Virtual Machine Cockpit screen, select the virtual machine, and scroll to the Disks panel, as shown in Figure 22-9:

Disks

Add disk

Device	disk	
Used	10 GiB	
Capacity	10 GiB	
Bus	virtio	
Access	Writeable	
Source	**File**	/var/lib/libvirt/images/demo-vm-guest.qcow2
Additional		

Remove   Edit

Figure 22-9

Although using the default storage pool is acceptable for testing purposes and early experimentation, it is recommended that additional pools be created for general virtualization use. To create a new storage pool, display the Storage Pools screen within Cockpit and click on the *Create storage pool* button to display the dialog shown in Figure 22-10:

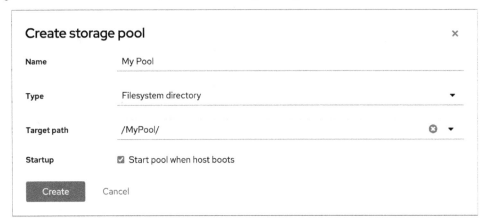

Figure 22-10

In the above example, a new storage pool is being created named MyPool using a file system partition mounted as /MyPool within the local filesystem (the topic of disk drives, partitions, and mount points is covered later in the chapter entitled *"Adding a New Disk Drive to a RHEL 9 System"*). Once created, the pool will be listed within the Cockpit storage pool screen and can contain storage volumes as new virtual machines are created.

22.5 Summary

This chapter has outlined using the Cockpit web-based interface to create and manage KVM-based virtual machines. The Cockpit interface has the advantage of not requiring access to a desktop environment running on the host system. An alternative option is using the *virt-manager* graphical tool outlined in the next chapter.

23. Creating KVM Virtual Machines on RHEL 9 using virt-manager

The previous chapter explored how to create KVM virtual machines on RHEL 9 using the Cockpit web tool. With the caveat that *virt-manager* may one day be discontinued once the Virtual Machines Cockpit extension is fully implemented, this chapter will cover using this tool to create new virtual machines.

23.1 Starting the Virtual Machine Manager

If you have not already done so, install the *virt-manager* package as follows:

```
# dnf install virt-manager
```

Next, launch Virtual Machine Manager from the command line in a terminal window by running *virt-manager*. Once loaded, the virtual machine manager will prompt for the password of the currently active user before displaying the following screen:

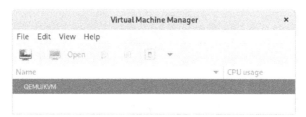

Figure 23-1

The main screen lists the current virtual machines running on the system. By default, the manager should be connected to the system libvirtd instance. If it is not, connect to the host system by right-clicking on the entry in the list and selecting *Connect* from the popup menu. To manage session-based virtual machines, select the *File -> Add Connection...* menu option to display the dialog shown in Figure 23-2:

Figure 23-2

Creating KVM Virtual Machines on RHEL 9 using virt-manager

Select QEMU/KVM user session from the Hypervisor menu and click the Connect button within this dialog. On returning to the main *virt-manager* screen, the QEMU/KVM session should now be listed as shown in Figure 23-1 above.

To create a virtual system, click on the new virtual machine button (the far left button in the toolbar) to display the first screen of the New VM wizard. In the Name field, enter a suitably descriptive name for the virtual system. On this screen, also select the location of the media from which the guest operating system will be installed. This can either be a CD or DVD drive, an ISO image file accessible to the local host, a network install using HTTP, FTP, NFS, or PXE, or the disk image from an existing virtual machine:

Figure 23-3

23.2 Configuring the KVM Virtual System

Clicking Forward will display a screen seeking additional information about the installation process. The displayed screen and information required will depend on selections made on the initial screen. For example, if a CD, DVD, or ISO is selected, this screen will ask for the specific location of the ISO file or physical media device. This screen also attempts to identify the type and version of the guest operating system (for example, the Windows version or Linux distribution) based on the specified installation media. If it is unable to do so, uncheck the *Automatically detect from installation media/source* option, type in the first few characters of the operating system name, and select an option from the list of possible matches:

Figure 23-4

Once these settings are complete, click the Forward button to configure CPU and memory settings. The optimal settings will depend on the number of CPUs and amount of physical memory present in the host, together with the requirements of other applications and virtual machines that will run in parallel with the new virtual machine:

Figure 23-5

On the next screen, options are available to create an image disk of a specified size, select a pre-existing volume, or create a storage volume of a specified format (raw, vmdk, ISO, etc.). Unless you have a specific need to use a particular format (for example, you might need to use vmdk to migrate to a VMware-based virtualization environment at a later date) or need to use a dedicated disk or partition, it is generally adequate to specify a size on this screen:

Creating KVM Virtual Machines on RHEL 9 using virt-manager

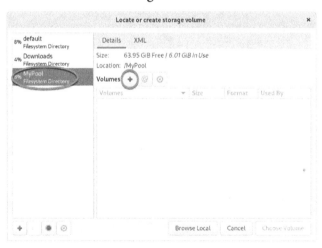

Figure 23-6

If the default settings are used here, the virtual machine will use a storage volume within the default storage pool for the virtual disk drive. To use the custom "MyPool" storage pool created earlier in the chapter, enable the *Select or create custom storage* option before clicking the *Manage...* button.

In the storage volume dialog, select the MyPool entry in the left-hand panel, followed by the + button in the main panel to create a new storage volume:

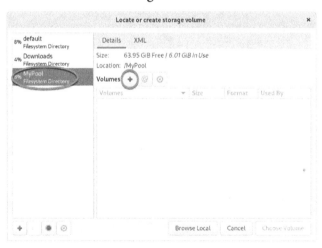

Figure 23-7

Note that the + button in the bottom left-hand corner of the dialog may also be used to create new storage pools as an alternative to using the Cockpit interface.

In the configuration screen (Figure 23-8), name the storage volume, select the volume size, and click on the *Finish* button to create the volume and assign it to the virtual machine:

Figure 23-8

Once these settings are configured, select the new volume and click the *Choose Volume* button. Then, click the Forward button once more. The final screen displays a summary of the configuration. Review the information displayed. Advanced options are also available to change the virtual network configuration for the guest, as shown in Figure 23-9:

Figure 23-9

23.3 Starting the KVM Virtual Machine

Click on the Finish button to begin the creation process. The virtualization manager will create the disk and configure the virtual machine before starting the guest system. Finally, the new virtual machine will appear in the main *virt-manager* window with the status set to *Running* as illustrated in Figure 23-10:

Figure 23-10

By default, the console for the virtual machine should appear in the virtual machine viewer window. To view the console of the running machine at any future time, ensure that it is selected in the virtual machine list and select the Open button from the toolbar. The virtual machine viewer should be ready for the installation process to begin:

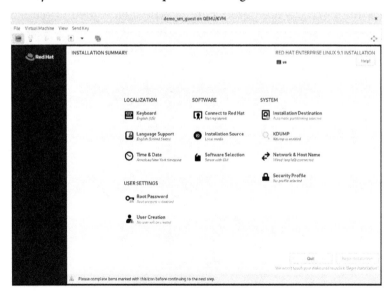

Figure 23-11

From now on, follow the installation instructions to install the guest OS in the KVM virtual machine.

23.4 Summary

There are several ways to create new KVM-based virtual machines on a RHEL 9 host system. This chapter uses the *virt-manager* graphical tool to create, configure, and run a guest operating system, including creating a new storage volume. With these basics covered, the next chapter will cover the creation of virtual machines from the command line.

24. Creating KVM Virtual Machines with virt-install and virsh

In the previous chapters, we explored the creation of KVM guest operating systems on a RHEL 9 host using Cockpit and the *virt-manager* graphical tool. This chapter will focus on creating KVM-based virtual machines using the *virt-install* and *virsh* command-line tools. These tools provide all the capabilities of the *virt-manager* and Cockpit options with the added advantage of being used within scripts to automate virtual machine creation. In addition, the *virsh* command allows virtual machines to be created based on a specification contained within a configuration file.

The *virt-install* tool is supplied to allow new virtual machines to be created by providing a list of command-line options. This chapter assumes that the necessary KVM tools are installed. Read the chapter *"Installing KVM Virtualization on RHEL 9"* for details on these requirements.

24.1 Running virt-install to build a KVM Guest System

The *virt-install* utility accepts a wide range of command-line arguments that provide configuration information related to the virtual machine being created. Some command-line options are mandatory (expressly, name, memory, and disk storage must be provided), while others are optional.

At a minimum, a *virt-install* command will typically need the following arguments:

- **--name** - The name to be assigned to the virtual machine.

- **--memory** - The amount of memory allocated to the virtual machine.

- **--disk** - The name and location of an image file for storage for the virtual machine. This file will be created by *virt-install* during the virtual machine creation unless the --import option is specified to indicate an existing image file is to be used.

- **--cdrom** or **--location** - Specifies the local path or the URL of a remote ISO image containing the installation media for the guest operating system.

A summary of all the arguments available for use when using *virt-install* can be found in the man page:

```
$ man virt-install
```

24.2 An Example RHEL 9 virt-install Command

With reference to the above command-line argument list, we can now look at an example command-line construct using the *virt-install* tool.

Note that to display the virtual machine and complete the installation, a *virt-viewer* instance must

Creating KVM Virtual Machines with virt-install and virsh

be connected to the virtual machine after the *virt-install* utility starts it. By default, *virt-install* will attempt to launch *virt-viewer* automatically once the virtual machine starts running. However, if *virt-viewer* is unavailable, *virt-install* will wait until a *virt-viewer* connection is established. For example, the *virt-viewer* session may be running locally on the host system if it has a graphical desktop, or a connection may be established from a remote client as outlined in the chapter entitled *"Creating KVM Virtual Machines on RHEL 9 using virt-manager"*.

The following command creates a new KVM virtual machine configured to run RHEL 9 using KVM para-virtualization. It creates a new 10GB disk image, assigns 2048MB of RAM to the virtual machine, and configures a virtual CD device for the installation media ISO image:

```
# virt-install --name demo_vm_guest --memory 2048 --disk path=/tmp/demo_vm_guest.
img,size=10 --network network=default --cdrom /tmp/rhel-baseos-9.1-x86_64-dvd.iso
```

As the creation process runs, the *virt-install* command will display status updates of the creation progress:

```
Starting install...
Allocating 'demo_vm_guest.img'                          |  10 GB  00:00:01
Running graphical console command: virt-viewer --connect qemu:///system --wait
demo_vm_guest
```

Once the guest system has been created, the *virt-viewer* screen will appear containing the operating system installer loaded from the specified installation media:

Figure 24-1

From this point, follow the standard installation procedure for the guest operating system.

24.3 Starting and Stopping a Virtual Machine from the Command-Line

Having created the virtual machine from the command line, it stands to reason that you may also need to start it from the command line in the future. This can be achieved using the *virsh* command-line utility, referencing the name assigned to the virtual machine during creation. For example:

```
# virsh start demo_vm_guest
```

Similarly, the virtual machine may be sent a shutdown signal as follows:

```
# virsh shutdown demo_vm_guest
```

Suppose the virtual machine fails to respond to the shutdown signal and does not begin a graceful shutdown. In that case, the virtual machine may be destroyed (with the attendant risks of data loss) using the destroy directive:

```
# virsh destroy demo_vm_guest
```

24.4 Creating a Virtual Machine from a Configuration File

The *virsh create* command can take as an argument the name of a configuration file on which to base the creation of a new virtual machine. The configuration file uses XML format. The easiest way to create a configuration file is to dump out the configuration of an existing virtual machine and modify it for the new one. This can be achieved using the *virsh dumpxml* command. For example, the following command outputs the configuration data for a virtual machine domain named *demo_vm_guest* to a file named *demo_vm_guest.xml*:

```
# virsh dumpxml demo_vm_guest > demo_vm_guest.xml
```

Once the file has been generated, load it into an editor to review and change the settings for the new virtual machine.

At the very least, the <name>, <uuid>, and image file path <source file> must be changed to avoid conflict with the virtual machine from which the configuration was taken. In the case of the UUID, this line can be deleted from the file.

The virtualization type, memory allocation, and number of CPUs, to name but a few options, may also be changed if required. Once the file has been modified, the new virtual machine may be created as follows:

```
# virsh create demo_vm_guest.xml
```

24.5 Summary

KVM provides the *virt-install* and *virsh* command-line tools as a quick and efficient alternative to using the Cockpit and *virt-manager* tools to create and manage virtual machine instances. These tools have the advantage that they can be used from within scripts to automate the creation and management of virtual machines. The *virsh* command also includes the option to create VM instances from XML-based configuration files.

25. Creating a RHEL 9 KVM Networked Bridge Interface

By default, the KVM virtualization environment on RHEL 9 creates a virtual network to which virtual machines may connect. It is also possible to configure a direct connection using a MacVTap driver. However, as outlined in the chapter entitled *"An Overview of Virtualization Techniques"* this approach does not allow the host and guest systems to communicate.

This chapter aims to cover the steps involved in creating a network bridge on RHEL 9, enabling guest systems to share one or more of the host system's physical network connections while still allowing the guest and host systems to communicate.

In the remainder of this chapter, we will explain how to configure a RHEL 9 network bridge for KVM-based guest operating systems.

25.1 Getting the Current Network Manager Settings

A network bridge can be created using the NetworkManager command-line interface tool (nmcli). The NetworkManager is installed and enabled by default on RHEL 9 systems and is responsible for detecting and connecting to network devices and providing an interface for managing networking configurations.

A list of current network connections on the host system can be displayed as follows:

```
# nmcli con show
NAME        UUID                                    TYPE      DEVICE
eno1        99d40009-6bb1-4182-baad-a103941c90ff    ethernet  eno1
virbr0      7cb1265e-ffb9-4cb3-aaad-2a6fe5880d38    bridge    virbr0
```

The above output shows that the host has an Ethernet network connection established via a device named eno1 and the default bridge interface named virbr0, which provides access to the NAT-based virtual network to which KVM guest systems are connected by default.

Similarly, the following command can be used to identify the devices (both virtual and physical) that are currently configured on the system:

```
# nmcli device show
GENERAL.DEVICE:                         eno1
GENERAL.TYPE:                           ethernet
GENERAL.HWADDR:                         AC:16:2D:11:16:73
GENERAL.MTU:                            1500
GENERAL.STATE:                          100 (connected)
GENERAL.CONNECTION:                     eno1
GENERAL.CON-PATH:                       /org/freedesktop/NetworkManager/
```

Creating a RHEL 9 KVM Networked Bridge Interface

```
ActiveConnection/1
WIRED-PROPERTIES.CARRIER:          on
IP4.ADDRESS[1]:                    192.168.86.59/24
IP4.GATEWAY:                       192.168.86.1
IP4.ROUTE[1]:                      dst = 0.0.0.0/0, nh = 192.168.86.1, mt =
100
IP4.ROUTE[2]:                      dst = 192.168.86.0/24, nh = 0.0.0.0, mt =
100
IP4.DNS[1]:                        192.168.86.1
IP4.DOMAIN[1]:                     lan
IP6.ADDRESS[1]:                    fe80::6deb:f739:7d67:2242/64
IP6.GATEWAY:                       --
IP6.ROUTE[1]:                      dst = fe80::/64, nh = ::, mt = 100
IP6.ROUTE[2]:                      dst = ff00::/8, nh = ::, mt = 256,
table=255

GENERAL.DEVICE:                    virbr0
GENERAL.TYPE:                      bridge
GENERAL.HWADDR:                    52:54:00:59:30:22
GENERAL.MTU:                       1500
GENERAL.STATE:                     100 (connected)
GENERAL.CONNECTION:                virbr0
GENERAL.CON-PATH:                  /org/freedesktop/NetworkManager/
ActiveConnection/2
IP4.ADDRESS[1]:                    192.168.122.1/24
IP4.GATEWAY:                       --
IP4.ROUTE[1]:                      dst = 192.168.122.0/24, nh = 0.0.0.0, mt
= 0
IP6.GATEWAY:                       --
.
.
```

The above partial output indicates that the host system on which the command was executed contains a physical Ethernet device (eno1) and a virtual bridge (virbr0).

The virsh command may also be used to list the virtual networks currently configured on the system:

```
# virsh net-list --all
 Name                 State      Autostart     Persistent
-----------------------------------------------------------
 default              active     yes           yes
```

Currently, the only virtual network present is the default network provided by virbr0. Now that some basic information about the current network configuration has been obtained, the next step is to create a network bridge connected to the physical network device (in this case, eno1).

25.2 Creating a Network Manager Bridge from the Command-Line

The first step in creating the network bridge is adding a new connection to the configuration. This can be achieved using the *nmcli* tool, specifying that the connection is to be a bridge and providing names for both the connection and the interface:

```
# nmcli con add ifname br0 type bridge con-name br0
```

Once the connection has been added, a bridge slave interface needs to be established between physical device eno1 (the slave) and the bridge connection br0 (the master) as follows:

```
# nmcli con add type bridge-slave ifname eno1 master br0
```

At this point, the NetworkManager connection list should read as follows:

```
# nmcli con show
NAME              UUID                                  TYPE      DEVICE
eno1              66f0abed-db43-4d79-8f5e-2cbf8c7e3aff  ethernet  eno1
virbr0            0fa934d5-0508-47b7-a119-33a232b03f64  bridge    virbr0
br0               59b6631c-a283-41b9-bbf9-56a60ec75653  bridge    br0
bridge-slave-eno1 395bb34b-5e02-427a-ab31-762c9f878908  ethernet  --
```

The next step is to start up the bridge interface. If the steps to configure the bridge are being performed over a network connection (i.e., via SSH) this step can be problematic because the current eno1 connection must be closed down before the bridge connection can be brought up. This means the current connection will be lost before the bridge connection can be enabled to replace it, potentially leaving the remote host unreachable.

If you are accessing the host system remotely, this problem can be avoided by creating a shell script to perform the network changes. This will ensure that the bridge interface is enabled after the eno1 interface is brought down, allowing you to reconnect to the host after the changes are complete. Begin by creating a shell script file named *bridge.sh* containing the following commands:

```
#!/bin/bash
nmcli con down eno1
nmcli con up br0
```

Once the script has been created, execute it as follows:

```
# sh ./bridge.sh
```

When the script executes, the connection will be lost when the eno1 connection is brought down. After waiting a few seconds, however, it should be possible to reconnect to the host once the br0 connection has been activated.

If you are working locally on the host, the two *nmcli* commands can be run within a terminal window without any risk of losing connectivity:

```
# nmcli con down eno1
# nmcli con up br0
```

Once the bridge is up and running, the connection list should now include both the bridge and the bridge-slave connections:

Creating a RHEL 9 KVM Networked Bridge Interface

```
# nmcli con show
NAME                UUID                                    TYPE       DEVICE
br0                 59b6631c-a283-41b9-bbf9-56a60ec75653    bridge     br0
bridge-slave-eno1   395bb34b-5e02-427a-ab31-762c9f878908    ethernet   eno1
virbr0              0fa934d5-0508-47b7-a119-33a232b03f64    bridge     virbr0
eno1                66f0abed-db43-4d79-8f5e-2cbf8c7e3aff    ethernet   --
```

Note that the eno1 connection is still listed but is no longer active. To exclude inactive connections from the list, use the --active flag when requesting the list:

```
# nmcli con show --active
NAME                UUID                                    TYPE       DEVICE
br0                 c2fa30cb-b1a1-4107-80dd-b1765878ab4f    bridge     br0
bridge-slave-eno1   21e8c945-cb94-4c09-99b0-17af9b5a7319    ethernet   eno1
virbr0              a877302e-ea02-42fe-a3c1-483440aae774    bridge     virbr0
```

25.3 Declaring the KVM Bridged Network

At this point, the bridge connection is on the system but is not visible to the KVM environment. Running the virsh command should still list the default network as being the only available network option:

```
# virsh net-list --all
 Name               State       Autostart    Persistent
---------------------------------------------------------------
 default            active      yes          yes
```

Before a virtual machine can use the bridge, it must be declared and added to the KVM network configuration. This involves the creation of a definition file and, once again, using the *virsh* command-line tool.

Begin by creating a definition file for the bridge network named *bridge.xml* that reads as follows:

```
<network>
  <name>br0</name>
  <forward mode="bridge"/>
  <bridge name="br0" />
</network>
```

Next, use the file to define the new network:

```
# virsh net-define ./bridge.xml
```

Once the network has been defined, start it and, if required, configure it to autostart each time the system reboots:

```
# virsh net-start br0
# virsh net-autostart br0
```

Once again, list the networks to verify that the bridge network is now accessible within the KVM environment:

```
# virsh net-list --all
```

Name	State	Autostart	Persistent
br0	active	yes	yes
default	active	yes	yes

25.4 Using a Bridge Network in a Virtual Machine

To create a virtual machine that uses the bridge network, use the *virt-install --network* option and specify the br0 bridge name. For example:

```
# virt-install --name demo_vm_guest --memory 1024 --disk path=/tmp/demo_vm_guest.img,size=10 --network network=br0 --cdrom /home/demo/rhel-baseos-9.1-x86_64-dvd.iso
```

When the guest operating system is running, it will appear on the same physical network as the host system and will no longer be on the NAT-based virtual network.

The bridge may also be selected for virtual machines within the Cockpit interface by editing the virtual machine, locating the Network interfaces section, and clicking the Edit button as highlighted in Figure 25-1 below:

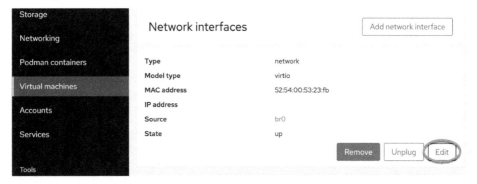

Figure 25-1

Within the resulting interface settings dialog, change the Interface type menu to Bridge to LAN and set the Source to br0 as shown in Figure 25-2:

Figure 25-2

Creating a RHEL 9 KVM Networked Bridge Interface

Similarly, when creating a new virtual machine using the *virt-manager* tool, the bridge will be available within the Network selection menu:

Figure 25-3

To modify an existing virtual machine so that it uses the bridge, use the *virsh edit* command. This command loads the XML definition file into an editor where changes can be made and saved:

```
# virsh edit GuestName
```

By default, the file will be loaded into the vi editor. To use a different editor, change the $EDITOR environment variable, for example:

```
# export EDITOR=gedit
```

To change from the default virtual network, locate the <interface> section of the file, which will read as follows for a NAT-based configuration:

```
<interface type='network'>
      <mac address='<your mac address here>'/>
      <source network='default'/>
      <model type='virtio'/>
      <address type='pci' domain='0x0000' bus='0x01' slot='0x00' function='0x0'/>
</interface>
```

Alternatively, if the virtual machine was using a direct connection, the entry may read as follows:

```
<interface type='direct'>
      <mac address='<your mac address here>'/>
      <source dev='eno1' mode='vepa'/>
      <model type='virtio'/>
      <address type='pci' domain='0x0000' bus='0x01' slot='0x00' function='0x0'/>
```

To use the bridge, change the source network property to read as follows before saving the file:

```
<interface type='network'>
      <mac address='<your mac address here>'/>
```

196

```
        <source network='br0'/>
        <model type='virtio'/>
        <address type='pci' domain='0x0000' bus='0x01' slot='0x00' function='0x0'/>
</interface>
```

If the virtual machine is already running, the change will not take effect until it is restarted.

25.5 Creating a Bridge Network using nm-connection-editor

If either local or remote desktop access is available on the host system, much of the bridge configuration process can be performed using the *nm-connection-editor* graphical tool. To use this tool, open a Terminal window within the desktop and enter the following command:

```
# nm-connection-editor
```

When the tool has loaded, the window shown in Figure 25-4 will appear listing the currently configured network connections (essentially the same output as that generated by the *nmcli con show* command):

Figure 25-4

To create a new connection, click on the '+' button in the window's bottom left-hand corner. Then, from the resulting dialog (Figure 25-5), select the Bridge option from the menu:

Figure 25-5

With the bridge option selected, click the Create button to proceed to the bridge configuration screen. Begin by changing both the connection and interface name fields to br0 before clicking on

Creating a RHEL 9 KVM Networked Bridge Interface

the Add button located to the right of the Bridge connections list, as highlighted in Figure 25-6:

Figure 25-6

From the connection type dialog (Figure 25-7), change the menu setting to Ethernet before clicking on the Create button:

Figure 25-7

Another dialog will now appear in which the bridge slave connection needs to be configured. Within this dialog, select the physical network to which the bridge is to connect (for example, eno1) from the Device menu:

Figure 25-8

Click on the Save button to apply the changes and return to the Editing br0 dialog (as illustrated in Figure 25-6 above). Within this dialog, click on the Save button to create the bridge. On returning to the main window, the new bridge and slave connections should now be listed:

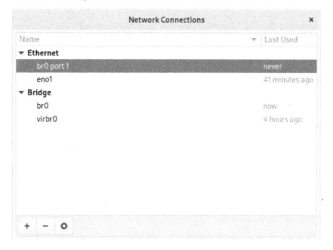

Figure 25-9

All that remains is to bring down the original eno1 connection and bring up the br0 connection using the steps outlined in the previous chapter (remembering to perform these steps in a shell script if the host is being accessed remotely):

```
# nmcli con down eno1
# nmcli con up br0
```

Creating a RHEL 9 KVM Networked Bridge Interface

It will also be necessary, as it was when creating the bridge using the command-line tool, to add this bridge to the KVM network configuration. To do so, repeat the steps outlined in the *"Declaring the KVM Bridged Network"* section above. Once this step has been taken, the bridge is ready to be used by guest virtual machines.

25.6 Summary

By default, KVM virtual machines are connected to a virtual network that uses NAT to provide access to the network to which the host system is connected. If the guests are required to appear on the network with their own IP addresses, they need to be configured to share the physical network interface of the host system. This chapter outlines that this can be achieved using the *nmcli* or *nm-connection-editor* tools to create a networked bridge interface.

26. Managing KVM using the virsh Command-Line Tool

In previous chapters, we have covered the installation and configuration of KVM-based guest operating systems on RHEL 9. This chapter explores additional areas of the *virsh* tool that have not been covered in previous chapters and how it may be used to manage KVM-based guest operating systems from the command line.

26.1 The virsh Shell and Command-Line

The virsh tool is both a command-line tool and an interactive shell environment. When used in the command-line mode, the command is issued at the command prompt with sets of arguments appropriate to the task.

To use the options as command-line arguments, use them at a terminal command prompt, as shown in the following example:

```
# virsh <option>
```

The *virsh* tool, when used in shell mode, provides an interactive environment from which to issue sequences of commands.

To run commands in the *virsh* shell, run the following command:

```
# virsh
Welcome to virsh, the virtualization interactive terminal.

Type:  'help' for help with commands
       'quit' to quit

virsh #
```

At the *virsh* # prompt, enter the options you wish to run. The following *virsh* session, for example, lists the current virtual machines, starts a virtual machine named FedoraVM, and then obtains another listing to verify the VM is running:

```
# virsh
Welcome to virsh, the virtualization interactive terminal.

Type:  'help' for help with commands
       'quit' to quit

virsh # list
 Id    Name                           State
```

```
----------------------------------------------------
 8      RHEL9VM                        running
 9      CentOS9VM                      running

virsh # start FedoraVM
Domain FedoraVM started

virsh # list
 Id    Name                         State
----------------------------------------------------
 8      RHEL9VM                        running
 9      CentOS9VM                      running
10      FedoraVM                       running

virsh#
```

The *virsh* tool supports a wide range of commands, a complete listing of which may be obtained using the help option:

```
# virsh help
```

Additional details on the syntax for each command may be obtained by specifying the command after the help directive:

```
# virsh help restore
  NAME
    restore - restore a domain from a saved state in a file

  SYNOPSIS
    restore <file> [--bypass-cache] [--xml <string>] [--running] [--paused]

  DESCRIPTION
    Restore a domain.

  OPTIONS
    [--file] <string>  the state to restore
    --bypass-cache     avoid file system cache when restoring
    --xml <string>     filename containing updated XML for the target
    --running          restore domain into running state
    --paused           restore domain into paused state
```

In the remainder of this chapter, we will look at some of these commands in more detail.

26.2 Listing Guest System Status

The status of the guest systems on a RHEL 9 virtualization host may be viewed at any time using the list option of the *virsh* tool. For example:

```
# virsh list
```

The above command will display output containing a line for each guest similar to the following:

```
virsh # list
 Id    Name                           State
----------------------------------------------------
 8     RHEL9VM                        running
 9     CentOS9VM                      running
 10    FedoraVM                       running
```

26.3 Starting a Guest System

A guest operating system can be started using the *virsh* tool combined with the start option followed by the name of the guest operating system to be launched. For example:

```
# virsh start myGuestOS
```

26.4 Shutting Down a Guest System

The shutdown option of the *virsh* tool, as the name suggests, is used to shut down a guest operating system:

```
# virsh shutdown guestName
```

Note that the shutdown option allows the guest operating system to perform an orderly shutdown when it receives the instruction. To instantly stop a guest operating system, the destroy option may be used (with the risk of file system damage and data loss):

```
# virsh destroy guestName
```

26.5 Suspending and Resuming a Guest System

A guest system can be suspended and resumed using the *virsh* tool's suspend and resume options. For example, to suspend a specific system:

```
# virsh suspend guestName
```

Similarly, to resume the paused system:

```
# virsh resume guestName
```

A suspended session will be lost if the host system is rebooted. Also, be aware that a suspended system continues to reside in memory. Therefore, to save a session such that it no longer takes up memory and can be restored to its exact state (even after a reboot), it is necessary to save and restore the guest.

26.6 Saving and Restoring Guest Systems

A running guest operating system can be saved and restored using the *virsh* utility. When saved, the current status of the guest operating system is written to disk and removed from system memory. A saved system may subsequently be restored at any time (including after a host system reboot).

To save a guest:

```
# virsh save guestName path_to_save_file
```

To restore a saved guest operating system session:

```
# virsh restore path_to_save_file
```

26.7 Rebooting a Guest System

To reboot a guest operating system:

```
# virsh reboot guestName
```

26.8 Configuring the Memory Assigned to a Guest OS

To configure the memory assigned to a guest OS, use the *setmem* option of the virsh command. For example, the following command reduces the memory allocated to a guest system to 256MB:

```
# virsh setmem guestName 256
```

Note that acceptable memory settings must fall within the memory available to the current Domain. This may be increased using the *setmaxmem* option.

26.9 Summary

The *virsh* tool provides various options for creating, monitoring, and managing guest virtual machines. As outlined in this chapter, the tool can be used in either command-line or interactive modes.

Chapter 27

27. An Introduction to Linux Containers

The preceding chapters covered the concept of virtualization, emphasizing creating and managing virtual machines using KVM. This chapter will introduce a related technology in the form of Linux Containers. While there are some similarities between virtual machines and containers, key differences will be outlined in this chapter, along with an introduction to the concepts and advantages of Linux Containers. The chapter will also overview some RHEL 9 container management tools. Once the basics of containers have been covered in this chapter, the next chapter will work through some practical examples of creating and running containers on RHEL 9.

27.1 Linux Containers and Kernel Sharing

In simple terms, Linux containers are a lightweight alternative to virtualization. A virtual machine contains and runs the entire guest operating system in a virtualized environment. The virtual machine, in turn, runs on top of an environment such as a hypervisor that manages access to the physical resources of the host system.

Containers work by using a concept referred to as kernel sharing, which takes advantage of the architectural design of Linux and UNIX-based operating systems.

To understand how kernel sharing and containers work, it helps first to understand the two main components of Linux or UNIX operating systems. At the core of the operating system is the kernel. The kernel, in simple terms, handles all the interactions between the operating system and the physical hardware. The second key component is the root file system which contains all the libraries, files, and utilities necessary for the operating system to function. Taking advantage of this structure, containers each have their own root file system but share the host operating system's kernel. This structure is illustrated in the architectural diagram in Figure 27-1 below.

This type of resource sharing is made possible by the ability of the kernel to dynamically change the current root file system (a concept known as change root or chroot) to a different root file system without having to reboot the entire system. Linux containers are essentially an extension of this capability combined with a container runtime, the responsibility of which is to provide an interface for executing and managing the containers on the host system. Several container runtimes are available, including Docker, lxd, containerd, and CRI-O. Earlier versions of RHEL used Docker by default, but Podman has supplanted this as the default in RHEL 9

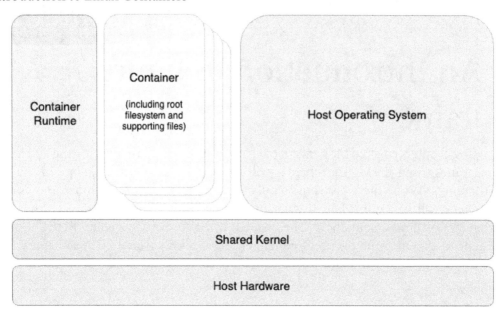

Figure 27-1

27.2 Container Uses and Advantages

The main advantage of containers is that they require considerably less resource overhead than virtualization allowing many container instances to be run simultaneously on a single server. They can be started and stopped rapidly and efficiently in response to demand levels. In addition, containers run natively on the host system providing a level of performance that a virtual machine cannot match.

Containers are also highly portable and can be easily migrated between systems. Combined with a container management system such as Docker, OpenShift, and Kubernetes, it is possible to deploy and manage containers on a vast scale spanning multiple servers and cloud platforms, potentially running thousands of containers.

Containers are frequently used to create lightweight execution environments for applications. In this scenario, each container provides an isolated environment containing the application together with all of the runtime and supporting files required by that application to run. The container can then be deployed to any other compatible host system that supports container execution and runs without any concerns that the target system may not have the necessary runtime configuration for the application - all of the application's dependencies are already in the container.

Containers are also helpful when bridging the gap between development and production environments. By performing development and QA work in containers, they can be passed to production and launched safely because the applications run in the same container environments in which they were developed and tested.

Containers also promote a modular approach to deploying large and complex solutions. Instead of developing applications as single monolithic entities, containers can be used to design applications as groups of interacting modules, each running in a separate container.

One possible drawback of containers is that the guest operating systems must be compatible with the version of the kernel being shared. It is not, for example, possible to run Microsoft Windows in a container on a Linux system. Nor is it possible for a Linux guest system designed for the 2.6 version of the kernel to share a 2.4 version kernel. These requirements are not, however, what containers were designed for. Rather than being seen as limitations, these restrictions should be considered some of the key advantages of containers in providing a simple, scalable, and reliable deployment platform.

27.3 RHEL 9 Container Tools

RHEL 9 provides several tools for creating, inspecting, and managing containers. The main tools are as follows:

- **buildah** – A command-line tool for building container images.

- **podman** – A command-line based container runtime and management tool. Performs tasks such as downloading container images from remote registries and inspecting, starting, and stopping images.

- **skopeo** – A command-line utility used to convert container images, copy images between registries and inspect images stored in registries without downloading them.

- **runc** – A lightweight container runtime for launching and running containers from the command line.

- **OpenShift** – An enterprise-level container application management platform consisting of command-line and web-based tools.

All of the above tools comply with the Open Container Initiative (OCI), a set of specifications designed to ensure that containers conform to the same standards between competing tools and platforms.

27.4 Container Catalogs, Repositories, and Registries

The Red Hat Container Catalog (RHCC) provides a set of pre-built images tested by Red Hat that can be downloaded and used as the basis for your own container images. The RHCC can be accessed at the following URL and allows searches to be performed for specific images:

https://catalog.redhat.com/software/containers/search

After completing a search, the catalog will display a list of matching repositories. A repository in this context is a collection of associated images. Figure 27-2, for example, shows a partial list of the container image repositories available for RHEL 9 related containers:

An Introduction to Linux Containers

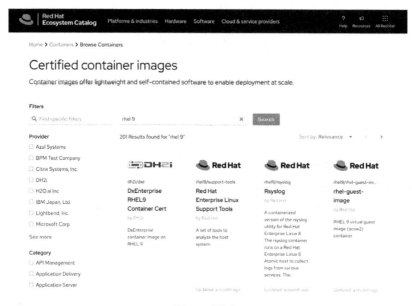

Figure 27-2

Selecting a repository from the list will display detailed information about the repository. When reviewing a repository in the catalog, key pieces of information are the repository name and the location of the registry where the repository is stored. Both specifications must be referenced when the container image is downloaded for use.

27.5 Container Networking

By default, containers are connected to a network using a Container Networking Interface (CNI) bridged network stack. In the bridged configuration, all the containers running on a server belong to the same subnet and, as such, can communicate with each other. The containers are also connected to the external network by bridging the host system's network connection. Similarly, the host can access the containers via a virtual network interface (usually named podman0) which will have been created as part of the container tool installation.

27.6 Summary

Linux Containers offer a lightweight alternative to virtualization and take advantage of the structure of the Linux and Unix operating systems. Linux Containers share the host operating system's kernel, with each container having its own root file system containing the files, libraries, and applications. As a result, containers are highly efficient and scalable and provide an ideal platform for building and deploying modular enterprise-level solutions. In addition, several tools and platforms are available for building, deploying, and managing containers, including third-party solutions and those provided by Red Hat.

28. Working with Containers on RHEL 9

Now that the basics of Linux Containers have been covered in the previous chapter, this chapter will demonstrate how to create and manage containers using the Podman, Skopeo, and Buildah tools on RHEL 9. By the end of this chapter, you will have a clearer understanding of how to create and manage containers on RHEL 9. In addition, you will have gained a knowledge foundation on which to continue exploring the power of Linux Containers.

28.1 Installing the Container Tools

Before starting with containers, the first step is to install all of the container tools outlined in the previous chapter using the following command:

```
# dnf install container-tools
```

28.2 Logging in to the Red Hat Container Registry

To begin with, a container will be created using an existing image provided within the Red Hat Container Registry. Before an image can be pulled from the registry to the local system, however, you must first log into the registry using your existing Red Hat credentials using the *podman* tool as follows:

```
# podman login registry.redhat.io
Username: yourusername
Password: yourpassword
Login Succeeded!
```

28.3 Pulling a Container Image

The RHEL 9 Universal Base Image (UBI) will be pulled from the registry for this example. Before pulling an image, however, information about the image repository can be obtained using the *skopeo* tool, for example:

```
# skopeo inspect docker://registry.redhat.io/ubi9/ubi-init
{
    "Name": "registry.redhat.io/ubi9/ubi-init",
    "Digest": "sha256:82352ed85d5dd55efd8d32a7eae998afded2769fc1b517cc4383301da19
36a58",
    "RepoTags": [
        "9.1.0-15",
        "9.1.0-12",
        "9.0.0-16",
        "9.0.0-19",
        "9.1.0",
```

```
            "9.0.0",
            "9.0.0-16.1655192132",
            "9.0.0-26.1666626006",
            "9.0.0-26.1665072052",
            "9.0.0-16.1655192132-source",
            "9.1.0-5.1669633213-source",
            "9.0.0-26.1666626006-source",
            "9.1.0-12-source",
            "9.1.0-5.1669025017-source",
            "9.1.0-5.1669633213",
            "9.0.0-26.1665072052-source",
            "9.1.0-5.1669025017",
            "9.1",
            "9.0.0-28",
            "9.0.0-29",
            "9.1.0-12.1675789285-source",
            "9.0.0-23",
            "9.0.0-26",
            "9.0.0-26-source",
            "9.0.0-28-source",
            "9.1.0-5-source",
            "9.0.0-29-source",
            "9.1.0-15-source",
            "9.1.0-5",
            "9.0.0-19-source",
            "9.0.0-16-source",
            "9.0.0-23-source",
            "9.1.0-12.1675789285",
            "latest"
    ],
    "Created": "2023-02-22T13:55:53.957676474Z",
    "DockerVersion": "",
    "Labels": {
        "architecture": "x86_64",
        "build-date": "2023-02-22T13:54:21",
        "com.redhat.component": "ubi9-init-container",
        "com.redhat.license_terms": "https://www.redhat.com/en/about/red-hat-end-
user-license-agreements#UBI",
        "description": "The Universal Base Image Init is designed to run an init
system as PID 1 for running multi-services inside a container. This base image is
freely redistributable, but Red Hat only supports Red Hat technologies through
subscriptions for Red Hat products. This image is maintained by Red Hat and
updated regularly."
```

.
.

This ubi-init image is the RHEL 9 base image for building minimal operating system containers and will be used as the basis for the example in this chapter.

Having verified that this is indeed the correct image, the following *podman* command will pull the image to the local system:

```
# podman pull docker://registry.redhat.io/ubi9/ubi-init
Trying to pull docker://registry.redhat.io/ubi9/ubi-init...Getting image source
signatures
Copying blob 340ff6d7f58c done
Copying blob 0e8ea260d026 done
Copying blob c3bd58a6898a done
Copying config a4933472b1 done
Writing manifest to image destination
Storing signatures
a4933472b168b6bd21bc4922dc1e72bb2805d41743799f5a823cdeca9a9a6613
```

Verify that the image has been stored by asking *podman* to list all local images:

```
# podman  images
REPOSITORY                         TAG      IMAGE ID       CREATED       SIZE
registry.redhat.io/ubi9/ubi-init   latest   a4933472b168   6 weeks ago   254 MB
```

Details about a local image may be obtained by running the *podman inspect* command:

```
# podman inspect registry.redhat.io/ubi9/ubi-init
```

This command should output the same information as the *skopeo* command performed on the remote image earlier in this chapter.

28.4 Running the Image in a Container

The image pulled from the registry is a fully operational image ready to run in a container without modification. To run the image, use the *podman run* command. In this case, the –rm option will be specified to indicate that we want to run the image in a container, execute one command and then have the container exit. In this case, the *cat* tool will be used to output the content of the */etc/passwd* file located on the container root filesystem:

```
# podman run --rm registry.redhat.io/ubi9/ubi-init cat /etc/passwd
root:x:0:0:root:/root:/bin/bash
bin:x:1:1:bin:/bin:/sbin/nologin
daemon:x:2:2:daemon:/sbin:/sbin/nologin
adm:x:3:4:adm:/var/adm:/sbin/nologin
lp:x:4:7:lp:/var/spool/lpd:/sbin/nologin
sync:x:5:0:sync:/sbin:/bin/sync
shutdown:x:6:0:shutdown:/sbin:/sbin/shutdown
halt:x:7:0:halt:/sbin:/sbin/halt
mail:x:8:12:mail:/var/spool/mail:/sbin/nologin
operator:x:11:0:operator:/root:/sbin/nologin
games:x:12:100:games:/usr/games:/sbin/nologin
```

```
ftp:x:14:50:FTP User:/var/ftp:/sbin/nologin
nobody:x:65534:65534:Kernel Overflow User:/:/sbin/nologin
systemd-coredump:x:999:997:systemd Core Dumper:/:/sbin/nologin
dbus:x:81:81:System message bus:/:/sbin/nologin
tss:x:59:59:Account used for TPM access:/dev/null:/sbin/nologin
systemd-oom:x:995:995:systemd Userspace OOM Killer:/:/usr/sbin/nologin
```

Compare the content of the */etc/passwd* file within the container with the */etc/passwd* file on the host system. Note that it lacks all of the additional users on the host confirming that the cat command was executed within the container environment. Also, note that the container started, ran the command, and exited within seconds. Compare this to the amount of time it takes to start a full operating system, perform a task, and shut down a virtual machine, and you begin to appreciate the speed and efficiency of containers.

To launch a container, keep it running, and access the shell, the following command can be used:

```
# podman run --name=mycontainer -it registry.redhat.io/ubi9/ubi-init /bin/bash
[root@dbed2be11730 /]#
```

In this case, an additional command-line option has been used to assign the name "mycontainer" to the container. Though optional, this makes the container easier to recognize and reference as an alternative to using the automatically generated container ID.

While the container is running, run *podman* in a different terminal window to see the status of all containers on the system

```
# podman ps -a
CONTAINER ID  IMAGE                             COMMAND     CREATED
STATUS             PORTS   NAMES
dbed2be11730  registry.redhat.io/ubi9/ubi:latest  /bin/bash  5 minutes ago  Up 2
minutes ago        mycontainer
```

To execute a command in a running container from the host, use the *podman exec* command, referencing the name of the running container and the command to be executed. The following command, for example, starts up a second bash session in the container named mycontainer:

```
# podman exec -it mycontainer /bin/bash
[root@dbed2be11730 /]#
```

Note that though the above example referenced the container name, the same result can be achieved using the container ID as listed by the *podman ps -a* command:

```
# podman exec -it dbed2be11730 /bin/bash
[root@dbed2be11730 /]#
```

Alternatively, the *podman attach* command will also attach to a running container and access the shell prompt:

```
# podman attach mycontainer
[root@dbed2be11730 /]#
```

Once the container is up and running, additional configuration changes can be made and packages installed like any other RHEL 9 system.

28.5 Managing a Container

Once launched, a container will continue to run until it is stopped via *podman*, or the command launched when the container was run exits. Running the following command on the host, for example, will cause the container to exit:

```
# podman stop mycontainer
```

Alternatively, pressing the Ctrl-D keyboard sequence within the last remaining bash shell of the container would cause both the shell and container to exit. Once it has exited, the status of the container will change accordingly:

```
# podman ps -a
CONTAINER ID  IMAGE                                  COMMAND    CREATED
STATUS                  PORTS   NAMES
dbed2be11730  registry.redhat.io/ubi9/ubi:latest  /bin/bash  9 minutes ago
Exited (0) 14 seconds ago          mycontainer
```

Although the container is no longer running, it still exists and contains all the configuration and file system changes. If you installed packages, made configuration changes, or added files, these changes will persist within "mycontainer". To verify this, restart the container as follows:

```
# podman start mycontainer
```

After starting the container, use the *podman exec* command again to execute commands within the container as outlined previously. For example, to once again gain access to a shell prompt:

```
# podman exec -it mycontainer /bin/bash
```

A running container may also be paused and resumed using the *podman pause* and *unpause* commands as follows:

```
# podman pause mycontainer
# podman unpause mycontainer
```

28.6 Saving a Container to an Image

Once the container guest system is configured to your requirements, there is a good chance that you will want to create and run more than one container of this particular type. To do this, the container needs to be saved as an image to local storage to be used as the basis for additional container instances. This is achieved using the *podman commit* command combined with the name or ID of the container and the name by which the image will be stored, for example:

```
# podman commit mycontainer myrhel_image
```

Once the image has been saved, check that it now appears in the list of images in the local repository:

```
# podman images
REPOSITORY                           TAG     IMAGE ID      CREATED        SIZE
localhost/myrhel_image               latest  4d207635db6c  9 seconds ago  239 MB
registry.redhat.io/ubi9/ubi-init     latest  a4933472b168  6 weeks ago    254 MB
```

The saved image can now be used to create additional containers identical to the original:

```
# podman run --name=mycontainer2 -it localhost/myrhel_image /bin/bash
```

28.7 Removing an Image from Local Storage

To remove an image from local storage once it is no longer needed, run the *podman rmi* command, referencing either the image name or ID as output by the *podman images* command. For example, to remove the image named myrhel_image created in the previous section, run *podman* as follows:

```
# podman rmi localhost/myrhel_image
```

Before an image can be removed, any containers based on that image must first be removed.

28.8 Removing Containers

Even when a container has exited or been stopped, it still exists and can be restarted anytime. If a container is no longer needed, it can be deleted using the *podman rm* command as follows after the container has been stopped:

```
# podman rm mycontainer2
```

28.9 Building a Container with Buildah

Buildah allows new containers to be built from existing containers, an image, or entirely from scratch. Buildah also includes the ability to mount the file system of a container so that it can be accessed and modified from the host.

The following *buildah* command, for example, will build a container from the RHEL 9 Base image (if the image has not already been pulled from the registry, *buildah* will download it before creating the container):

```
# buildah from registry.redhat.io/ubi9/ubi-init
```

The result of running this command will be a container named *ubi-init-working-container* that is ready to run:

```
# buildah run ubi-init-working-container cat /etc/passwd
```

28.10 Building a Container from Scratch

Building a container from scratch creates an empty container. Once created, packages may be installed to meet the requirements of the container. This approach is useful when creating a container that only needs the minimum of packages installed.

The first step in building from scratch is to run the following command to build the empty container:

```
# buildah from scratch
working-container
```

After the build is complete, a new container will be created named working-container:

```
# buildah containers
CONTAINER ID  BUILDER  IMAGE ID     IMAGE NAME                          CONTAINER
NAME
dbed2be11730     *       cb642e6a9917 registry.redhat.io/ubi9/ubi:latest dbed2be117
```

```
3000c099ff29c96eae59aed297b82412b240a8ed29ecec4d39a8ba
17df816ea0bb      *      a4933472b168 registry.redhat.io/ubi9/ubi-init:latest ubi-
init-working-container
65b424a31039      *                scratch                working-
container
```

The empty container is now ready to have some packages installed. Unfortunately, this cannot be performed within the container because not even the *bash* or *dnf* tools exist. So instead, the container filesystem needs to be mounted on the host system, and the packages are installed using *dnf* with the system root set to the mounted container filesystem. Begin this process by mounting the container's filesystem as follows:

```
# buildah mount working-container
/var/lib/containers/storage/overlay/20b46cf0e2994d1ecdc4487b89f93f6ccf41f72788da6
3866b6bf80984081d9a/merged
```

If the file system was successfully mounted, *buildah* will output the mount point for the container file system. Now that we have access to the container filesystem, the dnf command can install packages into the container using the *–installroot* option to point to the mounted container file system. The following command, for example, installs the bash, CoreUtils, and dnf packages on the container filesystem (where <container_fs_mount> is the mount path output previously by the *buildah mount* command) :

```
# dnf install --releasever=9.1 --installroot <container_fs_mount> bash coreutils
dnf
```

Note that the --releasever option indicates to *dnf* that the packages for RHEL 9.1 are to be installed within the container.

After the installation completes, unmount the scratch filesystem as follows:

```
# buildah umount working-container
```

Once *dnf* has performed the package installation, the container can be run, and the bash command prompt can be accessed as follows:

```
# buildah run working-container bash
bash-5.1#
```

28.11 Container Bridge Networking

As outlined in the previous chapter, container networking is implemented using the Container Networking Interface (CNI) bridged network stack. The following command shows the typical network configuration on a host system on which containers are running:

```
# ip a
1: lo: <LOOPBACK,UP,LOWER_UP> mtu 65536 qdisc noqueue state UNKNOWN group default
qlen 1000
    link/loopback 00:00:00:00:00:00 brd 00:00:00:00:00:00
    inet 127.0.0.1/8 scope host lo
       valid_lft forever preferred_lft forever
    inet6 ::1/128 scope host
```

```
        valid_lft forever preferred_lft forever
2: eno1: <BROADCAST,MULTICAST,UP,LOWER_UP> mtu 1500 qdisc fq_codel state UP group
default qlen 1000
    link/ether 00:23:24:52:52:57 brd ff:ff:ff:ff:ff:ff
    altname enp0s25
    inet 192.168.86.35/24 brd 192.168.86.255 scope global dynamic noprefixroute
eno1
        valid_lft 68525sec preferred_lft 68525sec
    inet6 fd7f:886f:716a:0:223:24ff:fe52:5257/64 scope global dynamic
noprefixroute
        valid_lft 1619sec preferred_lft 1619sec
    inet6 fe80::223:24ff:fe52:5257/64 scope link noprefixroute
        valid_lft forever preferred_lft forever
3: veth15d7e073@if2: <BROADCAST,MULTICAST,UP,LOWER_UP> mtu 1500 qdisc noqueue
master podman0 state UP group default qlen 1000
    link/ether 3e:3a:54:b8:d8:e1 brd ff:ff:ff:ff:ff:ff link-netns netns-658a3069-
5c69-185f-ef34-621107da5a71
    inet6 fe80::3c3a:54ff:feb8:d8e1/64 scope link
        valid_lft forever preferred_lft forever
6: podman0: <BROADCAST,MULTICAST,UP,LOWER_UP> mtu 1500 qdisc noqueue state UP
group default qlen 1000
    link/ether 3e:3a:54:b8:d8:e1 brd ff:ff:ff:ff:ff:ff
    inet 10.88.0.1/16 brd 10.88.255.255 scope global podman0
        valid_lft forever preferred_lft forever
    inet6 fe80::45e:83ff:fe68:4067/64 scope link
        valid_lft forever preferred_lft forever
```

In the above example, the host has an interface named eno1 connected to the external network with an IP address of 192.168.86.35. In addition, a virtual interface has been created named podman0 and assigned the IP address of 10.88.0.1. Running the same *ip* command on a container running on the host might result in the following output:

```
# ip a
1: lo: <LOOPBACK,UP,LOWER_UP> mtu 65536 qdisc noqueue state UNKNOWN group default
qlen 1000
    link/loopback 00:00:00:00:00:00 brd 00:00:00:00:00:00
    inet 127.0.0.1/8 scope host lo
        valid_lft forever preferred_lft forever
    inet6 ::1/128 scope host
        valid_lft forever preferred_lft forever
2: eth0@if3: <BROADCAST,MULTICAST,UP,LOWER_UP> mtu 1500 qdisc noqueue state UP
group default qlen 1000
    link/ether b6:fb:88:16:8b:5e brd ff:ff:ff:ff:ff:ff link-netnsid 0
    inet 10.88.0.8/16 brd 10.88.255.255 scope global eth0
        valid_lft forever preferred_lft forever
    inet6 fe80::b4fb:88ff:fe16:8b5e/64 scope link
        valid_lft forever preferred_lft forever
```

In this case, the container has an IP address of 10.88.0.8. Running the ping command on the host will verify that the host and containers are indeed on the same subnet:

```
# ping 10.88.0.8
PING 10.88.0.8 (10.88.0.8) 56(84) bytes of data.
64 bytes from 10.88.0.28: icmp_seq=1 ttl=64 time=0.056 ms
64 bytes from 10.88.0.28: icmp_seq=2 ttl=64 time=0.039 ms
.
.
.
```

We can also use the *podman network ls* command to obtain a list of container networks currently available on the host system:

```
# podman network ls
NETWORK ID     NAME         DRIVER
2f259bab93aa   podman       bridge
```

The following command can be used to display detailed information about a container network, in this case, the above *podman* network:

```
# podman network inspect podman
[
     {
          "name": "podman",
          "id": "2f259bab93aaaaa2542ba43ef33eb990d0999ee1b4b557b7be53c0b7a1bb9",
          "driver": "bridge",
          "network_interface": "podman0",
          "created": "2023-04-11T08:49:20.489892751-04:00",
          "subnets": [
               {
                    "subnet": "10.88.0.0/16",
                    "gateway": "10.88.0.1"
               }
          ],
          "ipv6_enabled": false,
          "internal": false,
          "dns_enabled": false,
          "ipam_options": {
               "driver": "host-local"
          }
     }
]
```

New container networks are created using the following syntax:

```
podman network create <network name>
```

For example, to create a new network named demonet, the following command would be used:

```
# podman network create demonet
```

Working with Containers on RHEL 9

The presence of the new network may be verified using the *podman network ls* command:

```
# podman network ls
NETWORK ID      NAME        DRIVER
9692930055dc    demonet     bridge
2f259bab93aa    podman      bridge
```

Once a network has been created, it can be assigned to a container as follows:

```
# podman network connect demonet mycontainer
```

Conversely, a container can be disconnected from a network using the *podman network disconnect* command:

```
# podman network disconnect demonet mycontainer
```

When the new container network is created, a configuration file is generated in the */etc/containers/networks* directory with the name <network name>.json. In the case of the above example, a file named *demonet.json* that reads as follows will have been created:

```
{
    "name": "demonet",
    "id": "9692930055dc6ceea5cc4d0720df548daa521fe62e23ca3659a9815664bca2f6",
    "driver": "bridge",
    "network_interface": "podman1",
    "created": "2023-04-10T16:54:35.618056082-04:00",
    "subnets": [
        {
            "subnet": "10.89.0.0/24",
            "gateway": "10.89.0.1"
        }
    ],
    "ipv6_enabled": false,
    "internal": false,
    "dns_enabled": true,
    "ipam_options": {
        "driver": "host-local"
    }
}
```

Modifications can be made to this file to change settings such as the subnet address range, IPv6 support, and network type (set to bridge for this example) for implementing different network configurations.

Finally, we can use the following command to delete the custom network:

```
# podman network rm demonet
```

28.12 Managing Containers in Cockpit

In addition to the command-line tools outlined in this chapter, Linux containers may be created and managed using the Cockpit web interface. Assuming that Cockpit is installed and enabled on the system (a topic covered in *"An Overview of the Cockpit Web Interface"*) and that the steps to log into the Red Hat Container Registry outlined at the start of the chapter have been completed, sign into Cockpit and select the *Podman Containers* option. If the Podman module is not installed within Cockpit, open a terminal window and run the following command:

```
# dnf install cockpit-podman
```

If necessary, click the button to start the Podman service, at which point the screen should resemble Figure 28-1:

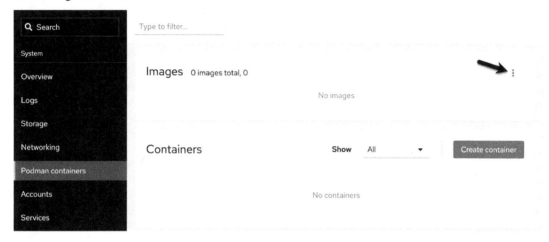

Figure 28-1

The first step is to download an image to use as the basis for a container (unless one has already been downloaded using the command-line tools). To perform the download, click the menu button marked by the arrow in Figure 28-1 above and select the Download new image option. When the search dialog appears, enter a keyword into the search dialog. Figure 28-2, for example, shows the result of searching for the RHEL 9 universal base images:

Search for an image   ×

Search for   ubi9   in   All registries   ▼

registry.access.redhat.com/ubi9/openjdk-17-runtime   rhcc_registry.access.redhat.com_ubi9/openjdk-17-runtime

registry.access.redhat.com/ubi9/openjdk-11-runtime   rhcc_registry.access.redhat.com_ubi9/openjdk-11-runtime

registry.access.redhat.com/ubi9   rhcc_registry.access.redhat.com_ubi9

registry.access.redhat.com/ubi9/toolbox   rhcc_registry.access.redhat.com_ubi9/toolbox

registry.access.redhat.com/ubi9/ubi-init   rhcc_registry.access.redhat.com_ubi9/ubi-init

Figure 28-2

Once the image has been located, select it and click the Download button to pull it from the registry. Once downloaded, it will appear in the images list as shown in Figure 28-3:

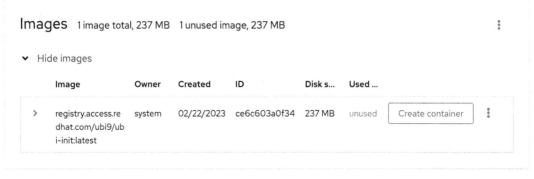

Figure 28-3

To run the image as a container, click on the *Create container* button and configure the container in the resulting dialog:

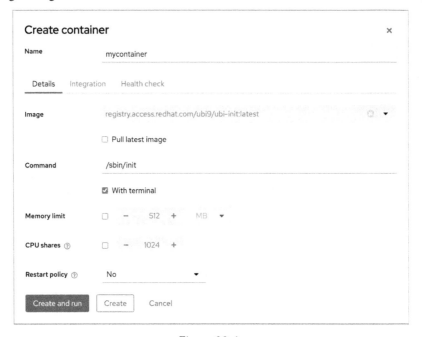

Figure 28-4

Note that options are provided to map ports on the host to ports on the container (useful, for example, if the container is hosting a web server), to limit the memory allocated to the container, and to specify volumes to use as the container storage. An option is also available to specify the program to run when the container starts. Once configured, click the *Create and run* button to launch the container.

Once running, the container will appear in the Containers section, as illustrated in Figure 28-5 below:

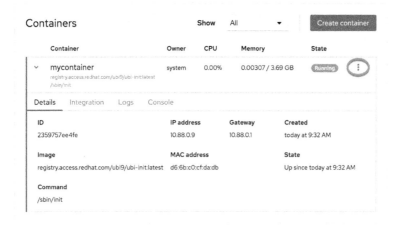

Figure 28-5

The highlighted menu button allows actions such as starting, stopping, pausing, and saving the container to be performed. In addition, the container may also now be accessed and managed from the command line using the steps outlined earlier in the chapter.

28.13 Summary

This chapter has worked through creating and managing Linux Containers on RHEL 9 using the *podman*, *skopeo*, and *buildah* tools together with the Cockpit web interface, including using container images obtained from a repository and the creation of a new image built entirely from scratch.

Chapter 29

29. Setting Up a RHEL 9 Web Server

The Apache web server is among the many packages that make up the RHEL 9 operating system. The scalability and resilience of RHEL 9 make it an ideal platform for hosting even the most heavily trafficked websites.

This chapter will explain how to configure a RHEL 9 system using Apache to act as a web server, including both secure (HTTPS) and insecure (HTTP) configurations.

29.1 Requirements for Configuring a RHEL 9 Web Server

To set up your own website, you need a computer (or cloud server instance), an operating system, a web server, a domain name, a name server, and an IP address.

In terms of an operating system, we will assume you are using RHEL 9. As previously mentioned, RHEL 9 supports the Apache web server, which can easily be installed once the operating system is up and running. In addition, a domain name can be registered with any domain name registration service.

If you are running RHEL 9 on a cloud instance, the IP address assigned by the provider will be listed in the server overview information. However, if you are hosting your own server and your internet service provider (ISP) has assigned a static IP address, you must associate your domain with that address. This is achieved using a name server, and all domain registration services will provide this service.

If you do not have a static IP address (i.e., your ISP provides you with a dynamic address that changes frequently), you can use one of several free Dynamic DNS (DDNS or DynDNS for short) services to map your dynamic IP address to your domain name.

Once you have configured your domain name and your name server, the next step is to install and configure your web server.

29.2 Installing the Apache Web Server Packages

The current release of RHEL typically does not install the Apache web server by default. To check whether the server is already installed, run the following command:

```
# rpm -q httpd
```

If rpm generates output similar to the following, the Apache server is already installed:

```
httpd-2.4.53-7.el9_1.5.x86_64
```

Alternatively, if rpm generates a "package httpd is not installed" message, the next step is to install it. To install Apache, run the following command at the command prompt:

```
# dnf install httpd
```

29.3 Configuring the Firewall

Before starting and testing the Apache web server, the firewall must be modified to allow the webserver to communicate with the outside world. By default, the HTTP and HTTPS protocols use ports 80 and 443, respectively, so depending on which protocols are being used, either one or both of these ports will need to be opened. When opening the ports, be sure to specify the firewall zone that applies to the internet-facing network connection:

```
# firewall-cmd --permanent --zone=<zone> --add-port=80/tcp
# firewall-cmd --permanent --zone=<zone> --add-port=443/tcp
```

After opening the necessary ports, be sure to reload the firewall settings:

```
# firewall-cmd --reload
```

On cloud-hosted servers, enabling the appropriate port for the server instance within the cloud console may also be necessary. Check the documentation for the cloud provider for steps to do this.

29.4 Port Forwarding

Suppose the RHEL 9 system hosting the web server sits on a network protected by a firewall (another computer running a firewall, router, or wireless base station containing built-in firewall protection). In that case, you must configure the firewall to forward ports 80 and 443 to your web server system. The mechanism for performing this differs between firewalls and devices, so check your documentation to find out how to configure port forwarding.

29.5 Starting the Apache Web Server

Once the Apache server is installed and the firewall configured, the next step is to verify that the server is running and start it if necessary.

To check the status of the Apache service from the command line, enter the following at the command prompt:

```
# systemctl status httpd
```

If the above command indicates that the httpd service is not running, it can be launched from the command line as follows:

```
# systemctl start httpd
```

If you would like the Apache httpd service to start automatically when the system boots, run the following command:

```
# systemctl enable httpd
```

29.6 Testing the Web Server

Once the installation is complete, the next step is verifying the web server is running.

If you have access (either locally or remotely) to the desktop environment of the server, start up a web browser and enter http://127.0.0.1 in the address bar (127.0.0.1 is the loop-back network address which tells the system to connect to the local machine). If everything is set up correctly, the browser should load the test page shown in Figure 29-1:

Figure 29-1

If the desktop environment is unavailable, connect either from another system on the same local network as the server, or use the external IP address assigned to the system if it is hosted remotely.

29.7 Configuring the Apache Web Server for Your Domain

The next step in setting up your web server is configuring it for your domain name. To configure the web server, begin by changing directory to *./etc/httpd*, which, in turn, contains several files and sub-directories. Change directory into the *conf* sub-directory, where you will find a file named *httpd.conf* containing the configuration settings for the Apache server.

Edit the *httpd.conf* file using your preferred editor with super-user privileges to ensure you have permission to access and modify the file. Once loaded, several settings need to be changed to match your environment.

The most common way to configure Apache for a specific domain is to add virtual host entries to the *httpd.conf* file. This allows a single Apache server to support multiple websites simply by adding a virtual host entry for each site domain. Within the *httpd.conf* file, add a virtual host entry for your domain as follows:

```
<VirtualHost *:80>
    ServerAdmin feedback@myexample.com
    ServerName www.myexample.com
    DocumentRoot /var/www/myexample
    ErrorLog logs/myexample_error_log
    CustomLog logs/myexample_access_log combined
</VirtualHost>
```

The ServerAdmin directive in the above virtual host entry defines an administrative email address for people wishing to contact the webmaster for your site. Change this to an appropriate email address where you can be contacted.

Next, the ServerName is declared so the web server knows the domain name associated with this virtual host.

Since each website supported by the server will have its own set of files, the DocumentRoot setting is used to specify the location of the files for this website domain. The tradition is to use /var/www/domain-name, for example:

```
DocumentRoot /var/www/myexample
```

Finally, entries are added for the access history and error log files.

Create the /var/www/<domain name> directory as declared in the httpd.conf file and place an index.html file in it containing some basic HTML. For example:

```
<html>
<title>Sample Web Page</title>
<body>
Welcome to MyExample.com
</body>
</html>
```

The last step is to restart the httpd service to make sure it picks up our new settings:

```
# systemctl restart httpd
```

Finally, check that the server configuration works by opening a browser window and navigating to the site using the domain name instead of the IP address. The web page that loads should be defined in the index.html file created above.

29.8 The Basics of a Secure Website

The web server and website created in this chapter use the HTTP protocol on port 80 and, as such, are considered to be insecure. The problem is that the traffic between the web server and the client (typically a user's web browser) is transmitted in clear text. In other words, the data is unencrypted and susceptible to interception. While not a problem for general web browsing, this is a severe weakness when performing tasks such as logging into websites or transferring sensitive information such as identity or credit card details.

These days, websites are expected to use HTTPS, which uses either Secure Socket Layer (SSL) or Transport Layer Security (TLS) to establish secure, encrypted communication between a web server and a client. This security is established through the use of public, private, and session encryption together with certificates.

To support HTTPS, a website must have a certificate issued by a trusted authority known as a Certificate Authority (CA). When a browser connects to a secure website, the web server sends back a copy of the website's SSL certificate, which also contains a copy of the site's public key. The browser then validates the authenticity of the certificate with trusted certificate authorities.

If the certificate is valid, the browser uses the public key sent by the server to encrypt a session

226

key and pass it to the server. The server decrypts the session key using the private key to send an encrypted acknowledgment to the browser. Once this process is complete, the browser and server use the session key to encrypt all subsequent data transmissions until the session ends.

29.9 Configuring Apache for HTTPS

By default, the Apache server does not include the necessary module to implement a secure HTTPS website. The first step, therefore, is to install the Apache mod_ssl module on the server system as follows:

```
# dnf install mod_ssl
```

Restart httpd after the installation completes to load the new module into the Apache server:

```
# systemctl restart httpd
```

Check that the module has loaded into the server using the following command:

```
# httpd -M | grep ssl_module
 ssl_module (shared)
```

Once the ssl module is installed, repeat the steps from the previous section of this chapter to create a configuration file for the website, this time using the *sites-available/default-ssl.conf* file as the template for the site configuration file.

Assuming the module is installed, the next step is to generate an SSL certificate for the website.

29.10 Obtaining an SSL Certificate

The certificate for a website must be obtained from a Certificate Authority. Several options are available at a range of prices. By far the best option, however, is to obtain a free certificate from Let's Encrypt at the following URL:

https://letsencrypt.org/

Obtaining a certificate from Let's Encrypt involves installing and running the Certbot tool. This tool will scan the Apache configuration files on the server and provides the option to generate certificates for any virtual hosts configured on the system. It will then generate the certificate and add virtual host entries to the Apache configuration for the corresponding websites.

Follow the steps on the Let's Encrypt website to download and install Certbot on your RHEL 9 system, then run the *certbot* tool as follows to generate and install the certificate:

```
# certbot --apache
```

After requesting an email address and seeking terms of service acceptance, Certbot will list the domains found in the *httpd.conf* file and allow the selection of one or more sites for which a certificate will be installed. Certbot will then perform some checks before obtaining and installing the certificate on the system:

```
Which names would you like to activate HTTPS for?
- - - - - - - - - - - - - - - - - - - - - - - - - - - - - - - - - - - - -
1: www.myexample.com
```

```
- - - - - - - - - - - - - - - - - - - - - - - - - - - - - - - - - - - - - -
Select the appropriate numbers separated by commas and/or spaces, or leave input
blank to select all options shown (Enter 'c' to cancel): 1
Obtaining a new certificate
Performing the following challenges:
http-01 challenge for www.myexample.com
Waiting for verification...
Cleaning up challenges
Created an SSL vhost at /etc/httpd/conf/httpd-le-ssl.conf
Deploying Certificate to VirtualHost /etc/httpd/conf/httpd-le-ssl.conf
Enabling site /etc/httpd/conf/httpd-le-ssl.conf by adding Include to root
configuration
```

Certbot will also create a new file named *httpd-le-ssl.conf* in the */etc/httpd/conf* directory containing a secure virtual host entry for each domain name for which a certificate has been generated. These entries will be similar to the following:

```
<IfModule mod_ssl.c>
<VirtualHost *:443>
    ServerAdmin feedback@myexample.com
    ServerName www.myexample.com
    DocumentRoot /var/www/myexample
    ErrorLog logs/myexample_error_log
    CustomLog logs/myexample_access_log combined


SSLCertificateFile /etc/letsencrypt/live/www.myexample.com/fullchain.pem
SSLCertificateKeyFile /etc/letsencrypt/live/www.myexample.com/privkey.pem
Include /etc/letsencrypt/options-ssl-apache.conf
</VirtualHost>
</IfModule>
```

Finally, Certbot will ask whether the server should redirect future HTTP web requests to HTTPS. In other words, if a user attempts to access http://www.myexample.com, the web server will redirect the user to https://www.myexample.com:

```
Please choose whether or not to redirect HTTP traffic to HTTPS, removing HTTP
access.
- - - - - - - - - - - - - - - - - - - - - - - - - - - - - - - - - - - - - -
1: No redirect - Make no further changes to the webserver configuration.
2: Redirect - Make all requests redirect to secure HTTPS access. Choose this for
new sites, or if you're confident your site works on HTTPS. You can undo this
change by editing your web server's configuration.
- - - - - - - - - - - - - - - - - - - - - - - - - - - - - - - - - - - - - -
Select the appropriate number [1-2] then [enter] (press 'c' to cancel): 2
```

If you are currently testing the HTTPS configuration and would like to keep the HTTP version live until later, select the No redirect option. Otherwise, redirecting to HTTPS is generally recommended.

Once the certificate has been installed, test it in a browser at the following URL (replacing myexample.com with your own domain name):

https://www.ssllabs.com/ssltest/analyze.html?d=www.myexample.com

If the certificate configuration is successful, the SSL Labs report will provide a high rating, as shown in Figure 29-2:

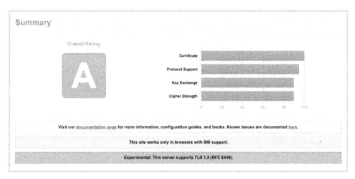

Figure 29-2

As a final test, open a browser window and navigate to your domain using the https:// prefix. The page should load as before, and the browser should indicate that the connection between the browser and server is secure (usually indicated by a padlock icon in the address bar, which can be clicked for additional information):

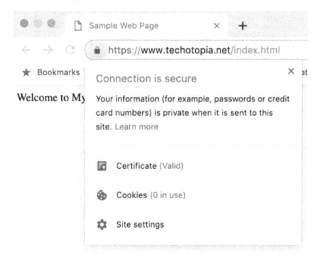

Figure 29-3

29.11 Summary

A RHEL 9 system can host websites by installing the Apache web server. Insecure (HTTP) and secure (HTTPS) websites can be deployed on RHEL 9. Secure websites use either Secure Socket

Layer (SSL) or Transport Layer Security (TLS) to establish encrypted communication between the web server and client through public, private, and session encryption, together with a certificate issued by a trusted Certificate Authority.

30. Configuring a RHEL 9 Postfix Email Server

Along with acting as a web server, email is one of the primary uses of a RHEL 9 system, particularly in business environments. Given the importance and popularity of email, it is surprising to some people to find out how complex the email structure is on a Linux system. This complexity can often be overwhelming to the RHEL 9 newcomer.

The good news is that much of the complexity is there to allow experienced email administrators to implement complicated configurations for large-scale enterprise installations. However, for most Linux administrators, setting up a basic email system is relatively straightforward so that users can send and receive electronic mail.

This chapter of Red Hat Enterprise Linux 9 Essentials will explain the basics of Linux-based email configuration and step through configuring a basic email environment. To provide the essentials, we will leave the complexities of the email system for more advanced books on the subject.

30.1 The Structure of the Email System

Several components make up a complete email system. Below is a brief description of each one:

30.1.1 Mail User Agent

The typical user will likely be most familiar with this part of the system. The Mail User Agent (MUA), or mail client, is the application that is used to write, send and read email messages. Anyone who has written and sent a message on any computer has used a Mail User Agent of one type or another.

Typical Graphical MUAs on Linux are Evolution, Thunderbird, and KMail. For those who prefer a text-based mail client, there are also the more traditional Pine and *mail* tools.

30.1.2 Mail Transfer Agent

The Mail Transfer Agent (MTA) is the part of the email system that transfers email messages from one computer to another (either on the same local network or over the internet to a remote system). Once configured correctly, most users will only directly interact with their chosen MTA if they wish to re-configure it. Many MTA choices are available for Linux, including Sendmail, Postfix, Fetchmail, Qmail, and Exim.

30.1.3 Mail Delivery Agent

Another part of the infrastructure typically hidden from the user, the Mail Delivery Agent (MDA), sits in the background and performs filtering of the email messages between the Mail Transfer Agent and the mail client (MUA). The most popular form of MDA is a spam filter to remove all unwanted email messages from the system before they reach the inbox of the user's mail client (MUA). Popular MDAs are Spamassassin and Procmail. It is important to note that some Mail User Agent applications (such as Evolution, Thunderbird, and KMail) include their own MDA filtering. Others, such as Pine and Basla, do not. This can be a source of confusion for the Linux beginner.

30.1.4 SMTP

SMTP is an acronym for Simple Mail Transport Protocol. The email systems use this protocol to transfer mail messages from one server to another. This protocol is the communication language that the MTAs use to talk to each other and transfer messages back and forth.

30.1.5 SMTP Relay

SMTP Relay is a protocol that allows an external SMTP server to send emails instead of hosting a local SMTP server. This will typically involve using a service such as Mailjet, SendGrid, or MailGun. These services avoid configuring and maintaining your own SMTP server and often provide additional benefits such as analytics.

30.2 Configuring a RHEL 9 Email Server

Many systems use the Sendmail MTA to transfer email messages; on many Linux distributions, this is the default Mail Transfer Agent. Unfortunately, Sendmail is a complex system that can be difficult for beginners and experienced users to understand and configure. It is also falling from favor because it is considered slower at processing email messages than many of the more recent MTAs available.

Many system administrators are now using Postfix or Qmail to handle email. Both are faster and easier to configure than Sendmail.

For this chapter, therefore, we will look at Postfix as an MTA because of its simplicity and popularity. However, if you prefer to use Sendmail, many books specialize in the subject and will do the subject much more justice than we can in this chapter.

As a first step, this chapter will cover configuring a RHEL 9 system to act as a full email server. Later in the chapter, the steps to use an SMTP Relay service will also be covered.

30.3 Postfix Pre-Installation Steps

The first step before installing Postfix is to ensure that Sendmail is not already running on your system. You can check for this using the following command:

```
# systemctl status sendmail
```

If sendmail is not installed, the tool will display a message similar to the following:

```
Unit sendmail.service could not be found.
```

If sendmail is running on your system, it is necessary to stop it before installing and configuring Postfix. To stop sendmail, run the following command:

```
# systemctl stop sendmail
```

The next step is to ensure that sendmail does not get restarted automatically when the system is rebooted:

```
# systemctl disable  sendmail
```

Sendmail is now switched off and configured to not auto-start when the system is booted. Optionally, to altogether remove sendmail from the system, run the following command:

```
# dnf remove sendmail
```

30.4 Firewall/Router Configuration

Since sending and receiving email messages involves network connections, the firewall must be configured to allow SMTP traffic. If firewalld is active, use the *firewall-cmd* tool will as follows:

```
# firewall-cmd --permanent --add-service=smtp
```

It will also be essential to configure any other firewall or router between the server and the internet to allow connections on ports 25, 143, and 587 and, if necessary, to configure port forwarding for those ports to the corresponding ports on the email server.

With these initial steps completed, we can now install Postfix.

30.5 Installing Postfix on RHEL 9

By default, the RHEL 9 installation process installs postfix for most configurations. To verify if postfix is already installed, use the following *rpm* command:

```
# rpm -q postfix
```

If rpm reports that postfix is not installed, it may be installed as follows:

```
# dnf install postfix
```

The *dnf* tool will download and install postfix and configure a special postfix user in the */etc/passwd* file.

30.6 Configuring Postfix

The main configuration settings for postfix are located in the */etc/postfix/main.cf* file. Many resources on the internet provide detailed information on postfix, so this section will focus on the basic options required to get email up and running. Even though the dnf installation set up some basic configuration options, it tends to miss some settings and guess incorrectly for others, so carefully review the *main.cf* file.

The key options in the *main.cf* file are as follows:

```
myhostname = mta1.domain.com
mydomain = domain.com
myorigin = $mydomain
mydestination = $myhostname, localhost.$mydomain, localhost, $mydomain
inet_interfaces = $myhostname
mynetworks = subnet
```

Other settings will have either been set up for you by the installation process or are only needed if you are feeling adventurous and want to configure a more sophisticated email system.

The format of myhostname is host.domain.extension. If, for example, your Linux system is named MyLinuxHost and your internet domain is MyDomain.com you would set the myhostname option as follows:

```
myhostname = mylinuxhost.mydomain.com
```

The mydomain setting is just the domain part of the above setting. For example:

```
mydomain = mydomain.com
```

The myorigin setting defines the name of the domain from which the output email appears to come from when it arrives in the recipient's inbox and should be set to your domain name:

```
myorigin = $mydomain
```

One of the most crucial parameters, mydestination relates to incoming messages and declares the domains for which this server is the final delivery destination. Any incoming email messages addressed to a domain name, not on this list will be considered a relay request which, subject to the mynetworks setting (outlined below), will typically result in a delivery failure.

The inet_interfaces setting defines the network interfaces on the system via which postfix is permitted to receive email and is generally set to all:

```
inet_interfaces = all
```

The mynetworks setting defines which external systems are trusted to use the server as an SMTP relay. Possible values for this setting are as follows:

- **host** - Only the local system is trusted. Attempts by all external clients to use the server as a relay will be rejected.

- **subnet** - Only systems on the same network subnet can use the server as a relay. If, for example, the server has an IP address of 192.168.1.29, a client system with an IP address of 192.168.1.30 could use the server as a relay.

- **class** - Any systems within the same IP address class (A, B, and C) may use the server as a relay.

Trusted IP addresses may be defined manually by specifying subnets, address ranges, or referencing pattern files. The following example declares the local host and the subnet 192.168.0.0 as trusted IP addresses:

```
mynetworks = 192.168.0.0/24, 127.0.0.0/8
```

For this example, set the property to subnet so that any other systems on the same local network as the server can send email via SMTP relay. In contrast, external systems are prevented from doing so:

```
mynetworks = subnet
```

30.7 Configuring DNS MX Records

When you register and configure your domain name with a registrar, several default values will have been configured in the DNS settings. One of these is the so-called Mail Exchanger (MX) record. This record defines where email addressed to your domain should be sent and is usually set by default to a mail server provided by your registrar. If you are hosting your own mail server, the MX record should be set to your domain or the IP address of your mail server. The steps to make this change will depend on your domain registrar but generally involves editing the DNS information for the domain and either adding or editing an existing MX record so that it points to your email server.

30.8 Starting Postfix on a RHEL 9 System

Once the */etc/postfix/main.cf* file is configured with the correct settings, it is now time to start up postfix. This can be achieved from the command line as follows:

```
# systemctl start postfix
```

If postfix was already running, make sure the configuration changes are loaded using the following command:

```
# systemctl reload postfix
```

To configure postfix to start automatically at system startup, run the following command:

```
# systemctl enable postfix
```

The postfix process should now start up. The best way to verify everything works is to check your mail log. This is typically in the */var/log/maillog* file and should now contain an entry resembling the following output:

```
Mar 25 11:21:48 demo-server postfix/postfix-script[5377]: starting the Postfix mail
system
Mar 25 11:21:48 demo-server postfix/master[5379]: daemon started -- version 3.3.1,
configuration /etc/postfix
```

As long as no error messages have been logged, you have successfully installed and started postfix and are ready to test the postfix configuration.

30.9 Testing Postfix

An easy way to test the postfix configuration is to send email messages between local users on the system. To perform a quick test, use the mail tool as follows (where name and mydomain are replaced by the name of a user on the system and your domain name, respectively):

```
# mail name@mydomain.com
```

When prompted, enter a subject for the email message and then type the message body text. To send the email message, press Ctrl-D. For example:

```
# mail demo@mydomain.com
Subject: Test email message
This is a test message.
EOT
```

Configuring a RHEL 9 Postfix Email Server

Rerun the mail command, this time as the other user, and verify that the message was sent and received:

```
$ mail
Heirloom Mail version 12.5 7/5/10. Type ? for help.
"/var/spool/mail/demo": 1 message 1 new
>N  1 root          Mon Mar 25 13:36  18/625   "Test email message"
&
```

Check the log file (*/var/log/maillog*) for errors if the message does not appear. Successful mail delivery will appear in the log file as follows:

```
Mar 25 13:41:37 demo-server postfix/pickup[7153]: 94FAF61E8F4A: uid=0 from=<root>
Mar 25 13:41:37 demo-server postfix/cleanup[7498]: 94FAF61E8F4A: message-
id=<20190325174137.94FAF61E8F4A@demo-server.mydomain.com>
Mar 25 13:41:37 demo-server postfix/qmgr[7154]: 94FAF61E8F4A: from=<root@mydomain.
com>, size=450, nrcpt=1 (queue active)
Mar 25 13:41:37 demo-server postfix/local[7500]: 94FAF61E8F4A: to=<neil@mydomain.
com>, relay=local, delay=0.12, delays=0.09/0.01/0/0.02, dsn=2.0.0, status=sent
(delivered to mailbox)
Mar 25 13:41:37 demo-server postfix/qmgr[7154]: 94FAF61E8F4A: removed
```

Once the local email is working, try sending an email to an external address (such as a GMail account). Also, test that incoming mail works by sending an email from an external account to a user on your domain. In each case, check the */var/log/maillog* file for explanations of any errors.

30.10 Sending Mail via an SMTP Relay Server

An SMTP Relay service is an alternative to configuring a mail server to handle outgoing email messages. As previously discussed, several services are available, most of which can be found by performing a web search for "SMTP Relay Service". Most of these services will require you to verify your domain in some way and will provide MX records with which to update your DNS settings. You will also be provided with a username and password, which must be added to the postfix configuration. The remainder of this section assumes that postfix is installed on your system and that all of the initial steps required by your chosen SMTP Relay provider have been completed.

Begin by editing the */etc/postfix/main.cf* file and configure the myhostname parameter with your domain name:

```
myhostname = mydomain.com
```

Next, create a new file in */etc/postfix* named *sasl_passwd* and add a line containing the mail server host provided by the relay service and the user name and password. For example:

```
[smtp.myprovider.com]:587 neil@mydomain.com:mypassword
```

Note that port 587 has also been specified in the above entry. Without this setting, postfix will default to using port 25, which is blocked by default by most SMTP relay service providers.

With the password file created, use the *postmap* utility to generate the hash database containing the mail credentials:

```
# postmap /etc/postfix/sasl_passwd
```

Before proceeding, take some additional steps to secure your postfix credentials:

```
# chown root:root /etc/postfix/sasl_passwd /etc/postfix/sasl_passwd.db
# chmod 0600 /etc/postfix/sasl_passwd /etc/postfix/sasl_passwd.db
```

Edit the *main.cf* file once again and add an entry to specify the relay server:

```
relayhost = [smtp.myprovider.com]:587
```

Remaining within the *main.cf* file, add the following lines to configure the authentication settings for the SMTP server:

```
smtp_use_tls = yes
smtp_sasl_auth_enable = yes
smtp_sasl_password_maps = hash:/etc/postfix/sasl_passwd
smtp_tls_CAfile = /etc/ssl/certs/ca-bundle.crt
smtp_sasl_security_options = noanonymous
smtp_sasl_tls_security_options = noanonymous
```

Finally, restart the postfix service:

```
# systemctl restart postfix
```

Once the service has restarted, try sending and receiving mail using either the mail tool or your preferred mail client.

30.11 Summary

A complete, end-to-end email system consists of a Mail User Agent (MUA), Mail Transfer Agent (MTA), Mail Delivery Agent (MDA), and the SMTP protocol. RHEL 9 provides several options in terms of MTA solutions, one of the more popular being Postfix. This chapter has outlined how to install, configure and test postfix on a RHEL 9 system to act as a mail server and send and receive email using a third-party SMTP relay server.

31. Adding a New Disk Drive to a RHEL 9 System

One of the first problems users and system administrators encounter is that systems need more disk space to store data. Fortunately, disk space is now one of the cheapest IT commodities. In this and the next chapter, we will look how to configure RHEL 9 to use the space provided when a new physical or virtual disk drive is installed.

31.1 Mounted File Systems or Logical Volumes

There are two ways to configure a new disk drive on a RHEL 9 system. One straightforward method is to create one or more Linux partitions on the new drive, create Linux file systems on those partitions and then mount them at specific mount points to be accessed. This approach will be covered in this chapter.

Another approach is adding new space to an existing volume group or creating a new one. When RHEL 9 is installed, a volume group named *rhel* is created. Within this volume group are three logical volumes named *root*, *home*, and *swap*, used to store the / and /home file systems and swap partitions, respectively. We can increase the disk space available to the existing logical volumes by configuring the new disk as part of a volume group. For example, using this approach, we can increase the size of the /home file system by allocating some or all of the space on the new disk to the home volume. This topic will be discussed in detail in *"Adding a New Disk to a RHEL 9 Volume Group and Logical Volume"*.

31.2 Finding the New Hard Drive

This tutorial assumes that a new physical or virtual hard drive has been installed and is visible to the operating system. Once added, the operating system should automatically detect the new drive. Typically, the disk drives in a system are assigned device names beginning hd, sd, or nvme, followed by a letter to indicate the device number. The first device might be */dev/sda*, the second */dev/sdb*, etc.

The following is the output from a typical system with only one disk drive connected to a SATA controller:

```
# ls /dev/sd*
/dev/sda   /dev/sda1   /dev/sda2
```

This shows that the disk drive represented by */dev/sda* is divided into two partitions, represented by */dev/sda1* and */dev/sda2*.

The following output is from the same system after a second hard disk drive has been installed:

```
# ls /dev/sd*
```

```
/dev/sda /dev/sda1 /dev/sda2 /dev/sdb
```

The new hard drive has been assigned to the device file */dev/sdb*. The drive has no partitions shown (because we have yet to create any).

At this point, we can create partitions and file systems on the new drive and mount them for access or add the disk as a physical volume as part of a volume group. To perform the former continue with this chapter; otherwise, read *"Adding a New Disk to a RHEL 9 Volume Group and Logical Volume"* for details on configuring Logical Volumes.

31.3 Creating Linux Partitions

The next step is to create one or more Linux partitions on the new disk drive. This is achieved using the *fdisk* utility, which takes as a command-line argument the device to be partitioned:

```
# fdisk /dev/sdb

Welcome to fdisk (util-linux 2.37.4).
Changes will remain in memory only, until you decide to write them.
Be careful before using the write command.

Device does not contain a recognized partition table.
Created a new DOS disklabel with disk identifier 0x64d68d00.

Command (m for help):
```

To view the current partitions on the disk, enter the p command:

```
Command (m for help): p
Disk /dev/sdb: 14.46 GiB, 15525216256 bytes, 30322688 sectors
Disk model: USB 2.0 FD
Units: sectors of 1 * 512 = 512 bytes
Sector size (logical/physical): 512 bytes / 512 bytes
I/O size (minimum/optimal): 512 bytes / 512 bytes
Disklabel type: dos
Disk identifier: 0x64d68d00
```

As we can see from the above *fdisk* output, the disk currently has no partitions because it was previously unused. The next step is to create a new partition on the disk, a task which is performed by entering n (for new partition) and p (for primary partition):

```
Command (m for help): n
Partition type
   p   primary (0 primary, 0 extended, 4 free)
   e   extended (container for logical partitions)
Select (default p): p
Partition number (1-4, default 1):
```

In this example, we only plan to create one partition, which will be partition 1. Next, we need to specify where the partition will begin and end. Since this is the first partition, we need it to start at the first available sector, and since we want to use the entire disk, we specify the last sector as the end. Note that if you wish to create multiple partitions, you can specify the size of each partition by sectors, bytes, kilobytes, or megabytes:

```
Partition number (1-4, default 1): 1
First sector (2048-30322687, default 2048):
Last sector, +/-sectors or +/-size{K,M,G,T,P} (2048-30322687, default 30322687):

Created a new partition 1 of type 'Linux' and of size 14.5 GiB.

Command (m for help):
```

Now that we have specified the partition, we need to write it to the disk using the w command:

```
Command (m for help): w
The partition table has been altered.
Calling ioctl() to re-read partition table.
Syncing disks.
```

If we now look at the devices again, we will see that the new partition is visible as */dev/sdb1*:

```
# ls /dev/sd*
/dev/sda /dev/sda1 /dev/sda2 /dev/sdb /dev/sdb1
```

The next step is to create a file system on our new partition.

31.4 Creating a File System on a RHEL 9 Disk Partition

We now have a new disk installed, it is visible to RHEL 9, and we have configured a Linux partition on the disk. The next step is to create a Linux file system on the partition so that the operating system can use it to store files and data. The easiest way to create a file system on a partition is to use the *mkfs.xfs* utility:

```
# mkfs.xfs -f /dev/sdb1
meta-data=/dev/sdb1              isize=512    agcount=4, agsize=947520 blks
         =                       sectsz=512   attr=2, projid32bit=1
         =                       crc=1        finobt=1, sparse=1, rmapbt=0
         =                       reflink=1    bigtime=1 inobtcount=1
data     =                       bsize=4096   blocks=3790080, imaxpct=25
         =                       sunit=0      swidth=0 blks
naming   =version 2             bsize=4096   ascii-ci=0, ftype=1
log      =internal log          bsize=4096   blocks=2560, version=2
         =                       sectsz=512   sunit=0 blks, lazy-count=1
realtime =none                  extsz=4096   blocks=0, rtextents=0
```

In this case, we have created an XFS file system. XFS is a high-performance file system that is the default filesystem type on RHEL 9 and includes several advantages in terms of parallel I/O performance and the use of journaling.

31.5 An Overview of Journaled File Systems

A journaling filesystem keeps a journal or log of the changes being made to the filesystem during disk writing that can be used to rapidly reconstruct corruptions that may occur due to events such as a system crash or power outage.

There are several advantages to using a journaling file system. First, the size and volume of data stored on disk drives have grown exponentially over the years. The problem with a non-journaled file system is that following a crash, the *fsck* (filesystem consistency check) utility has to be run. The *fsck* utility will scan the entire filesystem validating all entries and ensuring that blocks are allocated and referenced correctly. It will attempt to fix the problem if it finds a corrupt entry. The issues here are two-fold. First, the *fsck* utility will not always be able to repair the damage, and you will end up with data in the *lost+found* directory. An application uses this data, but the system no longer knows where it was referenced from. The other problem is the issue of time. Completing the *fsck* process on an extensive file system can take a long time, potentially leading to unacceptable downtime.

On the other hand, a journaled file system records information in a log area on a disk (the journal and log do not need to be on the same device) during each write. This is essentially an "intent to commit" data to the filesystem. The amount of information logged is configurable and ranges from not logging anything to logging what is known as the "metadata" (i.e., ownership, date stamp information, etc.) to logging the "metadata" and the data blocks that are to be written to the file. Once the log is updated, the system writes the actual data to the appropriate filesystem areas and marks an entry to say the data is committed.

After a crash, the filesystem can quickly be brought back online using the journal log, thereby reducing what could take minutes using *fsck* to seconds with the added advantage that there is considerably less chance of data loss or corruption.

31.6 Mounting a File System

Now that we have created a new file system on the Linux partition of our new disk drive, we need to mount it to be accessible and usable. To do this, we need to create a mount point. A mount point is simply a directory or folder into which the file system will be mounted. For this example, we will create a */backup* directory to match our file system label (although these values don't need to match):

```
# mkdir /backup
```

The file system may then be manually mounted using the *mount* command:

```
# mount /dev/sdb1 /backup
```

Running the *mount* command with no arguments shows us all currently mounted file systems (including our new file system):

```
# mount
proc on /proc type proc (rw,nosuid,nodev,noexec,relatime)
sysfs on /sys type sysfs (rw,nosuid,nodev,noexec,relatime,seclabel)
```

```
/dev/sdb1 on /backup type xfs (rw,relatime,seclabel,attr2,inode64,logbufs=8,logbs
ize=32k,noquota)
```

31.7 Configuring RHEL 9 to Mount a File System Automatically

To set up the system so that the new file system is automatically mounted at boot time, an entry needs to be added to the */etc/fstab* file. The format for an *fstab* entry is as follows:

```
<device>       <dir> <type> <options>      <dump> <fsck>
```

These entries can be summarized as follows:

- **<device>** - The device on which the filesystem will be mounted.

- **<dir>** - The directory that is to act as the mount point for the filesystem.

- **<type>** - The filesystem type (xfs, ext4 etc.)

- **<options>** - Additional filesystem mount options, for example, making the filesystem read-only or controlling whether any user can mount the filesystem. Run man mount to review a complete list of options. Setting this value to defaults will use the default settings for the filesystem (rw, suid, dev, exec, auto, nouser, async).

- **<dump>** - Dictates whether the content of the filesystem is to be included in any backups performed by the dump utility. This setting is rarely used and can be disabled with a 0 value.

- **<fsck>** - Whether the filesystem is checked by *fsck* after a system crash and the order in which filesystems are to be checked. For journaled filesystems such as XFS this should be set to 0 to indicate that the check is not required.

The following example shows an *fstab* file configured to automount our */backup* partition on the */dev/sdb1* partition:

```
/dev/mapper/rhel-root    /                         xfs       defaults       0 0
UUID=b4fc85a1-0b25-4d64-8100-d50ea23340f7 /boot                   xfs
defaults        0 0
/dev/mapper/rhel-home    /home                     xfs       defaults       0 0
/dev/mapper/rhel-swap    swap                      swap      defaults       0 0
/dev/sdb1                /backup                   xfs       defaults       0 0
```

The */backup* filesystem will now automount each time the system restarts.

31.8 Adding a Disk Using Cockpit

In addition to working with storage using the command-line utilities outlined in this chapter, it is also possible to configure a new storage device using the Cockpit web console. To view the current storage configuration, log into the Cockpit console and select the Storage option as shown in Figure 31-1:

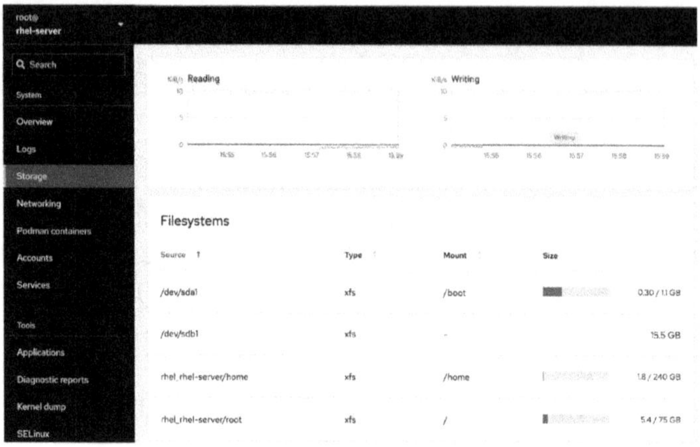

Adding a New Disk Drive to a RHEL 9 System

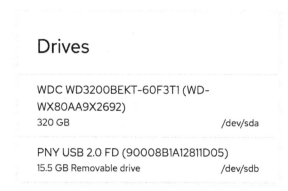

Figure 31-1

To locate the newly added storage, scroll to the bottom of the Storage page until the Drives section comes into view (note that the Drives section may also be located in the top right-hand corner of the screen):

Drives

WDC WD3200BEKT-60F3T1 (WD-
WX80AA9X2692)
320 GB   /dev/sda

PNY USB 2.0 FD (90008B1A12811D05)
15.5 GB Removable drive   /dev/sdb

Figure 31-2

In the case of the above figure, the new drive is the 15.5 GB drive. Select the new drive to display the Drive screen as shown in Figure 31-3:

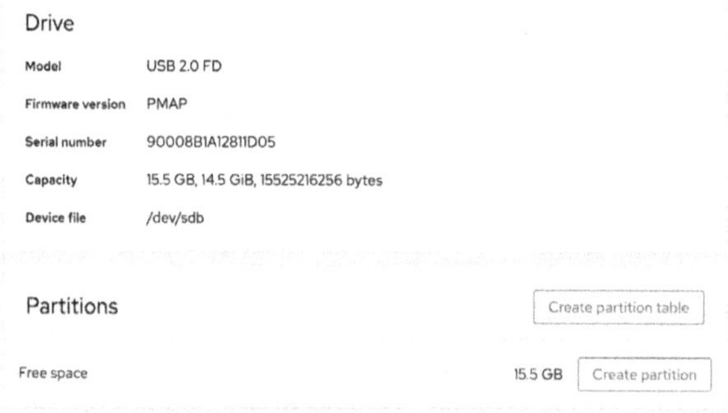

Drive

Model	USB 2.0 FD
Firmware version	PMAP
Serial number	90008B1A12811D05
Capacity	15.5 GB, 14.5 GiB, 15525216256 bytes
Device file	/dev/sdb

Partitions   Create partition table

Free space   15.5 GB   Create partition

Figure 31-3

Click on the *Create partition* button and use the dialog to specify how much space will be allocated to this partition, the filesystem type (XFS is recommended), and an optional label, filesystem mount point, and mount options. Note that additional partitions may be added to the drive if this new partition does not use all the available space. To change settings such as whether the filesystem is read-only or mounted at boot time, change the settings in the *Mount options* section:

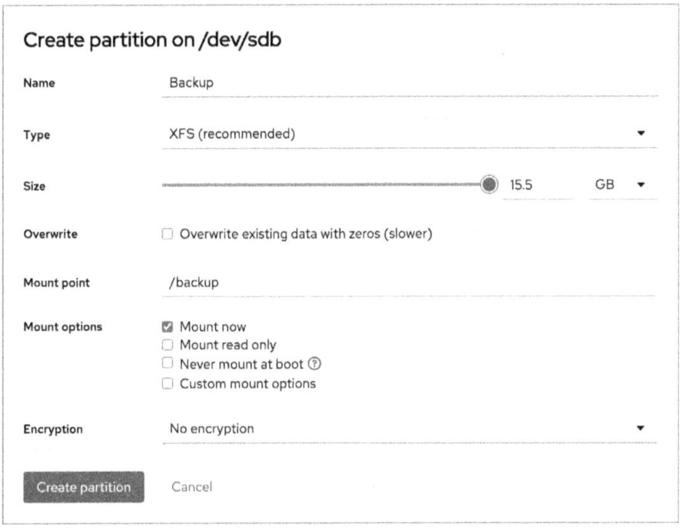

Figure 31-4

Once the settings have been selected, click the Create partition button to commit the change. Upon completion of the creation process, the new partition will be added to the disk, the corresponding filesystem will be created and mounted at the designated mount point, and appropriate changes will be made to the */etc/fstab* file.

31.9 Summary

This chapter has covered adding a physical or virtual disk drive to an existing RHEL 9 system. This is a relatively simple process of ensuring the new drive has been detected by the operating system, creating one or more partitions on the drive, and then making filesystems on those partitions. Although several filesystem types are available on RHEL 9, XFS is generally recommended. Once the filesystems are ready, they can be mounted using the mount command. So that the newly created filesystems mount automatically on system startup, additions can be made to the */etc/fstab* configuration file.

32. Adding a New Disk to a RHEL 9 Volume Group and Logical Volume

In the previous chapter, we looked at adding a new disk drive to a RHEL 9 system, creating a partition and file system, and then mounting that file system to access the disk. An alternative to creating fixed partitions and file systems is to use Logical Volume Management (LVM) to create logical disks comprising space from one or more physical or virtual disks or partitions. The advantage of using LVM is that space can be added to or removed from logical volumes without spreading data over multiple file systems.

Let us take, for example, the root (*/home*) file system of a RHEL 9-based server. Without LVM, this file system would be created with a specific size when the operating system is installed. If a new disk drive is installed, there is no way to allocate any of that space to the */home* file system. The only option would be to create new file systems on the new disk and mount them at particular mount points. In this scenario, you would have plenty of space on the new file system, but the */home* file system would still be nearly full. The only option would be to move files onto the new file system. With LVM, the new disk (or part thereof) can be assigned to the logical volume containing the root file system, thereby dynamically extending the space available.

In this chapter, we will look at the steps necessary to add new disk space to both a volume group and a logical volume to add additional space to the root file system of a RHEL 9 system.

32.1 An Overview of Logical Volume Management (LVM)

LVM provides a flexible and high-level approach to managing disk space. Instead of each disk drive being split into partitions of fixed sizes onto which fixed-size file systems are created, LVM provides a way to group disk space into logical volumes that can be easily resized and moved. In addition, LVM allows administrators to carefully control disk space assigned to different groups of users by allocating distinct volume groups or logical volumes to those users. When the space initially allocated to the volume is exhausted, the administrator can add more space without moving the user files to a different file system.

LVM consists of the following components:

32.1.1 Volume Group (VG)

The Volume Group is the high-level container with one or more logical and physical volumes.

32.1.2 Physical Volume (PV)

A physical volume represents a storage device such as a disk drive or other storage media.

Adding a New Disk to a RHEL 9 Volume Group and Logical Volume

32.1.3 Logical Volume (LV)

A logical volume is equivalent to a disk partition and, as with a disk partition, can contain a file system.

32.1.4 Physical Extent (PE)

Each physical volume (PV) is divided into equal size blocks known as physical extents.

32.1.5 Logical Extent (LE)

Each logical volume (LV) is divided into equal size blocks called logical extents.

Suppose we are creating a new volume group called VolGroup001. This volume group needs physical disk space to function, so we allocate three disk partitions */dev/sda1*, */dev/sdb1*, and */dev/sdb2*. These become physical volumes in VolGroup001. We would then create a logical volume called LogVol001 within the volume group comprising the three physical volumes.

If we run out of space in LogVol001, we add more disk partitions as physical volumes and assign them to the volume group and logical volume.

32.2 Getting Information about Logical Volumes

As an example of using LVM with RHEL 9, we will work through an example of adding space to the / file system of a standard RHEL 9 installation. Anticipating the need for flexibility in the sizing of the root partition, RHEL 9 sets up the / file system as a logical volume (called *root*) within a volume group called *rhel*. Before making any changes to the LVM setup, however, it is essential first to gather information.

Running the *mount* command will output information about a range of mount points, including the following entry for the root filesystem:

```
/dev/mapper/rhel-root on / type xfs (rw,relatime,seclabel,attr2,inode64,logbufs=8
,logbsize=32k,noquota)
```

Information about the volume group can be obtained using the *vgdisplay* command:

```
# vgdisplay
  --- Volume group ---
  VG Name               rhel
  System ID
  Format                lvm2
  Metadata Areas        1
  Metadata Sequence No  4
  VG Access             read/write
  VG Status             resizable
  MAX LV                0
  Cur LV                3
  Open LV               3
  Max PV                0
  Cur PV                1
```

```
Act PV                  1
VG Size                 <297.09 GiB
PE Size                 4.00 MiB
Total PE                76054
Alloc PE / Size         76054 / <297.09 GiB
Free  PE / Size         0 / 0
VG UUID                 8vZKNE-v6nY-uII2-NKk1-StmF-EkNp-NNKa9b
```

As we can see in the above example, the rhel volume group has a physical extent size of 4.00MiB and has a total of 297.09GB available for allocation to logical volumes. Currently, 76054 physical extents are allocated, equaling the total capacity. Therefore, we must add one or more physical volumes to increase the space allocated to any logical volumes in the *rhel* volume group. The *vgs* tool is also helpful for displaying a quick overview of the space available in the volume groups on a system:

```
# vgs
  VG              #PV #LV #SN Attr    VSize      VFree
  rhel     1   3   0 wz--n- <297.09g    0
```

Information about logical volumes in a volume group may similarly be obtained using the *lvdisplay* command:

```
# lvdisplay
  --- Logical volume ---
  LV Path                /dev/rhel/swap
  LV Name                swap
  VG Name                rhel
  LV UUID                RckIC8-T5Or-vZf9-Er1e-IqW7-Q7Uc-f9cpvj
  LV Write Access        read/write
  LV Creation host, time demoserver, 2023-04-10 14:11:15 -0400
  LV Status              available
  # open                 2
  LV Size                3.75 GiB
  Current LE             960
  Segments               1
  Allocation             inherit
  Read ahead sectors     auto
  - currently set to     256
  Block device           253:1

  --- Logical volume ---
  LV Path                /dev/rhel/home
  LV Name                home
  VG Name                rhel
  LV UUID                MMpQ05-Gry0-9qGg-zvGQ-Dszn-kIkd-ZpaqK6
  LV Write Access        read/write
  LV Creation host, time demoserver, 2023-04-10 14:11:15 -0400
```

Adding a New Disk to a RHEL 9 Volume Group and Logical Volume

```
LV Status              available
# open                 1
LV Size                <223.34 GiB
Current LE             57174
Segments               1
Allocation             inherit
Read ahead sectors     auto
- currently set to     256
Block device           253:2

--- Logical volume ---
LV Path                /dev/rhel/root
LV Name                root
VG Name                rhel
LV UUID                OFqABO-azjy-47DO-bzRo-ha2O-sHz5-jjMPcF
LV Write Access        read/write
LV Creation host, time demoserver, 2023-04-10 14:11:17 -0400
LV Status              available
# open                 1
LV Size                70.00 GiB
Current LE             17920
Segments               1
Allocation             inherit
Read ahead sectors     auto
- currently set to     256
Block device           253:0
```

As shown in the above example, 70 GiB of the space in volume group *rhel* is allocated to logical volume root (for the / file system), approximately 223.34 GiB to the home volume group (for /*home*), and 3.75 GiB to *swap* (for swap space).

Now that we know what space is being used, it is often helpful to understand which devices are providing the space (in other words, which devices are being used as physical volumes). To obtain this information, we need to run the *pvdisplay* command:

```
# pvdisplay
  --- Physical volume ---
  PV Name                /dev/sda2
  VG Name                rhel
  PV Size                <297.09 GiB / not usable 4.00 MiB
  Allocatable            yes (but full)
  PE Size                4.00 MiB
  Total PE               76054
  Free PE                0
  Allocated PE           76054
  PV UUID                siKTC2-fq47-LXTG-VWtc-Ma33-XRCm-5uF63v
```

250

Clearly, the space controlled by logical volume *rhel* is provided via a physical volume located on */dev/sda2*.

Now that we know more about our LVM configuration, we can add space to the volume group and the logical volume contained within.

32.3 Adding Additional Space to a Volume Group from the Command-Line

Just as with the previous steps to gather information about the current Logical Volume Management configuration of a RHEL 9 system, changes to this configuration can be made from the command line.

In the remainder of this chapter, we will assume that a new disk has been added to the system and that the operating system sees it as */dev/sdb*. We shall also assume this is a new disk with no existing partitions. If existing partitions are present, they should be backed up, and then the partitions should be deleted from the disk using the *fdisk* utility. For example, assuming a device represented by */dev/sdb* containing two partitions as follows:

```
# fdisk -l /dev/sdb
Disk /dev/sdb: 14.46 GiB, 15525216256 bytes, 30322688 sectors
Disk model: USB 2.0 FD
Units: sectors of 1 * 512 = 512 bytes
Sector size (logical/physical): 512 bytes / 512 bytes
I/O size (minimum/optimal): 512 bytes / 512 bytes
Disklabel type: dos
Disk identifier: 0x4c33060b


Device     Boot Start      End   Sectors  Size Id Type
/dev/sdb1          2048 30322687 30320640 14.5G 83 Linux
```

Once any filesystems on these partitions have been unmounted, they can be deleted as follows:

```
# fdisk /dev/sdb


Welcome to fdisk (util-linux 2.37.4).
Changes will remain in memory only, until you decide to write them.
Be careful before using the write command.


Command (m for help): d
Selected partition 1
Partition 1 has been deleted.


Command (m for help): w


The partition table has been altered.
Calling ioctl() to re-read partition table.
Syncing disks.
```

Adding a New Disk to a RHEL 9 Volume Group and Logical Volume

Before moving to the next step, remove any entries in the */etc/fstab* file for these filesystems so that the system does not attempt to mount them on the next reboot.

Once the disk is ready, the next step is to convert this disk into a physical volume using the *pvcreate* command (also wiping the dos signature if one exists):

```
# pvcreate /dev/sdb
WARNING: dos signature detected on /dev/sdb at offset 510. Wipe it? [y/n]: y
  Wiping dos signature on /dev/sdb.
  Physical volume "/dev/sdb" successfully created.
```

If the creation fails with a message that reads "Device /dev/<device> excluded by a filter", it may be necessary to wipe the disk using the *wipefs* command before creating the physical volume:

```
# wipefs -a /dev/sdb
/dev/sdb: 8 bytes were erased at offset 0x00000200 (gpt): 45 46 49 20 50 41 52 54
/dev/sdb: 8 bytes were erased at offset 0x1ffffffe00 (gpt): 45 46 49 20 50 41 52
54
/dev/sdb: 2 bytes were erased at offset 0x000001fe (PMBR): 55 aa
/dev/sdb: calling ioctl to re-read partition table: Success
```

With the physical volume created, we now need to add it to the volume group (in this case, rhel) using the *vgextend* command:

```
# vgextend rhel /dev/sdb
  Volume group "rhel" successfully extended
```

The new physical volume has now been added to the volume group and is ready to be allocated to a logical volume. To do this, we run the *lvextend* tool providing the size by which we wish to extend the volume. In this case, we want to extend the size of the *home* logical volume by 14 GB. Note that we need to provide the path to the logical volume, which can be obtained from the *lvdisplay* command (in this case, */dev/rhel/home*):

```
# lvextend -L+14G /dev/rhel/home
  Size of logical volume rhel/home changed from <223.34 GiB (57174 extents) to
<237.34 GiB (60758 extents).
  Logical volume rhel/home successfully resized.
```

The last step is to resize the file system residing on the logical volume to use the additional space. The way this is performed will depend on the filesystem type, which can be identified using the following *df* command and checking the Type column:

```
# df -T /home
Filesystem                  Type 1K-blocks     Used Available Use% Mounted on
/dev/mapper/rhel-home00     xfs  234070356 1669596 232400760   1% /home
```

If */home* is formatted using the XFS filesystem, it can be resized using the *xfs_growfs* utility:

```
# xfs_growfs /home
meta-data=/dev/mapper/rhel-home isize=512    agcount=4, agsize=14636544 blks
        =                       sectsz=512   attr=2, projid32bit=1
        =                       crc=1        finobt=1, sparse=1, rmapbt=0
```

```
                =                       reflink=1      bigtime=1 inobtcount=1
data            =                       bsize=4096     blocks=58546176, imaxpct=25
                =                       sunit=0        swidth=0 blks
naming          =version 2              bsize=4096     ascii-ci=0, ftype=1
log             =internal log           bsize=4096     blocks=28587, version=2
                =                       sectsz=512     sunit=0 blks, lazy-count=1
realtime =none                          extsz=4096     blocks=0, rtextents=0
data blocks changed from 58546176 to 62216192
```

If, on the other hand, the filesystem is of type ext2, ext3, or ext4, the *resize2fs* utility should be used instead when performing the filesystem resize:

```
# resize2fs /dev/rhel/home
```

Once the resize completes, the file system will have been extended to use the additional space provided by the new disk drive. All this has been achieved without moving a single file or restarting the server. As far as users on the system are concerned, nothing has changed (except that there is now more disk space).

32.4 Adding Additional Space to a Volume Group Using Cockpit

In addition to the command-line utilities outlined so far in this chapter, it is also possible to access information about logical volumes and make volume group and logical volume changes from within the Cockpit web interface using the Storage page, as shown in Figure 32-1:

Figure 32-1

If the Storage option is not listed, the *cockpit-storaged* package will need to be installed, and the cockpit service restarted as follows:

```
# dnf install cockpit-storaged
# systemctl restart cockpit.socket
```

Once the Cockpit service has restarted, log back into the Cockpit interface, at which point the

Adding a New Disk to a RHEL 9 Volume Group and Logical Volume

Storage option should now be visible.

To add a new disk drive to an existing volume group from within the Cockpit console, start at the above Storage page and click on a filesystem associated with the volume group to be extended from the list marked A above.

On the resulting screen, click on the + button highlighted in Figure 32-2 below to add a physical volume:

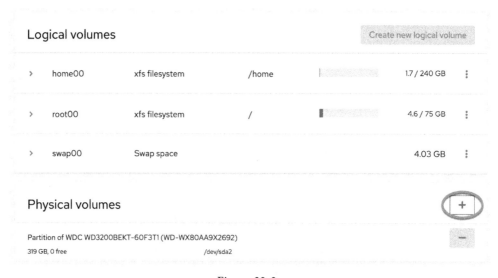

Figure 32-2

Select the new drive to be added to the volume group and click on the Add button:

Figure 32-3

On returning to the volume group screen, scroll down to the logical volume to be extended and click on it to unfold additional information. Figure 32-4, for example, shows details of the *home* logical volume:

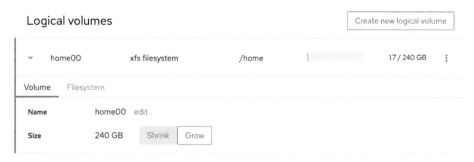

Figure 32-4

To extend the logical volume using the new space, click the *Grow* button and use the slider in the resulting dialog to select how much space should be added to the volume. Then, click the *Grow* button to commit the change (the available space can be shared among different volume groups if required):

Figure 32-5

Once these steps are complete, the volume group will have been configured to use the newly added space.

32.5 Summary

Volume groups and logical volumes provide an abstract layer on top of the physical storage devices on a RHEL 9 system to provide a flexible way to allocate the space provided by multiple disk drives. This allows disk space allocations to be made and changed dynamically without the need to repartition disk drives and move data between filesystems. This chapter has outlined the basic concepts of volume groups and logical and physical volumes while demonstrating how to manage these using command-line tools and the Cockpit web interface.

33. Adding and Managing RHEL 9 Swap Space

An essential part of maintaining the performance of a RHEL 9 system involves ensuring that adequate swap space is available comparable to the memory demands placed on the system. Therefore, this chapter provides an overview of swap management on RHEL 9.

33.1 What is Swap Space?

Computer systems have a finite amount of physical memory available to the operating system. When the operating system approaches the available memory limit, it frees up space by writing memory pages to disk. When the operating system requires any of those pages, they are read back into memory. The disk area allocated for this task is referred to as *swap space*.

33.2 Recommended Swap Space for RHEL 9

The swap recommended for RHEL 9 depends on several factors, including the amount of memory in the system, the workload imposed on that memory, and whether the system is required to support hibernation. The current guidelines for RHEL 9 swap space are as follows:

Amount of installed RAM	Recommended swap space	Recommended swap space if hibernation enabled
2GB or less	Installed RAM x 2	Installed RAM x 3
2GB - 8GB	Installed RAM x 1	Installed RAM x 2
8GB - 64GB	At least 4GB	Installed RAM x 1.5
64GB or more	At least 4GB	Hibernation not recommended

Table 33-1

When a system enters hibernation, the current system state is written to the hard disk, and the host machine is powered off. When the machine is subsequently powered on, the system's state is restored from the hard disk drive. This differs from suspension, where the system state is stored in RAM. The machine then enters a sleep state whereby power is maintained to the system RAM while other devices are shut down.

33.3 Identifying Current Swap Space Usage

The current amount of swap used by a RHEL 9 system may be identified in several ways. One option is to output the */proc/swaps* file:

```
# cat /proc/swaps
Filename          Type          Size          Used          Priority
```

```
/dev/dm-1    partition    3932156      0              -2
```

Alternatively, the *swapon* command may be used:

```
# swapon
NAME        TYPE        SIZE USED PRIO
/dev/dm-1 partition 3.7G    0B    -2
```

To view the amount of swap space relative to the overall available RAM, the *free* command may be used:

```
# free
              total        used        free      shared  buff/cache   available
Mem:        3601420     1577696     1396172      404412     1273236     2023724
Swap:       3932156           0     3932156
```

33.4 Adding a Swap File to a RHEL 9 System

Additional swap space may be added to the system by creating a file and assigning it as swap. Begin by creating the swap file using the dd command. The size of the file can be changed by adjusting the *count* variable. The following command line, for example, creates a 2.0 GB file:

```
# dd if=/dev/zero of=/newswap bs=1024 count=2000000
2000000+0 records in
2000000+0 records out
2048000000 bytes (2.0 GB, 1.9 GiB) copied, 29.3601 s, 69.8 MB/s
```

Before converting the file to a swap file, it is essential to make sure the file has secure permissions set:

```
# chmod 0600 /newswap
```

Once a suitable file has been created, it needs to be converted into a swap file using the *mkswap* command:

```
# mkswap /newswap
Setting up swapspace version 1, size = 1.9 GiB (2047995904 bytes)
no label, UUID=28d314e9-492f-46f8-bdcf-3a734c4426db5
```

With the swap file created and configured, it can be added to the system in real-time using the *swapon* utility:

```
# swapon /newswap
```

Re-running *swapon* should now report that the new file is now being used as swap:

```
# swapon
NAME        TYPE        SIZE USED PRIO
/dev/dm-1 partition 3.7G    1M    -2
/newswap   file       1.9G   0B    -3
```

The swap space may be removed dynamically by using the *swapoff* utility as follows:

```
# swapoff /newswap
```

Finally, modify the */etc/fstab* file to automatically add the new swap at system boot time by adding the following line:

```
/newswap    swap    swap    defaults 0 0
```

33.5 Adding Swap as a Partition

As an alternative to designating a file as swap space, entire disk partitions may also be designated as swap. The steps to achieve this are the same as those for adding a swap file. Before allocating a partition to swap, ensure that any existing data on the corresponding filesystem is either backed up or no longer needed and that the filesystem has been unmounted.

Assuming that a partition exists on a disk drive represented by */dev/sdb1*, for example, the first step would be to convert this into a swap partition, once again using the *mkswap* utility:

```
# mkswap /dev/sdb1
Setting up swapspace version 1, size = 14.5 GiB (15524163584 bytes)
no label, UUID=306b7fee-eb20-4679-9f14-f94548683557
```

Next, add the new partition to the system swap and verify that it has indeed been added:

```
# swapon /dev/sdb1
[root@demoserver ~]# swapon
NAME        TYPE        SIZE USED PRIO
/dev/dm-1 partition   3.7G 996K   -2
/dev/sdb1 partition 14.5G   0B   -3
```

Once again, the */etc/fstab* file may be modified to automatically add the swap partition at boot time as follows:

```
/dev/sdb1    swap    swap    defaults 0 0
```

33.6 Adding Space to a RHEL 9 LVM Swap Volume

On systems using Logical Volume Management, an alternative to adding swap via file or disk partition is to extend the logical volume used for the swap space.

The first step is to identify the current amount of swap available and the volume group and logical volume used for the swap space using the *lvdisplay* utility (for more information on LVM, refer to the chapter entitled *"Adding a New Disk to a RHEL 9 Volume Group and Logical Volume"*):

```
# lvdisplay
  --- Logical volume ---
  LV Path                /dev/rhel/swap00
  LV Name                swap00
  VG Name                rhel
  LV UUID                EbOScj-1qXw-bB9d-LU61-ZjdC-L7u5-Uhj8De
  LV Write Access        read/write
  LV Creation host, time demoserver, 2023-04-12 09:34:29 -0400
  LV Status              available
  # open                 2
  LV Size                3.75 GiB
  Current LE             960
```

```
Segments                 1
Allocation               inherit
Read ahead sectors       auto
 - currently set to      256
Block device             253:1
     .
     .
     .
```

Clearly, the swap resides on a logical volume named *swap00* which is part of the volume group named *rhel*. The next step is to verify if there is any space available on the volume group that can be allocated to the swap volume:

```
# vgs
  VG   #PV #LV #SN Attr   VSize   VFree
  rhel  2   3   0 wz--n- 197.66g <22.00g
```

If the amount of space available is sufficient to meet additional swap requirements, turn off the swap and extend the swap logical volume to use as much of the available space as needed to meet the system's swap requirements:

```
# swapoff /dev/rhel/swap
# lvextend -L+8GB /dev/rhel/swap
    Logical volume rhel/swap successfully resized.
```

Next, reformat the swap volume and turn the swap back on:

```
# mkswap /dev/rhel/swap
mkswap: /dev/rhel/swap: warning: wiping old swap signature.
Setting up swapspace version 1, size = 12 GiB (12754874368 bytes)
no label, UUID=241a4818-e51c-4b8c-9bc9-1697fc2ce26e

# swapon /dev/rhel/swap
```

Having made the changes, check that the swap space has increased:

```
# swapon
NAME        TYPE       SIZE USED PRIO
/dev/dm-1 partition   12G   0B   -2
```

33.7 Adding Swap Space to the Volume Group

In the above section, we extended the swap logical volume to use space already available in the volume group. If no space is available in the volume group, it must be added before extending the swap.

Begin by checking the status of the volume group:

```
# vgs
  VG              #PV #LV #SN Attr   VSize    VFree
  rhel             1   3   0 wz--n- <297.09g    0
```

The above output indicates that no space is available within the volume group. However, suppose we have a requirement to add 14 GB to the swap on the system. This will require the addition of more space to the volume group. For this example, it will be assumed that a disk that is 16 GB in size and represented by *dev/sdb* is available for addition to the volume group. Therefore, the first step is to turn this partition into a physical volume using *pvcreate*:

```
# pvcreate /dev/sdb
  Physical volume "/dev/sdb" successfully created.
```

If the creation fails with a message similar to "Device /dev/sdb excluded by a filter", it may be necessary to wipe the disk before creating the physical volume:

```
# wipefs -a /dev/sdb
/dev/sdb: 8 bytes were erased at offset 0x00000200 (gpt): 45 46 49 20 50 41 52 54
/dev/sdb: 8 bytes were erased at offset 0x1fffffe00 (gpt): 45 46 49 20 50 41 52
54
/dev/sdb: 2 bytes were erased at offset 0x000001fe (PMBR): 55 aa
/dev/sdb: calling ioctl to re-read partition table: Success
```

Next, the volume group needs to be extended to use this additional physical volume:

```
# vgextend rhel /dev/sdb
  Volume group "rhel" successfully extended
```

At this point, the *vgs* command should report the addition of space from *dev/sdb* to the volume group:

```
# vgs
  VG              #PV #LV #SN Attr   VSize    VFree
  rhel             2   3   0 wz--n- 311.54g <14.46g
```

Now that the additional space is available in the volume group, the swap logical volume may be extended to utilize the space. But first, turn off the swap using the *swapoff* utility:

```
# swapoff /dev/rhel/swap00
```

Next, extend the logical volume to use the new space:

```
# lvextend -L+14GB /dev/rhel/swap00
  Size of logical volume rhel/swap00 changed from 3.75 GiB (960 extents) to 17.75
GiB (4544 extents).
  Logical volume rhel/swap00 successfully resized.
```

Re-create the swap on the logical volume:

```
# mkswap /dev/rhel/swap00
mkswap: /dev/rhel/swap: warning: wiping old swap signature.
Setting up swapspace version 1, size = 11.9 GiB (12754874368 bytes)
no label, UUID=241a4818-e51c-4b8c-9bc9-1697fc2ce26e
```

Next, turn swap back on:

```
# swapon /dev/rhel/swap
```

Finally, use the *swapon* command to verify the addition of the swap space to the system:

```
# swapon
```

```
NAME        TYPE        SIZE USED PRIO
/dev/dm-1 partition 17.7G    0B   -2
```

33.8 Summary

Swap space is vital to any operating system when memory resources become constrained. By swapping out memory areas to disk, the system can continue to function and meet the needs of the processes and applications running on it.

RHEL 9 has a set of guidelines recommending the amount of disk-based swap space that should be allocated depending on the amount of RAM installed in the system. When these recommendations prove insufficient, additional swap space can be added to the system, typically without rebooting. This chapter outlines that swap space can be added as a file, disk, or disk partition or by extending existing logical volumes configured as swap space.

34. RHEL 9 System and Process Monitoring

An essential part of running and administering a RHEL 9 system involves monitoring the overall system health regarding memory, swap, storage, and processor usage. This includes knowing how to inspect and manage the system and user processes running in the background. This chapter will outline some tools and utilities that can be used to monitor system resources and processes on a RHEL 9 system.

34.1 Managing Processes

Even when a RHEL 9 system appears idle, many *system processes* will run silently in the background to keep the operating system functioning. For example, when you execute a command or launch an app, *user processes* are started, running until the associated task is completed.

To obtain a list of active user processes you are currently running within the context of a single terminal or command-prompt session, use the *ps* command as follows:

```
$ ps
  PID TTY          TIME CMD
10395 pts/1    00:00:00 bash
13218 pts/1    00:00:00 ps
```

The output from the *ps* command shows that two user processes are running within the context of the current terminal window or command prompt session, the bash shell into which the command was entered, and the *ps* command itself.

To list all active processes running for the current user, use the *ps* command with the -a flag. This command will list all running processes that are associated with the user regardless of where they are running (for example, processes running in other terminal windows):

```
$ ps -a
    PID TTY          TIME CMD
   5442 tty2     00:00:00 gnome-session-b
   6350 pts/0    00:00:00 sudo
   6354 pts/0    00:00:00 su
   6355 pts/0    00:00:00 bash
   9849 pts/2    00:00:00 nano
   9850 pts/1    00:00:00 ps
```

As shown in the above output, the user is running processes related to the GNOME desktop, the shell session, the *nano* text editor, and the *ps* command.

To list the processes for a specific user, run *ps* with the -u flag followed by the user name:

```
# ps -u john
  PID TTY          TIME CMD
  914 ?        00:00:00 systemd
  915 ?        00:00:00 (sd-pam)
  970 ?        00:00:00 gnome-keyring-d
  974 tty1     00:00:00 gdm-x-session
  .

  .
```

Note that each process is assigned a unique process ID which can be used to stop the process by sending it a termination (TERM) signal via the *kill* command. For example:

```
$ kill 13217
```

The advantage of ending a process with the TERM signal is that it allows the process to exit gracefully, potentially saving any data that might otherwise be lost.

If the standard termination signal does not terminate the process, repeat the *kill* command with the -9 option. This command sends a KILL signal which should cause even frozen processes to exit but does not give the process a chance to exit gracefully, possibly resulting in data loss:

```
$ kill -9 13217
```

To list all of the processes running on a system (including all user and system processes), execute the following command:

```
$ ps -ax
   PID TTY      STAT   TIME COMMAND
     1 ?        Ss     0:22 /usr/lib/systemd/systemd rhgb --switched-root
     2 ?        S      0:00 [kthreadd]
     3 ?        I<     0:00 [rcu_gp]
     4 ?        I<     0:00 [rcu_par_gp]
     5 ?        I<     0:00 [netns]
```

To list all processes and include information about process ownership, CPU, and memory use, execute the *ps* command with the -aux option:

```
$ ps -aux
USER          PID %CPU %MEM    VSZ   RSS TTY       STAT START   TIME COMMAND
root            2  0.0  0.0      0     0 ?         S    09:59   0:00 [kthreadd]
root            3  0.0  0.0      0     0 ?         I<   09:59   0:00 [rcu_gp]
root            4  0.0  0.0      0     0 ?         I<   09:59   0:00 [rcu_par_gp]
root            5  0.0  0.0      0     0 ?         I<   09:59   0:00 [netns]
root            7  0.0  0.0      0     0 ?         I<   09:59   0:00 [kworker/0:0H-
events_highpri]
root            9  0.0  0.0      0     0 ?         I<   09:59   0:00 [kworker/0:1H-
events_highpri]
  .

  .
demo         9788  0.1  1.4 763248 50480 ?         Ssl  15:05   0:00 /usr/libexec/
```

```
gnome-terminal-serv
demo       9814  0.0  0.1 224108  5664 pts/2   Ss  15:05  0:00 bash
demo       9849  0.0  0.0 222412  3588 pts/2   S+  15:06  0:00 nano
demo       9873  0.0  0.1 233416  6280 pts/1   R+  15:08  0:00 ps -aux
```

A Linux process can start its own sub-processes (referred to as *spawning*), resulting in a hierarchical parent-child relationship between processes. To view the process tree, use the *ps* command and include the -H option. Below is part of the tree output for a *ps -aH* command execution:

```
$ ps -aH
    PID TTY          TIME CMD
  10036 pts/3    00:00:00 ps
   6350 pts/0    00:00:00 sudo
   6354 pts/0    00:00:00   su
   6355 pts/0    00:00:00     bash
   5442 tty2     00:00:00 gnome-session-b
```

Process information may also be viewed via the System Monitor tool from the GNOME desktop. This tool can either be launched by searching for "System Monitor" within the desktop environment or from the command line as follows:

```
$ gnome-system-monitor
```

Once the System Monitor has launched, select the Processes button located in the toolbar to list the processes running on the system, as shown in Figure 34-1 below:

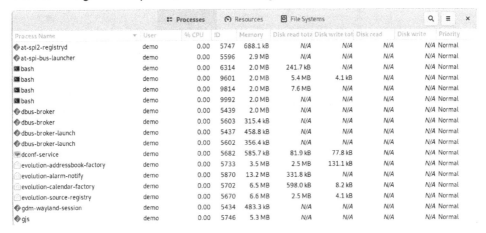

Figure 34-1

To change the processes listed (for example, to list all processes or just your own processes), use the menu as illustrated in Figure 34-2:

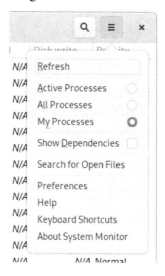

Figure 34-2

To filter the list of processes, click on the search button in the title bar and enter the process name into the search field:

Figure 34-3

To display additional information about a specific process, select it from the list and click on the button located in the bottom right-hand corner (marked A in Figure 34-4) of the dialog:

Figure 34-4

A dialog similar to that marked B in the above figure will appear when the button is clicked. Select a process from the list and click the End Process button (C) to terminate it.

To monitor CPU, memory, swap, and network usage, click on the Resources button in the title bar to display the screen shown in Figure 34-5:

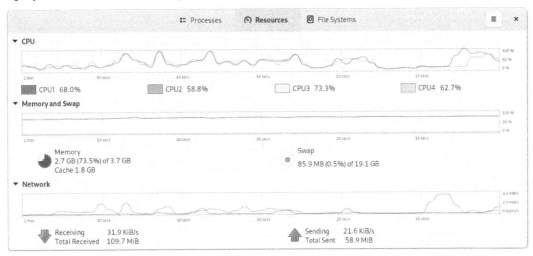

Figure 34-5

Similarly, a summary of storage space used on the system can be viewed by selecting the File Systems toolbar button:

Figure 34-6

34.2 Real-time System Monitoring with top

As the chapter *"An Overview of the Cockpit Web Interface"* outlined, the Cockpit web interface can perform basic system monitoring. The previous section also explained how the GNOME System Monitor tool could be used to monitor processes and system resources. This chapter also explored how the *ps* command can provide a snapshot of the processes running on a RHEL 9 system. However, the *ps* command does not provide a real-time view of the processes and resource usage on the system. The *top* command is an ideal tool for real-time monitoring of system resources and processes from the command prompt.

When running, *top* will list the processes running on the system ranked by system resource usage (with the most demanding process in the *top* position). The upper section of the screen displays memory and swap usage information together with CPU data for all CPU cores. All of this output is constantly updated, allowing the system to be monitored in real-time:

```
top - 15:43:28 up  5:44,  5 users,  load average: 0.00, 0.25, 0.35
Tasks: 272 total,   1 running, 271 sleeping,   0 stopped,   0 zombie
%Cpu(s):  0.2 us,  0.1 sy,  0.0 ni, 99.6 id,  0.0 wa,  0.1 hi,  0.0 si,  0.0 st
MiB Mem :   3517.0 total,    225.0 free,   2458.0 used,   1645.1 buff/cache
MiB Swap:  18176.0 total,  18081.8 free,     94.2 used.   1059.0 avail Mem

  PID USER      PR  NI    VIRT    RES    SHR S  %CPU  %MEM     TIME+ COMMAND
 5543 demo      20   0 4836608 219372 120288 S   0.3   6.1   0:39.00 gnome-shell
 6442 cockpit+  20   0  508744   6056   4792 S   0.3   0.2   0:44.53 cockpit-tls
 6501 root      20   0  546104  64464   7212 S   0.3   1.8   0:45.45 cockpit-bridge
11384 demo      20   0 2862632 224700 107288 S   0.3   6.2   0:26.87 Isolated Web Co
    1 root      20   0  173116  17208  10168 S   0.0   0.5   0:26.43 systemd
    2 root      20   0       0      0      0 S   0.0   0.0   0:00.02 kthreadd
    3 root       0 -20       0      0      0 I   0.0   0.0   0:00.00 rcu_gp
    4 root       0 -20       0      0      0 I   0.0   0.0   0:00.00 rcu_par_gp
    5 root       0 -20       0      0      0 I   0.0   0.0   0:00.00 netns
    7 root       0 -20       0      0      0 I   0.0   0.0   0:00.00 kworker/0:0H-events_highpri
    9 root       0 -20       0      0      0 I   0.0   0.0   0:00.11 kworker/0:1H-events_highpri
   10 root       0 -20       0      0      0 I   0.0   0.0   0:00.00 mm_percpu_wq
   12 root      20   0       0      0      0 I   0.0   0.0   0:00.00 rcu_tasks_kthre
   13 root      20   0       0      0      0 I   0.0   0.0   0:00.00 rcu_tasks_rude_
   14 root      20   0       0      0      0 I   0.0   0.0   0:00.00 rcu_tasks_trace
   15 root      20   0       0      0      0 S   0.0   0.0   0:00.03 ksoftirqd/0
   16 root      20   0       0      0      0 I   0.0   0.0   0:06.98 rcu_preempt
   17 root      rt   0       0      0      0 S   0.0   0.0   0:00.02 migration/0
   19 root      20   0       0      0      0 S   0.0   0.0   0:00.00 cpuhp/0
   20 root      20   0       0      0      0 S   0.0   0.0   0:00.00 cpuhp/1
   21 root      rt   0       0      0      0 S   0.0   0.0   0:00.13 migration/1
   22 root      20   0       0      0      0 S   0.0   0.0   0:00.03 ksoftirqd/1
   24 root       0 -20       0      0      0 I   0.0   0.0   0:00.00 kworker/1:0H-events_highpri
   25 root      20   0       0      0      0 S   0.0   0.0   0:00.00 cpuhp/2
   26 root      rt   0       0      0      0 S   0.0   0.0   0:00.13 migration/2
```

Figure 34-7

To limit the information displayed to the processes belonging to a specific user, start *top* with the -u option followed by the user name:

```
$ top -u john
```

For a complete listing of the features available in *top*, press the keyboard 'h' key or refer to the man page:

```
$ man top
```

34.3 Command-Line Disk and Swap Space Monitoring

Disk space can be monitored from within Cockpit and using the GNOME System Monitor. To identify disk usage from the command line, however, the *df* command provides a helpful and quick overview:

```
# df -h
Filesystem                    Size  Used Avail Use% Mounted on
devtmpfs                      4.0M     0  4.0M   0% /dev
tmpfs                         1.8G     0  1.8G   0% /dev/shm
tmpfs                         704M  9.6M  694M   2% /run
/dev/mapper/rhel-root00        70G  6.3G   64G   9% /
/dev/mapper/rhel-home00       224G  1.8G  222G   1% /home
/dev/sda1                    1014M  290M  725M  29% /boot
tmpfs                         352M  144K  352M   1% /run/user/1000
```

To review current swap space and memory usage, run the *free* command:

```
# free
              total        used        free      shared  buff/cache   available
Mem:        3823720      879916     1561108      226220     1382696     2476300
```

To continuously monitor memory and swap levels, use the *free* command with the -s option, specifying the delay in seconds between each update (keeping in mind that the *top* tool may provide a better way to view this data in real time):

```
$ free -s 1
Mem:       3823720      879472     1561532      226220     1382716     2476744
Swap:      2097148           0     2097148


             total        used        free      shared  buff/cache   available
Mem:       3823720      879140     1559940      228144     1384640     2475152
Swap:      2097148           0     2097148
```
.
.

To monitor disk I/O from the command line, consider using the *iotop* command, which can be installed as follows:

```
# dnf install iotop
```

Once installed and executed (*iotop* must be run with system administrator privileges), the tool will display a real-time list of disk I/O on a per-process basis:

```
Total DISK READ :     0.00 B/s | Total DISK WRITE :      0.00 B/s
Actual DISK READ:     0.00 B/s | Actual DISK WRITE:      0.00 B/s
   TID  PRIO  USER     DISK READ DISK WRITE>     COMMAND
     1 be/4 root        0.00 B/s    0.00 B/s systemd rhgb --switched-root --system --deserialize 31
     2 be/4 root        0.00 B/s    0.00 B/s [kthreadd]
     3 be/4 root        0.00 B/s    0.00 B/s [rcu_gp]
     4 be/4 root        0.00 B/s    0.00 B/s [rcu_par_gp]
     5 be/4 root        0.00 B/s    0.00 B/s [netns]
     7 be/4 root        0.00 B/s    0.00 B/s [kworker/0:0H-events_highpri]
     9 be/4 root        0.00 B/s    0.00 B/s [kworker/0:1H-events_highpri]
    10 be/4 root        0.00 B/s    0.00 B/s [mm_percpu_wq]
    12 be/4 root        0.00 B/s    0.00 B/s [rcu_tasks_kthre]
    13 be/4 root        0.00 B/s    0.00 B/s [rcu_tasks_rude_]
    14 be/4 root        0.00 B/s    0.00 B/s [rcu_tasks_trace]
    15 be/4 root        0.00 B/s    0.00 B/s [ksoftirqd/0]
    16 be/4 root        0.00 B/s    0.00 B/s [rcu_preempt]
    17 be/4 root        0.00 B/s    0.00 B/s [migration/0]
    19 be/4 root        0.00 B/s    0.00 B/s [cpuhp/0]
    20 be/4 root        0.00 B/s    0.00 B/s [cpuhp/1]
    21 be/4 root        0.00 B/s    0.00 B/s [migration/1]
    22 be/4 root        0.00 B/s    0.00 B/s [ksoftirqd/1]
    24 be/4 root        0.00 B/s    0.00 B/s [kworker/1:0H-events_highpri]
    25 be/4 root        0.00 B/s    0.00 B/s [cpuhp/2]
    26 be/4 root        0.00 B/s    0.00 B/s [migration/2]
    27 be/4 root        0.00 B/s    0.00 B/s [ksoftirqd/2]
    29 be/4 root        0.00 B/s    0.00 B/s [kworker/2:0H-events_highpri]
    30 be/4 root        0.00 B/s    0.00 B/s [cpuhp/3]
    31 be/4 root        0.00 B/s    0.00 B/s [migration/3]
    32 be/4 root        0.00 B/s    0.00 B/s [ksoftirqd/3]
    34 be/4 root        0.00 B/s    0.00 B/s [kworker/3:0H-events_highpri]
    37 be/4 root        0.00 B/s    0.00 B/s [kdevtmpfs]
```

Figure 34-8

34.4 Summary

Even a system that appears to be doing nothing will have many system processes running in the background. Activities performed by users on the system will result in additional processes being started. Processes can also spawn their own child processes. Each process will use some system resources, including memory, swap space, processor cycles, disk storage, and network bandwidth. This chapter has explored a set of tools that can be used to monitor both process and system resources on a running system and, when necessary, kill errant processes that may be impacting the performance of a system.

Index

Symbols

A

B

Index

Index

Index

Q

R

S

Index

Index

www.ingramcontent.com/pod-product-compliance
Lightning Source LLC
LaVergne TN
LVHW080113070326
832902LV00015B/2567